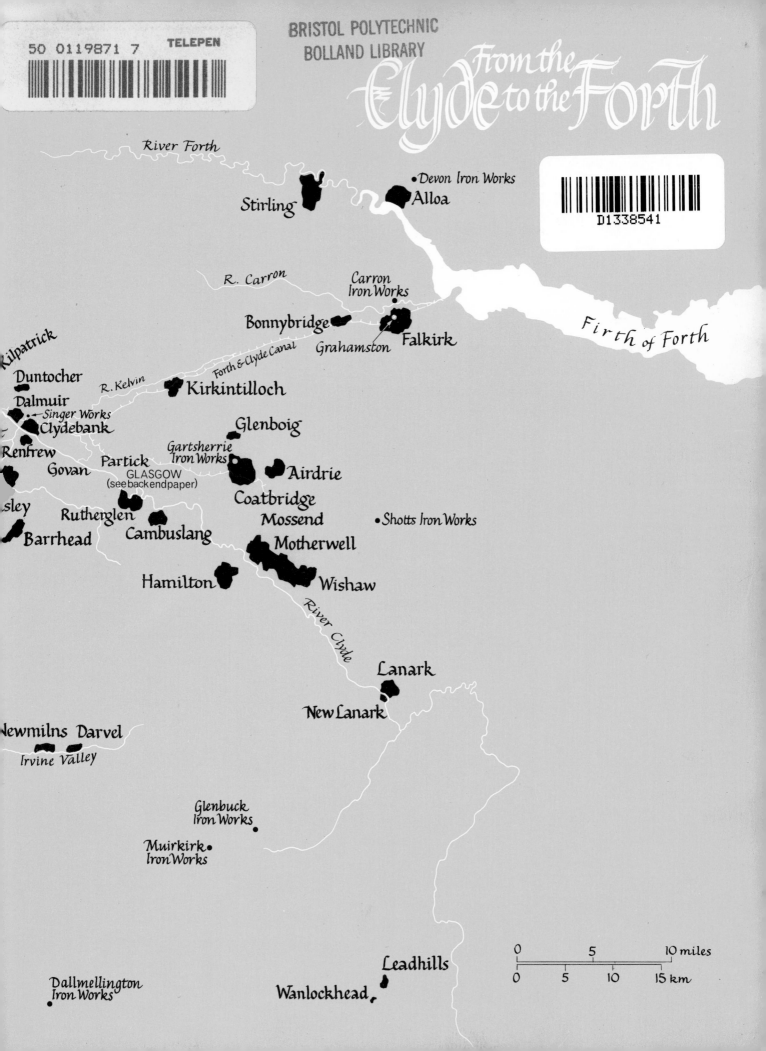

From the Clyde to the Forth

River Forth

Stirling

• Devon Iron Works

Alloa

R. Carron

Carron
Iron Works

Bonnybridge

Grahamston

Falkirk

Firth of Forth

Forth & Clyde Canal

Kilpatrick

Duntocher

Dalmuir

R. Kelvin

Kirkintilloch

Singer Works

Clydebank

Renfrew

Govan

Partick

GLASGOW
(see back endpaper)

Glenboig

Gartsherrie
Iron Works

Airdrie

sley

Rutherglen

Barrhead

Cambuslang

Coatbridge

Mossend

Motherwell

• Shotts Iron Works

Hamilton

Wishaw

River Clyde

Lanark

New Lanark

Newmilns Darvel

Irvine Valley

Glenbuck
Iron Works •

Muirkirk •
Iron Works

Dallmellington
Iron Works •

Leadhills

Wanlockhead •

0		5		10 miles
0	5	10		15 km

WORKSHOP OF THE BRITISH EMPIRE

Engineering and Shipbuilding in
the West of Scotland

WORKSHOP OF THE BRITISH EMPIRE

Engineering and Shipbuilding in

the West of Scotland

Michael S. Moss
Archivist, University of Glasgow

John R. Hume

Heinemann Educational Books Ltd
LONDON EDINBURGH MELBOURNE AUCKLAND TORONTO
HONG KONG SINGAPORE KUALA LUMPUR NEW DELHI
NAIROBI JOHANNESBURG LUSAKA IBADAN
KINGSTON

ISBN 0 435 32590 6
© Michael S. Moss and John R. Hume 1977
First published 1977

Published by Heinemann Educational Books Ltd
48 Charles Street, London W1X 8AH

Filmset and printed in Great Britain by
BAS Printers Limited, Wallop, Hampshire

for
John Imrie
&
James Campbell

Preface

Of the 'basic' industries in Britain, engineering and shipbuilding have probably fared least well at the hands of economic historians. Apart from Professor Saul's pioneering article in the *Economic History Review,* 1967, recent writing has been concerned mainly with the contrast between American and British engineering in the nineteenth century. There are many histories of engineering – or of its various branches – but they are largely concerned with evolutionary patterns of technical change. In the best of them, such as L.T.C. Rolt's excellent *Tools for the Job* (London: Batsford, 1965), some attempt has been made to relate changes in technique to changing economic circumstances, but such relationships remain vague. Certain attitudes pervade both types of writing. Authors are obsessed with technical change as a measure of effectiveness, ignoring the possibility that continued operation of certain basic processes can maintain whole branches of industry on a profitable basis with only marginal technical change. Another school, led by Professor R. Floud, suggests that foreign competition was detrimental to British engineering before 1914, and that British manufacturers were remiss in not adopting the techniques of the foreigner to compete in the same markets. As far as the West of Scotland is concerned, we would suggest that, up to 1914 foreign competition was largely ineffective in making inroads into the most important sectors of the engineering and shipbuilding industries, and that where competition was encountered, or where new products of foreign origin were introduced, the response of the region was vigorous and effective.

In 1832, Macaulay reviewed a three-volume life of Lord Burleigh, by the then Regius Professor of Modern History at Oxford, in these words: 'Compared with the labour of reading through these volumes, all other labour, the labour of thieves on the treadmill, of children in factories, of negroes in sugar plantations is an agreeable recreation.' Unfortunately, the work of many present day business and economic historians, with their delight in statistical reconditeness, is open to similar comparison. In writing this history of West of Scotland shipbuilding and engineering we have tried to redress the balance in favour of the narrative approach to the subject. By the use of photographs of works, shop floors, and products we have sought to underline our belief that within an industry the disparity in products, the capacity of individual firms, and linkages, makes statistical comparisons difficult and possibly odious. Moreover, of the series of company records that survive in the West of Scotland few are complete, and of these most are for exceptional firms. It would be unwise to generalize from their particular detailed analysis.

We have described the general development of the heavy industries of the West of Scotland, with a thorough examination of the particular firms of Andrew Barclay Sons & Co. (locomotive manufacturers and general engineers), Kilmarnock (Chapter 4) and the Fairfield and John Brown Shipbuilding and Engineering Companies (Chapter 6). In the introduction we outline what we believe to be the chief factors affecting these industries, relying on the later chapters to support our conclusions. While we consider these to be substantially correct, their confirmation requires careful and specific scrutiny of the development of many other West of Scotland firms. The work is based on our work for the Western Survey of the National Register of Archives (Scotland) which is described in Chapter 8.

Michael S. Moss
John R. Hume

1977

Contents

PREFACE   *page* *vii*

ACKNOWLEDGEMENTS   *x*

LIST OF ILLUSTRATIONS   *xiii*

Part One: Ironfounding and Engineering

CHAPTER ONE: *Introduction*   3

CHAPTER TWO: *Ironfounding*   11

CHAPTER THREE: *Engineering*   27

CHAPTER FOUR:
Andrew Barclay Sons & Co. Ltd
Locomotive manufacturers and engineers   68

Part Two: Shipbuilding

CHAPTER FIVE: *Shipbuilding*   87

CHAPTER SIX:
The Fairfield and John Brown Shipbuilding and
Engineering Companies   113

Part Three: Other Industries

CHAPTER SEVEN: *Other industries*   147

Part Four: Survey Techniques, References, and Further Reading

CHAPTER EIGHT:
The Techniques of the Western Survey of the
National Register of Archives (Scotland)   155

REFERENCES   178

SUGGESTIONS FOR FURTHER READING   183

INDEX   186

Acknowledgements

The authors wish to thank all those who, during the compilation of this book, and in their work for the Western Survey, helped them to find historical records and photographs, and patiently answered their many questions, which must often have seemed foolish and naive. In particular, they would like to thank: all those ironfounding firms that co-operated in their survey of the industry in Scotland; John Bates, Secretary of the National Register of Archives (Scotland); John Butt for his support and encouragement and his critical comments; James Campbell for reading the manuscript; M. Clarke and the staff of A. & W. Smith & Co. Ltd; Professor S.G. Checkland of the Department of Economic History, University of Glasgow, for reading Chapter 1; R.F. Dell, the Strathclyde Regional archivist and his staff; T.M. Devine for help and critical comments on Chapter 1; C. Donald of McGrigor Donald & Co.; Professor A.A.M. Duncan of the Department of Scottish History, University of Glasgow; C. Anderson of William Beardmore & Co. Ltd, and his staff; S.R. Elson of the University of Strathclyde for all his help in arranging the exhibition 'Pride in Your Work', without which this book would not have been possible; J.S. Forsyth of Armitage Shanks Ltd; Mrs E. Frame of the Andersonian Library, University of Strathclyde; A. Gilchrist, A. Ross, and the staff of Govan Shipbuilders Ltd; I.M. Graham of John Brown & Co. Ltd; Edwin Green, archivist of the Midland Bank Group, for encouragement and critical advice; R. Henderson and R. Hutchinson of MacKenzie Roberton & Co.; A.W. Hubbard of Blairs Ltd; John Imrie, the Keeper of the Records of Scotland, for all his help and encouragement, his comments on Chapter 8, and permission to quote from the UCS records; T. Jackson of Scotstoun Marine Ltd; S. Kewney and the staff of Andrew Barclay Sons & Co. Ltd; J.T. Lang of Wickam Lang Ltd; W. Lind for his enthusiastic support and unending supply of detailed and useful information; Sir William Lithgow, W.G. Adair, and the late J. White of the Scott-Lithgow group, without whose advice and frankness it would not have been possible to write Chapters 5 and 6; David Lyon of the National Maritime Museum; Professor S.G.E. Lythe, Professor of Economic History, University of Strathclyde; G. Macdonald of Bannatyne, Kirkwood, France & Co.; J. Macgregor of Fullerton, Hodgart & Barclay Ltd; J.G. McGregor of Murray & Paterson Ltd; H. McKellar of Hugh Smith (Glasgow) Ltd; J.L. Meyer for information on the Fairfield connection with Holland; D. Murray of Maclay, Murray and Spens; R.P. Paton of William Paton Ltd; Professor P. Payne of the Department of Economic History at the University of Aberdeen for reading and commenting on the manuscript and for allowing the authors to use his paper on rationalization in the Scottish steel industry; J. Peach of Ferguson

Brothers (Port Glasgow) Ltd; H.D. Picken of James Picken & Sons; Sylvia Price, who is researching on labour in the Clyde Shipbuilding industry before 1914 at the University of Edinburgh; T. Scott of the Glasgow Head Office of the Bank of Scotland; J.H. Sime, the technical archivist at the Scottish Record Office; A. Slaven of the Department of Economic History at the University of Glasgow for advice, friendship, and encouragement; Robert C. Smith, chairman of the Business Archives Council of Scotland; J.F. Stephen, A.A.M. Stephen, and T.R. Evans of Alexander Stephen & Sons Ltd; H.A. Stewart of the Grahamston Iron Co. Ltd; J. Thomson of the Dick Institute, Kilmarnock; Jean Verth, who was researching on Clyde Shipbuilding between the wars at the University of Glasgow; W.G. Wallace of Charles Connel & Co. Ltd; H. Waugh of Weir Pumps Ltd; the Committee of the Western Survey of the National Register of Archives (Scotland); T. Walden and A.S.E. Browning of the Glasgow Art Gallery and Museums; and T.E. Woodsend of Eadie Bros Ltd.

The authors would also like to thank the following firms and institutions for permission to reproduce photographs:

Aimers, MacLean & Co. Ltd: Figure 8.16.
T. & R. Annan & Sons: Figures 5.4, 8.19.
Armitage-Shanks Ltd: Figure 7.5.
Sir William Arrol & Co. Ltd: Figures 5.15 (a)-(f).
Andrew Barclay Sons & Co. Ltd: Figures 2.16, 4.1-4.21, 8.2(b), 8.6.
Barclay Curle & Co. Ltd: Figures 5.1(a) and (b), 5.25.
William Beardmore & Co. Ltd: Figures 3.10, 5.21, 8.15.
Blairs Ltd: Figure 8.4.
Blantyre Engineering Co. Ltd: Figure 3.2.
Carron Co.: Figures 2.1, 2.3, 2.4, 2.17.
Clifton & Baird Ltd: Figure 8.11.
James Davie & Son, Cornford: Figures 2.10(a) and (b).
Andrew Fleming Ltd: Figures 8.10(a) and (b).
Fullerton, Hodgart & Barclay Ltd: Figures 2.15, 3.24, 3.25, 8.9.
H.R. Gibbs, Esq.: Figure 5.1(a).
Glasgow Art Galleries and Museum, Museum of Transport: Figures 8.5(a)-(c).
Glynwed Foundries Ltd: Figures 2.18, 2.19, 2.20.
Govan Shipbuilders Ltd: Figure 6.3.
Grahamston Iron Co. Ltd: Figure 2.2.
Captain J. Inglis: Figure 5.2.
Keeper of the Records of Scotland,
    British Rail collection: Figures 1.1, 3.23(a) and (b).
    Upper Clyde Shipbuilders collection:
    John Brown Shipbuilding and En-

gineering Co. Ltd: Figures 3.26, 5.6(a) and (b), 5.13, 5.19, 5.20(a), 5.27, 6.4, 6.5(a) and (b), 6.6, 6.10(a) and (b), 6.12, 6.14, 6.16, 6.18, 6.19, 6.20, 6.21, 8.7, 8.14(a).
    Fairfield Shipbuilding and Engineering Co. Ltd: Figures 5.5, 5.16, 5.26, 6.2, 6.9, 6.11, 6.13(a) and (b), 6.15(a) and (b), 6.17.
    Lobnitz Co. Ltd: Figure 5.12.
Kelvin Marine Ltd: Figure 8.13.
Adam Knox & Sons Ltd: Figure 8.22.
W.J. & W. Lang Ltd: Figure 7.1.
W. Lind, Esq.: Figures 1.2, 5.17, 5.18, 6.8.
Lion Foundry Co. Ltd: Figures 2.14(a)-(c).
Lithgows Ltd: Figure 5.10.
Mitchell Library, Glasgow,
    Graham collection: Figure 3.12.
    North British Locomotive Co. collection: Figures 1.3, 3.9, 3.13, 3.14, 3.15, 3.16, 3.17, 3.18, 3.19, 8.2(c).
Murray & Paterson Ltd: Figure 3.21.
National Maritime Museum,
    William Denny and Bros collection: Figures 3.8, 3.15, 5.7, 5.24, 8.14(b).
North Western Museum of Science and Industry,
    Thomas Shanks collection: Figure 3.20.
William Paton Ltd: Figure 7.2.
James Picken & Sons, Figures 7.3(a) and (b).
R.Y. Pickering & Co. Ltd: Figure 3.11.
W. Ralstons Ltd: Figures 5.11(a) and (b), 5.23(a) and (b), 8.20.

Science Museum,
North British Locomotive Co. collection: Figure 8.2(a).
Scotts Shipbuilding and Engineering Co. Ltd: Figures 5.1, 5.8, 5.20(b).
Scottish Machine Tool Corporation: Figures 3.22, 8.1, 8.12.
A. and W. Smith Co. Ltd: Figures 3.3, 3.4, 3.5, 3.6, 8.8.
Smith and Wellstood Ltd: Figure 8.3.

Alexander Stephen & Sons Ltd: Figures 5.14(a) and (b).
Templeton Carpets Ltd: Figure 7.4.
The Court of the University of Glasgow: Figure 7.6.
University of Strathclyde, Department of History: Figures 1.4, 2.5, 2.6, 2.7, 2.8, 2.9, 2.12, 2.13, 3.1, 3.22, 6.22, 8.17, 8.18, 8.21 (a)-(c), 8.23, 8.24(a) and (b), 8.25.
Wilson Pipe Fittings Ltd: Figure 2.11.
Yarrow & Co. Ltd: Figures 5.15(a)-(f).

List of Illustrations

1.1 A *Royal Scot* class locomotive with a 2 foot gauge locomotive
1.2 P.S. *Rasmara* on trials
1.3 Forth Bridge under construction
1.4 Frontispiece of the catalogue of Walter Macfarlane & Co.
2.1 Foundry yard at Carron Co.
2.2 The frontispiece of a Grahamston Iron Co. catalogue
2.3 Charging a cupola at Carron Co.
2.4 Tapping a cupola at Carron Co.
2.5 Two solid-bottom cupolas
2.6 Mould for a centrifugal pump body
2.7 A ship's propeller mould
2.8 Ramming up a drysand mould
2.9 Pouring a mould
2.10 (a) Interior and (b) yard of the Stirling Foundry
2.11 Machine shop at the Barrowfield Foundry
2.12 Trade card of Walter Macfarlane & Co.
2.13 Page from the catalogue of Walter Macfarlane & Co.
2.14 Three illustrations from the catalogue of Jackson, Brown & Hudson: (a) spiral staircase, (b) urinal, and (c) iron gate and railings
2.15 40-ton casting being transported
2.16 Locomotive castings
2.17 Moulding bombs
2.18 Grinding shop
2.19 Stove fitting shop
2.20 *Kaffir* pot warehouse
3.1 Large slotting machine
3.2 Steel pithead frame
3.3 Steam driven six roller sugar cane mill
3.4 Vacuum pan, condenser, and wet vacuum pump
3.5 Historical chart of British sugar machinery manufacturing firms
3.6 Copper rum still
3.7 Two sets of triple-expansion sewage-pumping engines
3.8 Denny & Co.'s heavy machine shop
3.9 Forge at the Queen's Park Locomotive Works
3.10 Forging a hollow propeller shaft
3.11 Wood-framed side-and-end door coal wagon

3.12 Hydepark Locomotive Works, Springburn
3.13 Locomotive built by the Glasgow Railway Engineering Co.
3.14 Lady tracers at work
3.15 Bristol BE2C fighter
3.16 Whitelegg 'Baltic' locomotive
3.17 Class 15F 4-8-2 locomotive
3.18 Diesel hydraulic A1A-A1A locomotive
3.19 Modified-Fairlie locomotive
3.20 Large lathe
3.21 Heavy steam driven combined guillotine and open-ended shearing machine
3.22 Set of shell-plate bending rolls
3.23 Forth Bridge: (a) central girder on drill road and (b) Queensferry Main Pier
3.24 Duplex hydraulic pumping engine
3.25 Group of mobile hydraulic cranes
3.26 180-ton hammer-head crane
4.1 Horizontal winding engine
4.2 0-4-0 ST locomotive
4.3 No. 2 shop Caledonia foundry
4.4 Steam navvy
4.5 Piano tank locomotive
4.6 Graph of locomotive production
4.7 Graph of turnover
4.8 New boiler shop Caledonia foundry
4.9 Erecting shop Caledonia foundry
4.10 0-4-0 ST locomotive
4.11 Three compound engines
4.12 (a) Crane locomotive and (b) traction engine hauling locomotive
4.13 Erecting shop Caledonia foundry
4.14 0-6-2 and 0-4-2 T locomotives
4.15 Four standard locomotives
4.16 Group of 0-6-0 well tank locomotives
4.17 Fireless locomotive hauling trucks
4.18 Six 0-4-0 well tank locomotives
4.19 LMS locomotive
4.20 Two diesel locomotives
4.21 Steam hammer
5.1 (a) Scotts' West Burn yard, Greenock and (b) Barclay Curle's yard, Stobcross
5.2 P.S. *Margery*
5.3 Tod & MacGregor's Meadowside yard
5.4 P.S. *Persia* on the stocks
5.5 *Empress of Scotland* on trials

5.6   (a) *City of Paris* in Clydebank fitting-out basin and (b) first-class saloon of the *City of New York*
5.7   Test-tank at William Denny & Bros, Dumbarton
5.8   Sailing ship on the ways at Scotts' Cartsburn yard, Greenock
5.9   *Devonshire*
5.10   *Clan Galbraith*
5.11   (a) Launch of *Dunera* and (b) *Dunera* on trials
5.12   Dredger–*André Rebouças*–at Renfrew
5.13   Berth of the *Queen Mary* at Clydebank
5.14   (a) Mansion house at Linthouse and (b) the Linthouse shipyard with mansion house converted to offices
5.15   (a) Site of Yarrow's yard, (b) trench for wet basin at Yarrow's yard, (c) Yarrow's engineers shop under construction, (d) Yarrow's boiler shop, (e) Yarrow's wet basin, and (f) launch of the *Para* at Yarrow
5.16   *Fuerst Bismarck*
5.17   *King Edward*
5.18   *Jutlandia*
5.19   Brown-Curtis turbine at Clydebank
5.20   (a) H.M.A.S. *Australia* on the ways at Clydebank and (b) fitting the main armament to H.M.S. *Colossus*
5.21   H.M.S. *Agamemnon* at Beardmores' Dalmuir yard
5.22   (a) Artist's impression of the Fairfield yard and (b) layout drawing of the Fairfield yard
5.23   (a) Berths and (b) fitting-out basin at Harland and Wolff's Govan yard
5.24   *Robert the Bruce*
5.25   Barclay Curle's West yard
5.26   Naval craft in the Fairfield fitting-out basin
5.27   *Ivernia*
6.1   Drawing of the *Ban-Righ*
6.2   Drawing of the *Cotopaxi*
6.3   Elevation drawing of the engine of H.M.S. *Constance*
6.4   Drawing of the *Claymore*
6.5   (a) *Glen Sannox* and (b) *Duchess of Rothesay*
6.6   Triple-expansion engines at Clydebank
6.7   West yard at Clydebank
6.8   *Campania* on trials
6.9   Deck view of H.M.S. *Good Hope*
6.10   (a) The *Carmania* leaving Clydebank and (b) the turbine casings for the *Lusitania*

6.11   *Ermine* on the ways at Fairfield
6.12   Girls testing condenser tubes at Clydebank
6.13   (a) and (b) Turbines for H.M.S. *Colombo* at Fairfield
6.14   Submarine oil engines being built at Clydebank
6.15   (a) Early stage of construction of the *Montrose* at Fairfield and (b) the cabin-class dining room of the *Montrose*
6.16   H.M.S. *Hood* with 'W' and 'V' class destroyers at Clydebank
6.17   *Letitia* fitting out at Fairfield
6.18   *Queen Mary* on the ways
6.19   *Queen Mary* on trials
6.20   Clydebank fitting-out basin
6.21   *Queen Elizabeth 2* on trials
6.22   Launch of *Alisa* from Clydebank
7.1   W.J. & W. Lang's Seedhill Tannery
7.2   Group of 'Paton's angels'
7.3   Interior of the Abercorn Ropeworks
7.4   Weaving chenille axminster carpets
7.5   An advertisement for Shanks' Patent Water Closets
7.6   Lord Kelvin with a compass of his design
8.1   Advertisement for a scrap cutting machine
8.2   (a) Order for Neilson & Co. locomotive No. 123, (b) pipe work arrangement for Neilson & Co. locomotive No. 123, (c) Neilson & Co. locomotive No. 123
8.3   Smith & Wellstood's *Doric* range
8.4   Drawing of 500 gallon rum still made by W. & A. McOnie
8.5   (a)–(c) Elevations of the engines of P.S. *King Orry*
8.6   Detailed drawing of a Porter governor
8.7   *City of New York's* hull under construction at Clydebank
8.8   15-roller sugar mill at A. & W. Smith & Co. Ltd
8.9   Compound side-by-side Corliss engine
8.10   (a) Horse-drawn laundry van and (b) motor laundry van
8.11   End-milling machine
8.12   Rail-bending machine
8.13   Bergius Co. fitting shop
8.14   (a) Portable hydrauling riveting machine and (b) welders at work
8.15   Fire-brigade at Beardmore's Dalmuir yard
8.16   Semi-portable single-cylinder horizontal engine with workmen
8.17   2-6-2 tank locomotive being loaded on to a ship

8.18 Copper converter at Rio Tinto mines, Spain

8.19 Glasgow Central Station with the New Year's crowd

8.20 Erecting shop of Duncan Stewart & Co.

8.21 (a)–(c) Adam Knox's works, Glasgow

8.22 Layout drawing of Adam Knox's works

8.23 Jeffrey Bros foundry, Langholm

8.24 (a) Open sand mould and (b) machine-made moulds

8.25 Brass finisher's lathe

'Engineering has done more than war and diplomacy; it has done more than the Church and the Universities; it has done more than abstract philosophy and literature. . . . There can be nothing mean or coarse in Engineering. . . . After all, Engineering is the science of life, and of living prosperously and worthily.'

[*The opening editorial of* Engineering, *vol. 1, 1866*]

Ironfounding and
Engineering

Introduction

CHAPTER ONE

Figure 1.1 *A view from the south cantilever of the Forth Bridge taken on 2 May 1889. The Forth Bridge built by Tancred Arrol & Co. Ltd, and designed by Sir John Fowler represents the skill of Glasgow structural engineers at its best. This striking view shows the centre cantilever nearing completion. The steam crane on the the top member was used to lift steelwork into position.*

'Workshop of the British Empire' is, perhaps, an ambitious claim for the Clyde Valley, yet the ships and machinery turned out by the yards and engineering works of West-central Scotland during the late nineteenth century formed a tangible expression of the imperial idea. Bridges (Figure 1.1), piers, gas-works machinery, machine tools, sanitary appliances, and architectural ironwork from the West of Scotland poured into the markets of the Empire. Before the First World War, more than 80 per cent of the world output of sugar-crushing and refinery machinery was made in Glasgow (see page 31), 71 per cent of the locomotives produced in 1895–9 by the Glasgow locomotive builders, the largest group in Europe (Figure 1.3) (see page 4) were for overseas customers, mainly in the colonies. Most shipping companies serving imperial routes had long-standing connections with Clyde shipbuilders – from 1870 until 1913 18 per cent of the world output of ships came from the river (Figure 1.2). King George V was crowned Emperor of India at the Delhi Durbar in 1911 in a prefabricated cast-iron hall made by Walter Macfarlane's Saracen ironworks (Figure 1.4).

Figure 1.2 P.S. Rasmara *on trials in the Firth of Clyde. Made of steel by A. & J. Inglis of Pointhouse in 1890, the* Rasmara *was the last paddle steamer built for the British India Steam Navigation Co. 'B.I.', a Glasgow Company, had nearly all their vessels built on the Clyde, especially at the yard of Barclay Curle & Co., who boasted that there was always a 'B.I.' boat building in the yard. See Figures 5.11 (a) and (b), on page 95).*

Laying the Foundations

The West of Scotland became an industrial centre in the late eighteenth century. Imports of tobacco, sugar, cotton, and dyestuffs from America, India, and the West Indies were balanced by re-exports to the continent, and by exports of manufactured products, especially iron goods, boots and shoes, and cloth. In response to both continental and home demand, the cotton industry grew rapidly from about 1780, drawing its raw material from the West Indies and America and relying on cheap labour, established links with the North of England, and an existing expertise in the manufacture and merchanting of linen goods. By 1791 there were about 15 000 looms belonging to Glasgow manufacturers alone. Although most of the technology originated in England, local proficiency in building and maintaining looms, spinning machinery, water wheels, steam engines, and drive shafts was transferred readily to other branches of machine making (see pages 23, 30, 86, and 113). Significantly, the engine of the *Comet*, the first commercially viable steamship, was intended for a factory, and most of the pioneering marine engineers were trained as millwrights. Other skills required for the expansion of industry, such as shipwrighting, cartwrighting, and mining, already existed. These spread as scarcity forced wages to rise, so encouraging new entrants to these trades.

The water-power potential of Renfrewshire and other lowland counties was a precondition for the establishment of the cotton trade, and the rich mineral resources of the area eased the shift to steam power when water resources proved inadequate for expansion. Coal mining was a long-established industry, and

Figure 1.3 *A London Midland & Scottish Railway* Royal Scot *class locomotive – actually 6120 – posing outside the Queens Park Works of the North British Locomotive Co., in 1927 with a 2 foot gauge Darjeeling & Himalayan Railway locomotive in the foreground.*

Figure 1.4 *The frontispiece of the sixth edition of the catalogue of Walter Macfarlane & Co.'s Saracen Foundry, showing a 'Perspective View of Central thoroughfare with examples of architectural and sanitary castings', 1883.*

grew to meet an urban demand, which was increasingly industrial in character. Until the 1840s mining equipment was simple, apart from steam pumping engines, but, after the shallow seams had been exhausted, new techniques were developed to tap deeper reserves. Winding and hauling engines, pumps, and ventilating machinery became more sophisticated as the century advanced, and new manufacturers were attracted into the market for mining equipment (see page 68). The transport needs of the mineowners in the eighteenth century led to turnpike road construction, canal building, and the introduction of wooden waggonways on the Newcastle pattern. From the 1820s iron railways, eventually worked by locomotives, extended the boundaries of profitable coal production. These railways created a demand for locomotives manufactured by local engineering firms, a handful of which became specialists (see page 43). Coal mining resulted in the discovery of other minerals, especially ironstone and fireclay.

The demand for iron was relatively insignificant until the 1820s. Ironworks were few in number and small in scale and their products expensive in comparison with other construction materials. The availability of railway and canal transport made the large-scale exploitation of the ironstone of the Monklands area to the east of Glasgow worthwhile in the 1830s. Thereafter, further extensions of the railway network allowed more remote deposits of ironstone and coal to be worked, especially in Ayrshire. By 1850 the hot blast process had so cheapened local iron that its use became commonplace in West of Scotland shipbuilding and engineering (see page 86). Local ironstone production reached a peak in the 1870s and then declined, owing to the exhaustion of easily worked deposits and to increasing demand for low-phosphorus iron for acid steel making.

The development of steamboats after 1812 (see page 86) solved the transport problem of the sheltered Clyde estuary, with its numerous inlets. Traditional social and trading links with Ireland and North-west England encouraged local pioneers in the 1820s and 1830s to develop sea-going steamships, opening the way after 1840 for the growth of marine engineering and shipbuilding on the Clyde. Though communications within the region by rail, steamer, canal, and road were good by the 1830s, the West of Scotland was still remote from other British industrial centres. This allowed for specialization in manufacture, the development of strong ties between local firms and home and overseas customers, and the creation of an independent labour market. This position began to be eroded after the completion of rail links to England in the 1840s. Nevertheless, in the engineering and shipbuilding industries, until after the First World War, lower wages, and the availability of cheap raw materials, outweighed any technical advantage possessed by other regions, encouraging local enterprise, and attracting investment from outside the region.

The heavy industrial firms of the West of Scotland did not specialize before 1830. While traditional skills in wooden shipbuilding persisted until the 1840s, engineering techniques and products were common to most firms. The typical firm consisted of a foundry, a few simple machine tools, and an erecting shop, all controlled by a small partnership, composed of merchants supplying capital and time-served engineers. Firms commonly shared facilities for making large components. Low-pressure steam technology required engines and components which were, by later standards, massive and so circulating capital among the producers was large in proportion to fixed capital. The largest firms were invariably those producing the largest products. There was nothing corresponding to such mass production engineering industries as the small-arms manufacture of the late nineteenth century. Since much of the capital employed came from undistributed profit, nominal capital was frequently small and owned by interested individuals who did not expect high yields from their holdings and allowed the capitalization of their profits. The public company was exceptional and most firms were either partnerships, or more commonly after about 1890 private limited companies. Even after taking out limited liability, partnerships continued without formal agreement since loans and mortgages were often secured by personal guarantees provided by the former partners. In the period up to 1914 this type of management and capital structure was typical in shipbuilding and heavy engineering.

Booms and Slumps

The rapid alternations from intense economic activity to severe depression, that were characteristic of the nineteenth century, shaped the financial policy of the majority of firms. With a growing proportion of capital invested in plant, a firm's survival depended, as the century progressed, on its ability to subsist with very few orders for periods of months or even years. Manufacturers sought to avoid the worst effects of booms and slumps by assuming, directly or indirectly, the dual roles of producer and consumer (see pages 89 and 118). The risk of loss was reduced by specialization which increased profits by providing protected markets. Only in severe depressions was there much direct competition between local firms (see pages 99 and 118). During depressions creditors were frequently prepared to wait for settlement of accounts, or to allow debtors to capitalize them (see pages 70 and 118). Manufacturers, with cash in hand or effective credit, were willing to maintain a flow of orders, by providing customers with 'acceptances' – by becoming parties to bills of exchange – or by other forms of credit, sometimes for large sums. They would occasionally accept payment for products, often technically advanced, in shares (see pages 89 and 94) or part payment in obsolescent equipment. Some of the relationships built up in these ways were severed by the amalgamation of customers during the early years of this century, and by the strain of the First World War. The continued and generalized nature of the post-war depression in world trade further weakened the links both with customers and between producers in the West of Scotland's heavy industry. The artificial demand created by the Second World War and the 1950s boom delayed, until the 1960s, effective modernization of plant and rationalization of products to fit a changing pattern of international trade.

The response of companies to slumps was conditioned by their financial position. Firms with access to liquid capital or with written-down fixed capital and low overheads were able to undercut more heavily-committed competitors and take advantage of low prices to replace or extend their plant. Where firms had liquidity problems, they were vulnerable to takeover at a reduced valuation by their creditors or by firms looking for opportunities for vertical integration (see pages 75, 109, and 122). In the event of failure it was uncommon in the nineteenth century for a works to close permanently, although changes in ownership were frequent. The way out of a depression for the specialist company often appeared to be the introduction of new techniques reducing costs to either their customers or themselves (see pages 107, 119, and 125). This was sometimes achieved only to the detriment of the firm's profitability. The rapid and uneven pace of technical change posed problems as the successful introduction of new techniques by a competitor could make fixed capital valueless (see page 12). As innovation in particular specializations advanced, manufacturers, as they committed themselves to productive methods that were less versatile, ceased to be able to resort to general markets during slumps. Products for the general market were themselves altered by the effects of depressions. As competition grew stronger and linkages weaker, the necessity of reducing prices and costs caused many engineering and shipbuilding firms to introduce standard lines, which customers, although used to tailor-made products, were prepared to accept because of the price advantage.

Business trends also influenced the management structure of firms in the West of Scotland. Companies established in the early nineteenth century, though apparently managed by individual 'engineers' or 'shipbuilders', were often run by a group of senior managers with divided functions. The 'sole partner' was usually responsible for links with customers and financial management, the works manager ran the factory, and design was handled by the chief draughtsman acting in consultation with senior colleagues. Since the 1820s at least, many of the successful businessmen in the heavy industries were mainly concerned with financial management and relationships with customers. Slumps in the second half of the century changed this pattern. The need for a wider capital base resulted in larger partnerships. These required more detailed accounting, especially more comprehensive and precise balance sheets, to satisfy 'outside' partners, and revised order and design procedures, partly to meet the growing complexity of products and partly to identify areas of inefficiency. Standards of profitability and accountability which satisfied a 'sole partner' were not adequate for men familiar with the returns of joint-stock companies. Except in the large public company, the change to limited liability did not effectively disturb the balance of control, or markedly extend the capital base. The directors' freedom of action was only circumscribed by post-1911 changes in social and company legislation.

As nineteenth century slumps affected most sectors of the economy, the concomitant unemployment did not normally disperse the work force of any one company. In the knowledge that unemployment meant privation, employees were willing to accept wage reductions, which were agreed between employers and employees on a district or industry basis. Labour disputes were generally a feature of booms rather than depressions, and reflected a scarcity of skilled labour. During the First World War, because of the severe labour shortage, wage rates in all sectors rose dramatically, and enhanced expectations on the part of employees made a return to pre-war levels impractical. In the 1920s and 1930s the traditional pattern of labour relations was replaced by continuing unrest, symptomatic of an over-supply of skilled labour. The worst effects of unemployment were somewhat mitigated by social legislation. Trade Unions, though established and recognized by employers in the West of Scotland shipbuilding and engineering industries as early as the 1860s, faced during the war by a general threat to their more skilled members from dilution (the replacement of skilled by semi-skilled workers, especially women), became more aware of their power and less understanding of the difficulties of the owners and managers. The resulting bad reputation of West of Scotland heavy industry for poor labour relations reinforced other, and inherent, forces depressing the economy of the region after 1920. Recently, its significance has been over emphasized in explaining the rapid decline of the region's heavy industry, disguising and exaggerating the problems associated with the exhaustion of local mineral fields and the difficulties of rationalization.

Businessmen found it even more difficult to manage upswings in economic activity. As demand increased as a boom progressed, raw materials became scarce and expensive, delivery dates lengthened, wage rates went up, and costs and quoted prices rose in consequence. Eventually prices reached the point where few buyers could be found, labour unrest made delivery dates impossible to achieve, and the boom collapsed. These problems were exacerbated by unsatisfied demand calling into being new firms either re-using outmoded equipment, with low capital costs, or with up-to-date cost saving equipment representing the best practice of existing firms. Encouraged by rising demand, established companies frequently increased their productive capacity. The temptation was to over extend to meet demand projected on the basis of output at the peak of the boom (see pages 64, 77, 105, and 131). The pressure from demand during booms discouraged the introduction of new techniques, unless they could be readily assimilated. Other outlets were found for investing surplus income in the public sector. The multiplier effect of increased wages and profits encouraged the formation of social capital, often financed by employers, such as workers' housing schemes, town halls, schools, churches, and recreational institutes. The consequent advances in living and working conditions were seldom completely eroded by subsequent depressions.

Going Downhill

Because of the long life-expectancy of their products, shipbuilders and engineers were more aware of the inevitability of the pre-1914 trade cycle than other employers. Such awareness was helpful, as the effective management of boom conditions could provide the opportunity for the accumulation of capital reserves to withstand depressions by meeting fixed charges and retaining a nucleus of skilled workers. Unfortunately, the certainty of consistent profits during the First World War created in most firms a false sense of security that was carried forward into the post-war boom. This attitude resulted in an over-optimistic assessment of future market trends and the wholesale investment of reserves in fixed capital, leaving little liquid cash.

The First World War and the consequent over-expansion of capacity under government control to meet demands for armaments, reinforced by shrinking traditional markets and failing liquidity, exacerbated the classical nineteenth century pattern of trade cycles. This gave rise to an increased measure of government regulation and finance. The seriousness of the 1931-32 depression was, in part, a consequence of the failure of the inter-war economy to stimulate the accumulation of cash reserves. Despite a recovery between 1935 and 1958 in the cash base of most of the firms that survived the 1920s and 1930s depression, the fiscal policies of both political parties in the 1950s and 1960s has prevented any extensive return to the pre-1920 system of financing new investment. Instead of being paid for out of undistributed profits, capitalization needs are now met by loans at high rates of interest.

Post-1945 nationalization was implemented in the belief that public ownership would produce higher standards of public service and increase efficiency. This was to be achieved by rationalization, reinforced by economies of scale. Industries, like railways and coal mining, in which investment had been restricted by poor returns on capital, were to be revitalized by access to public funds. These objectives were partially realized in those industries producing a narrow range of products or services, like coal or railways, but were less successful where producer-customer links were strong. The resulting debate between the Labour and Conservative parties over the merits of nationalization, apart from the service industries, delayed the emergence of a mixed economy in Britain until the 1960s. This has been detrimental to West of Scotland heavy industry. Prolonged uncertainty in the steel and shipbuilding sectors deterred private investment, and when government support was forthcoming it tended to be motivated by short-term political considerations, over-ruling the economic value of rationalization-by-nationalization.

In the late 1950s and early 1960s a political consensus was reached favouring a collective approach to the problems of the region's heavy industries. During the first and second Wilson administrations (1964-70) a real attempt was made to encourage their rationalization by amalgamation, closures, and the national-ization of steel. Unfortunately, the attractiveness of large-scale enterprise deterred government from making aid readily available to medium-sized firms, at a time when fiscal policy was effectively denying them traditional sources of capital. The Heath government's initially severe attitude towards 'lame ducks' was tempered by the exigencies of the failure of Rolls Royce, in 1970, and Upper Clyde Shipbuilders, in 1971. The collective approach was consequently maintained. However, future prospects remain uncertain with the apparent collapse of political agreement on the mixed economy. The demand for ships and engineering products from the developing Scottish offshore oil industry may sustain the residual heavy industry in the West of Scotland; but geographically North-east England, with a better equipped steel industry, is in a stronger position to exploit this market. The future prosperity of West of Scotland heavy industry, except for those firms producing high value/low cost products, must depend on considerable cash injections or direction of orders from either the government or the EEC and, probably, the acceptance by the Trade Unions of a low-wage economy for the region.

CHAPTER TWO

Ironfounding

Although some castings were made, most of the output of the early seventeenth and eighteenth century iron-smelting plants in the West of Scotland, such as those at Bonawe and Craleckan in Argyllshire, was in the form of pig for sale in England. Early iron castings that survive in the West of Scotland, like the furnace lintels at Bonawe and Craleckan, dating from the 1750s, were made by the associated English ironworks. It is, therefore, remarkable that ironfounding was introduced on such a large scale by the incorporation of Carron Co. in 1759. Carron's initial output included plough plates, axle bushes, pots and pans, anvils, and railings. Subsequently, steam-engine cylinders, pipes, stoves, grates, sugar-boiling pans, and ordnance came to dominate production (Figure 2.1). Despite the difficulty of controlling the quality of castings, particularly for ordnance, Carron's success encouraged the growth of ironfounding and iron smelting in West-central Scotland. Muirkirk in Ayrshire (established 1787) made gearwheels and castings for textile machinery and railways, the nearby Glenbuck (established *c.* 1795) cast many of the tram plates for the Kilmarnock and Troon Railway (built in 1811), and Shotts Ironworks (established 1802)

Figure 2.1 *The foundry yard of Carron Co. c. 1870, with the 'triangle' used for lifting heavy castings. Note that this is itself made of cast-iron sections. Products of the foundry, including sugar-boiling pans and grates are visible. Note the pantiled roofs, which were common in foundry buildings, as they allowed the fumes produced during casting to escape. A few examples still survive.*

became famous for a wide range of cast goods, including architectural work. During the Napoleonic wars the casting of cannon and cannon balls absorbed almost all their production. These integrated ironworks used iron either straight from the blast furnace, or melted it in an air furnace (a reverberatory furnace) and employed moulding techniques similar in principle to those standard throughout the nineteenth century. Carron & Co. had sixteen air furnaces and three cupolas in 1792. When Devon Ironworks, Clackmannanshire, was advertised for sale in 1853 it had a 'large foundry with moulding shops'[1].

Ironfounding became a business in its own right in Scotland in the 1790s. At that time John Napier was making ordnance at his forge in Dumbarton, which had two steam engines and a blowing engine. Cannon cast in Clyde Iron Works were also bored there. The Napier family built two foundries in Glasgow at Howard Street and at Camlachie in 1802 and 1812. In 1825, *Pigot's Directory of Scotland* listed more than seventy iron foundries scattered throughout the larger Scottish towns. Glasgow had eighteen, Edinburgh five, and Ayr, Aberdeen, and Greenock three each, compared with forty-seven in London, twenty-five in Birmingham, and eighteen in Manchester. The Scottish foundries at the time made various products. Edinburgh firms made architectural castings, such as rainwater goods, railings, and lamp-posts, which can still be seen in profusion in the 'New Town' and west end of the city. The output of Glasgow foundries was largely engineering castings, especially components for steam engines, but they also turned out rainwater goods, water mains, castings for the gas industry, stoves, and columns for mills and workshops. At least thirteen of the Glasgow ironfounders listed in *Pigot* were also engineers, including such well-known names as David and Robert Napier (the sons of John Napier), James Cook, pioneer of sugar-machinery manufacture, H. & R. Baird of the Canal Foundry, and Houldsworth & Fairbairn of the Anderston Foundry. These engineering foundries made equipment which contained a high proportion of castings, like sugar mills, stationary and marine steam engines, water wheels, drive shafts for mills, and textile machinery.

Materials and Foundry Techniques

The expansion of Scottish ironfounding during the early nineteenth century not only reflected a rising demand for castings in the region, but also a fall in the price of pig iron, the principal raw material. Even at a time when its chemical constitution was unknown to the practical ironfounder, the physical properties of a particular grade of pig iron could markedly affect its saleability and price. For light castings, and other castings where detail was more important than strength, No. 1 pig iron was the best, as it had a relatively low melting point, was fluid when melted, and did not contract very much on cooling. During the nineteenth century, and later, 'Scotch No. 1' enjoyed a premium in price. In 1810, it cost £9 as against £8 per ton for No. 2. No. 1 was sometimes mixed with scrap to make a higher number iron. No. 2, harder and stronger, was used for more robust ornamental castings, and No. 3, tougher and harder still, for machine parts and products like tram plates. No. 4, the strongest grade of foundry iron, was used for heavy castings, where little machining was required, particularly for girders, bed plates, engine beams, and plain columns. Other grades of iron, collectively known as 'forge pig', were used for making wrought iron by the puddling process. No. 1 pig iron had a high carbon content and had most of this element distributed on the boundaries of the iron crystals as graphite. The weakness of the graphite layers made it fragile. The presence of other elements, especially silicon, sulphur, phosphorus, and manganese modify the properties of iron in different ways. For instance, phosphorus makes it more fluid, but harder, and manganese produces softer iron, and reduces the incidence of blowholes in castings.

The proportion of other elements depends largely on the composition of the ores from which the iron is smelted, but can be altered by smelting and remelting techniques. Smelting at low temperatures reduces the extent to which other elements are absorbed. Thus the cold blast, universally employed before 1828, tended to produce less No. 1 pig and low-phosphorus iron. The introduction of the hot blast process, invented by J. Beaumont Neilson in Glasgow in that year, raised the proportion of No. 1 pig which could be produced, reduced the quantity of fuel used per ton of iron smelted, allowed coal to be used without coking, and increased the rate of smelting in a given size of furnace. From the 1830s, partly as a result of the adoption of the hot blast process, Scottish ironmasters became the leading makers of foundry pig iron in Britain. William Baird & Co. were possibly the largest single manufacturers of foundry iron in the world. In 1876, at Gartsherrie, the principle Baird works, about 80 per cent of the output was 'No. 1 Gartsherrie', the rest being marked No. 2 and No. 3 and selling at a lower price. In the firm's thirty-seven furnaces, mostly in Ayrshire, about 300 000 tons of iron were made annually in the early 1870s, about a quarter of Scottish pig iron production. The mixing of pig irons to give superior castings developed during the nineteenth century. Mixing remained a matter of experience rather than of science. It was usual to mix No. 1 and No. 3 irons for general foundry needs. In 1900, John Sharp commented 'it is rare to employ only one kind of iron in the foundry'[2]. During the late nineteenth century, Scottish pig iron was sold in lots comprising two-fifths of No. 3 and three-fifths No. 1 iron.

The three methods of melting which had been developed by 1800 – the blast-furnace, air furnace, and cupola – produced molten iron for different purposes. The blast-furnace was little used in ironfounding except perhaps to supply very large quantities of iron for heavy, rough castings. Until the 1880s, Carron Co. used iron from the furnaces in its High Foundry for large castings like tunnel segments. Air furnaces by contrast were widely used until the invention of the cupola, supposedly by William Wilkinson, in about 1794. Thereafter they were occasionally retained for melting large quantities of iron. By 1866, in the heavy Kinning Park Foundry, Glasgow, the 50-ton air furnace was 'seldom used', four 'large' cupolas being preferred[3] (Figure 2.2). The advantage of the cupola (Figures 2.3 and 2.4) is its versatility. It can provide a steady flow of iron or a sizeable volume of metal at any one time especially if a receiver is added. Cupolas were easy to design and build (Figure 2.5) and their cheapness and simplicity allowed small foundries to develop. By 1840 there were fifty-two foundries listed in the Glasgow directory ranging from the small works, probably making rainwater goods, to the large engineering foundries. In 1849, the Hercules Foundry, Dobbies Loan, Glasgow was advertised at £1440 upset price and the large and well-equipped Camlachie Foundry at £4500[4].

Three materials for mould-making were known by the end of the eighteenth century. Loam – a mixture of sand, clay, and a fibrous material (commonly horse-dung, chopped straw or sawdust) – was used for moulding articles with circular sections like cannon, pots, sugar-boiling pans, cylinders, bells, and pipes. The normal procedure was to make a rough brick foundation, to apply a coating of moist loam and to use a revolving template to sweep out the internal shape of the mould or the external shape of the core. The finished parts of the mould then had to be dried in a stove before final assembly. Not only the moulds themselves but the cores which formed the voids in finished castings could be made from this

Figure 2.2   *The frontispiece of a Grahamston Iron Co. catalogue of c. 1880. This shows a solid-bottom cupola of large capacity, with operatives charging coke and removing molten iron in a hand shank (ladle) and a barrow ladle, modern equivalents of which are still used. The man behind the ladle holds an iron rod with a fireclay plug for stopping up the tapping hole.*

Figure 2.3 *Charging a cupola of the Carron Co. with pig iron in the 1930s. The sand-cast pig would have been made by the company.*

Figure 2.4 *(Right)* *Tapping a cupola of the Carron Co. in the 1930s, with a barrow ladle very similar to the Grahamston Iron Co. specimen in Figure 2.2.*

Figure 2.5 *(Far right)* *Two old solid-bottom cupolas in a Border foundry, now disused. Note the similarity between these and that in Figure 2.2, on page 14; brick tops are now uncommon. (Photograph taken in 1971.)*

easily-worked material (Figure 2.6). In a mould for a large hollow object, the loam-coated brick core gives as the metal contracts on cooling, preventing the cracking and distortion of the casting. Loam moulding obviated the need for expensive wooden patterns, and for large castings of special types still has advantages. It is used for making ships' propellers (Figure 2.7) and large chemical reaction vessels which are to be enamelled or rubber lined. Similarly, drysand – a sand-clay mixture moulded when moist and dried in a stove – can be used to make moulds without patterns, as it is plastic enough to be worked with a trowel or other tools. It is particularly suitable for large castings, as it needs little skill to ram (pack) the sand in the mould (Figure 2.8) and the finished mould can resist the wash and weight of large volumes of molten iron. It has been largely superseded in recent years by artificially hardened sands which do not require to be dried in stoves. In 1866, the Kinning Park Foundry in Glasgow had nine drying stoves varying from 24 to 30 feet in length and 8 to 20 feet in width, provided with rails and carriages for moving moulds and cores weighing up to 20 tons.

The majority of castings have been made, at least since the early nineteenth century, in greensand moulds. Greensand is not green in colour, but green in the sense of being unbaked or unfired. It consists of a mixture of sand with coal dust and a little water. The coal dust at the surface of the mould burns as it comes in contact with the molten metal, producing a thin layer of gas which prevents the iron flowing in between the particles of sand, leaving a fine finish. Blacking – a suspension of finely-ground carbon in water or an inflammable solvent – is frequently applied to the inside surface of the mould to give the same effect. To be successful a greensand mould has to be carefully rammed. If the sand is compacted too much, the gases produced during casting do not diffuse through the sand and the metal may blow out of the mould while it is being poured (Figure 2.9). If it is not compacted enough, the pressure of metal may distort the

Figure 2.6 *(Above left) A mould in preparation in 1971 for a centrifugal pump body showing the cores, which determine the volume and position of the voids in the finished casting.*

Figure 2.7 *(Above right) A mould for a cast-iron propeller in Strang's foundry, Hurlford, near Kilmarnock, in 1971. The blades are moulded separately using guided formers. The mould is supported by bricks covered in loam.*

16

Figure 2.8 *Ramming up a drysand mould in the Chapel Street, Airdrie, foundry of William Martyn & Co., in 1971. The drying stove is in the background.*

Figure 2.9 *Pouring a large mould. The man on the left is tilting the ladle, while the one on the right is controlling the overhead crane from which the ladle is suspended. (Photograph taken in 1971.)*

(a)

(b)

Figure 2.10 *Two views of the Stirling Foundry of James Davie & Son, c. 1900. (a) shows the interior of the moulding shop with wooden 'foundry' cranes, one in operation on the right, and moulders at work on the left. Note the fluted columns supporting the roof – an unusual touch of elegance. (b) shows the yard with some typical products including pipes, lamp-posts, and one of the columns for the Scottish Co-operative Wholesale Society's Shieldhall Works, Glasgow. Pantile roofs are again in evidence.*

mould or the metal may percolate through the sand giving the casting a hard skin, which is difficult to machine. Greensand moulding is a highly skilled occupation and the failure rate of hand-made moulds is comparatively high. This encouraged the introduction of moulding machines, which reduced the labour involved, increased the speed of the process, and provided more reliable moulds. Machine moulding was developed in the late nineteenth century, and is particularly applicable to the mass-production of, for example, sewing machine and textile machinery components, and gas, and later electric, cooker parts. J. & T. Boyd, spinning machinery makers in Shettleston, mechanized their foundry in the 1890s.

18

Figure 2.11 *View of the machine shop at the Barrowfield Foundry, Glasgow, of Wilson's Pipe Fittings in the 1930s. This was one of the smaller pipe foundries. The firm moved to Irvine in the 1960s and still specializes in marine pipe work.*

Specialization

It is hard (through lack of information (see page 27)) to document the growth of specialization in the foundry industry in the West of Scotland. From about 1810 the links between smelting, engineering, and ironfounding were gradually loosened, though the Shotts Iron Co. and Carron Co. retained engineering foundries in association with blast furnaces until 1947 and 1963 respectively. By the 1850s, as well as a number of general foundries of varying sizes (Figure 2.10), there were already specialist firms, particularly for pipe and architectural work. In the second half of the nineteenth century the largest tonnage of castings made in the West of Scotland was in the form of pipes (Figure 2.11). The majority of these were for supplying water, but some were for gas supply and sewage schemes. Among the early pipe founders was Robert Napier, who made pipes for the Glasgow Water Company at his Camlachie Foundry in the 1820s. Until 1840, when D.Y. Stewart of Montrose patented a pipe-moulding machine, all pipes were hand moulded. Stewart moved to Glasgow in the following year to set up a pipe works, and during the next thirty years ten firms in the city became

19

specialist producers. Thousands of tons of their products were exported all over the world. In 1876, the largest firms, Thomas Edington & Sons and R. Laidlaw & Son, could turn out over 2000 tons of finished pipes a month and it was reckoned that Glasgow 'might be regarded as the headquarters of this branch of the iron trades'[5]. The total annual capacity of the industry was reckoned to be about 120 000 tons. In 1877, McFarlane, Strang & Co., a newcomer to the pipe-founding industry, set up works beside the Forth and Clyde canal. By 1888, the firm employed nearly 1000 men and had 'executed contracts for the largest sizes of pipes (4 feet internal diameter), in tonnages up to 50 000 for British, Colonial, and Foreign markets'[6]. Large contracts were sometimes tendered for jointly. In the 1870s, an 80 000 ton order for Rio de Janeiro, worth about £1 million on delivery, was shared amongst the three largest firms. Shaw & McInnes of Firhill Iron Works, established in 1858, is the only Glasgow firm still making pipes. The firm now concentrates on special pipe fittings.

Architectural ironfounding in the West of Scotland was begun as a separate speciality in 1850 by Walter Macfarlane at his Saracen Lane Foundry off the Gallowgate in Glasgow. The foundry moved to Washington Street in 1862 (Figure 2.12) and then to a green-field site at Possilpark, which covered seven and a half acres in 1876 and fourteen in 1891. By then the company employed over 1200 men and its catalogue of about 2000 quarto pages contained

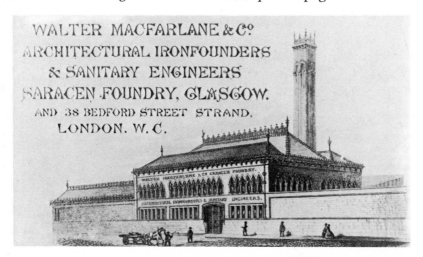

Figure 2.12 *A trade card of the famous firm of architectural ironfounders, Walter Macfarlane & Co., showing their Washington Street foundry in the 1850s. The Gothic architecture was highly regarded by contemporaries.*

Figure 2.13 *A page from the 1883 catalogue of the architectural ironfounders, Walter Macfarlane & Co., illustrating 'the application of Ironwork to Public Interiors, Halls, Museums, Libraries, Saloons, Banks, etc.'*

Figure 2.14 *Three illustrations from the first catalogue (c. 1885) of Jackson, Brown & Hudson, Lion Foundry, Kirkintilloch. (a) Shows a spiral staircase, built up from standard sections round a central column. (The foundry still makes simplified staircases of this type.) (b) A urinal, typical of the period. (A few examples still survive.) (c) An iron gate and railings, one of a wide range of standard designs made for local builders. Most of these were removed for scrap during the last war.*

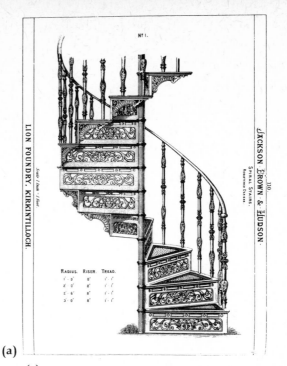

(a)

(b)

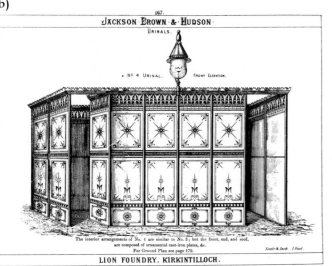

(c)

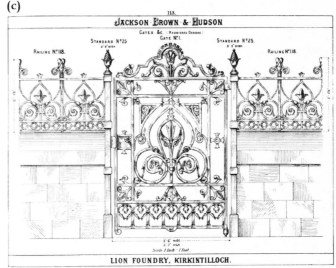

illustrations of 6000 products (Figure 2.13). As early as 1876 John Mayer commented: 'Macfarlane's castings are favourably known in every civilized nation in the world'[7]. Walter Macfarlane had several imitators and by 1876 it could be confidently stated that 'the manufacture [of architectural and sanitary castings] has become quite a feature of the iron industries of Glasgow'[7]. The most notable was George Smith & Co.'s Sun Foundry, which made sanitary apparatus (see Figure 7.5, on page 149) as well as a wide range of ornamental and architectural castings. Many of this firm's products can still be seen in the streets of most towns in the West of Scotland. In the 1880s, Kirkintilloch became a centre of the industry with the establishment of the Star and Lion Foundries. The first partners in the Lion Foundry were three of Walter Macfarlane's foremen and much of their early work closely resembled that of the Saracen Foundry (Figure 2.14). Several of the smaller general foundries of central Scotland made rainwater and ornamental goods.

40 Tons.
FROM.
FULLERTON. HODGART. & BARCLAY.
LIMITED.
PAISLEY.

40 TONS.

Figure 2.15 *A 40-ton casting for a machine bedplate being removed from Fullerton, Hodgart & Barclay's Vulcan Foundry, Paisley, c. 1900, by two traction engines. This was about the largest casting the firm could make.*

Figure 2.16 *A posed display of locomotive castings in the foundry yard at the Caledonia Foundry of Andrew Barclay Sons & Co., Kilmarnock (see Chapter 4), c. 1905. From left to right are: driving wheel centres, smokebox saddles, chimneys, brake blocks, steam pipes, axleboxes, cylinders, and sandboxes. This firm still operates a foundry.*

Some of the largest castings made by the combined engineering/ironfounding firms were for the low-pressure side-lever engines for the last and largest transatlantic paddle steamers of the 1850s. With the introduction of the compound engine after 1854 (see page 114), cylinder castings became more complex and engine builders began to rely on outside suppliers. This encouraged the separation of engineering and ironfounding, 'the tendency of this specialization [being] undoubtedly to produce better goods, and at a more economical rate'[8]. By 1876, there were about six independent heavy foundries in Glasgow making castings for sugar machinery, tanks and pans, retorts, parts for marine engines, gearing, machine tool bedplates (Figure 2.15), and bridge castings. Some engineering firms, like the Fairfield Shipbuilding and Engineering Co. and the North British Locomotive Co., even if they bought in castings that were difficult to make, continued to operate their own foundries, in several cases until the 1960s (Figure 2.16).

Ironfounding in Decline

The Scottish ironfounding industry declined from the 1890s with the disappearance of cheap pig iron as native resources of iron ore were exhausted. The First World War (Figures 2.17 to 2.20) was a watershed in this, as in so many other branches of industry, in the region; rising wages and raw material costs, and foreign competition, all contributed to the industry's difficulties. Pig iron, which averaged about £3 per ton in 1914, had risen to £10–£11 in 1920, and real

Figure 2.17 *An uncanny sight. Bombs being moulded in one of Carron Co.'s foundries during the 1914–18 war. The spherical objects are the cores, which had been dried in the movable core ovens in the right background. The cavities and, hence the cores, had to be absolutely smooth to prevent the premature explosion of the charge.*

Figure 2.18 *The grinding shop of the Falkirk Iron Works, in 1911, where castings were finished by hand.*

wages had risen by 200 to 300 per cent. Erosion of traditional markets was mentioned in the *Glasgow Herald* supplement on shipbuilding, engineering, and commerce in 1917. Commenting on the fortunes of the cast-iron pipe industry, in which Glasgow's position had been distinguished, with more than 50 per cent of U.K. output in 1907, the paper referred to the loss of export orders to other suppliers owing to restrictions imposed by the Ministry of Munitions, high transport charges, and infrequent sailings. This speciality never recovered, while architectural and ornamental ironfounding declined with changing architectural taste reinforced by the low level of building activity in the 1920s. Some foundries made brave attempts to adjust to the new aesthetic criteria by producing cast-iron building-front panels. Similarly, the fortunes of the engineering castings industry slumped with the general decline in the level of industrial activity. There was an element of substitution, which became more important after the Second World War, in which steel castings, and more significantly welded-steel fabrications, replaced iron castings. Men who should know say that the level of skill in moulding deteriorated, particularly after the last war.

Reactions to changing circumstances varied widely. One approach was to form a restrictive trade association. The National Light Castings Association was set up in 1912 with the typical pattern of production quotas and price fixing. The Scottish Ironfounders' Association was a similar grouping for machinery castings, and there were other specialized associations, such as the Garden Roller

Figure 2.19   *The stove fitting shop, of the Falkirk Iron Works, in 1911, with enamelled stoves at various stages of assembly.*

Figure 2.20   *A corner of the 'Kaffir' pot warehouse of the Falkirk Iron Works, in 1911. The pots were stored here before despatch, mainly to Africa and the Middle East.*

Association. More formal links came with the setting up of Allied Ironfounders in 1929, and of Federated Foundries in 1935, and in recent years many of the surviving firms have been incorporated in the Glynwed group. In each of these cases a degree of rationalization and modernization followed amalgamation. In a very few instances, especially in larger integrated firms, in which the foundry was an adjunct to some branch of engineering, rising fixed costs were countered by building new foundries, with improved mechanical handling or mechanized moulding (see Figure 8.24 (b), on page 175). Owing to the nature of their work, some firms, like J. & T. Boyd of Shettleston and the Singer Manufacturing Co., had introduced mechanical moulding before the war, but G. & J. Weir's Argus Foundry at Thornliebank, and Harland & Wolff's gigantic Clyde Foundry in Govan were different in concept. In the event the full potential of the Argus Foundry was not realized owing to friction with the unions, and the Clyde Foundry was rarely used to capacity as the demand for marine engine castings never met that anticipated in the first flush of the post-1918 boom. Another response was the setting up of small foundries. The simple techniques and low fixed-capital requirements of the ironfounding industry at its most basic level have always made entry into the industry easy, and there has always been a place for the small firm with low overheads. This is still the case to-day, for example, a tiny foundry set up in a row of converted cottages near Dalry in Ayrshire in the late 1960s is a flourishing small-scale business.

In the face of altered conditions, some companies modified their products. The stove and domestic range firms radically changed their designs from the inter-war period, introducing slow-burning, enclosed cookers and stoves with vitreous enamel finishes. The Lion Foundry turned to making Post Office and engineering castings, while Robert MacLaren & Co., pipe founders, began making thermostats. Price cutting and competition, resulting from the dwindling market for cast-iron products, has induced engineering firms to close their own foundries and put out work to specialist firms.

The Scottish ironfounding industry in recent years has, however, retained much of its variety. Of the fifty or so foundries active in the West of Scotland and in the Falkirk area *circa* 1970, about a quarter were tied foundries operating in more or less close association with engineering firms. Another quarter were specialist foundries on a large scale, using mechanized moulding and pouring to mass-produce relatively small castings. The remaining half were independent small and medium-sized firms, varying widely in techniques and output. These groups were not clearly-defined, as some firms in the first category made castings for sale, while firms in the second group produced 'fitted' goods like stoves. The position of the industry has changed rapidly since 1970. No fewer than nine foundries have closed in the last five years.

CHAPTER THREE

Engineering

The origins of engineering in the West of Scotland are obscure, but are closely linked with those of the ironfounding and iron smelting industries. The early Newcomen engines in Scotland were almost certainly made by English craftsmen, and the English-financed blast furnaces at Bonawe and Craleckan, built in the early 1750s, have marked resemblances to contemporary English examples. There were, however, indigenous traditions of millwrighting and clockmaking (gear cutting) which threw up several of the West of Scotland engineering pioneers.

The Basic Skills

Clockmakers were needed to build the water frames and mules used for cotton spinning from *c.* 1780, and most of the early cotton mill proprietors employed their own technicians (see page 68). In 1795, there were twelve clockmakers, twenty smiths, nine millwrights, nineteen joiners, ten turners, and fifteen hammermen at New Lanark, the famous cotton mill of David Dale and Robert Owen. James Smith, manager of James Finlay & Co.'s Deanston Mill, Perthshire, as late as the 1820s and 1830s enjoyed a reputation as a mule-builder and general millwright, until his employers objected to the work he did for other cotton firms. His most notable work was the 70 feet 2 inch diameter waterwheel built in 1841 for the Shaws Water Cotton Spinning Co., Greenock, one of the largest waterwheels ever constructed, developing 192 horsepower at 75 per cent efficiency.

When iron and steel replaced wood as a material for building textile machinery, parts such as frames could easily be made from wooden patterns by casting, instead of individually by joiners. The planes, metal-turning lathes, and drills necessary to work the metal parts of textile machinery were, however, expensive and scarce, making it desirable to concentrate production in one place. This stimulated the millwrights to set up their own independent factories, entirely devoted to making machinery. By the early years of the nineteenth century, William Dunn of Duntocher had opened a specialist textile machine factory in Glasgow and others, most notably the Houldsworths, set up works to supply such machinery in general. However, in the face of competition from Lancashire firms, West of Scotland engineers stopped making spinning machinery in the 1860s and as a result, the Houldsworths' Anderston Foundry, in common with a number of other firms, began to build power looms. The specialist textile engineering firms never completely dominated local markets; Templetons, the carpet weavers, continued to make their own looms (see Figure 7.6, on page 150) and other machinery until the 1960s.

From the late seventeenth century the millwright craft in the West of Scotland developed from the work of constructing gearing and waterwheels for corn mills. By the end of the eighteenth century millwrights were making much larger waterwheels for cotton and flax mills, with more complex transmission systems, as at New Lanark, where each of the original mills had three waterwheels, driving two vertical shafts, with horizontal shafts on each of five floors to drive the water frames and their associated machinery. These men were also making wooden machinery for bleaching, dyeing, and calico printing. During the early 1800s the expansion of industry in the West of Scotland attracted millwrights from the east, where the skill had developed more widely in response to the demands of the linen industry. David Elder, whose family were millwrights in Fife, was perhaps the greatest of the West of Scotland millwright/engineers. He worked in Paisley and Glasgow before becoming Robert Napier's manager at Camlachie Foundry in 1821, where he continued as a millwright until after the 1840s when marine engineering became the dominant part of the business. As with other and more famous engineers such as Maudslay, Clement, and Nasmyth, he developed machine tools to suit the products of the firm (Figure 3.1).

Figure 3.1 *A large slotting machine, known as* Jumbo, *buil about 1840, in Robert Napier's Lancefield Engine Works. This was almost certainly designed b David Elder. The design of the frame castings is unusual by lat standards. Note the gallery workshop in the background, a typical feature of marine engine works of the mid-nineteenth century.*

Millwrighting remained a significant industry in its own right in the region until the mid-1850s. Randolph, Elliot & Co., the millwright firm in which David Elder's son, John bought a partnership in 1852,was founded in 1834 by Charles Randolph, born in Stirling. Randolph was educated in Glasgow University and the Andersonian University before serving his apprenticeship with Robert Napier at Camlachie and Lancefield. After a period in Manchester, where he worked in two millwright shops, he set up his own works in Glasgow, and developed an extensive practice in Glasgow, Selkirkshire, and Dundee. After John Elliot joined Randolph in 1839, the business was extended to Northern Ireland. In the 1840s 'for a considerable period the greater part of the millwright work done in Scotland was done in [their works]'[1].

West of Scotland firms did not, however, have a monopoly of local trade. When the Finlay cotton mills were modernized in the 1820s, James Smith was responsible for refurbishing the Deanston Mills but the two great waterwheels at Catrine Mills in Ayrshire were designed by Sir William Fairbairn, who at that time was working in Manchester. Even where the original machinery was bought from outside West-central Scotland, components and replacement parts were often cheaper if made locally, largely because of the high transport costs. The Boulton and Watt engines installed in the West of Scotland usually incorporated many parts made in the region.

From 1759 onwards the introduction of coke-smelting to the iron industry of West-central Scotland had important implications for local engineering. Coke-smelting made more pig iron available, but, in doing so, used up more iron ore and coal which in turn placed a heavier demand on the mining industry, encouraging engineers to develop mining machinery (Figure 3.2)—particularly water or steam powered pumps and winding engines (see page 69). William Symington, pioneer of steam navigation, built a number of pumping engines, at

Figure 3.2   The trial erection of ... steel pithead frame for Ramsay ...t, in Midlothian, at the works ... the Blantyre Engineering Co. ...d, c. 1930. In the background ... a typical cupola.

least one of which was installed at a lead mine in Wanlockhead, Lanarkshire. In the 1760s, John Roebuck, a partner in Carron Co., employed James Watt on his own behalf, and the Company itself retained John Smeaton, the leading engineer of his day, to invent new mining equipment, particularly pumping engines. The routine maintenance and repair of these new mining machines by local millwrights helped the understanding of the techniques of their construction to spread quickly through the region. The fact that eight engineers were involved in the construction of the first thirty-eight marine engines in Glasgow during the 1810s suggests that the techniques and the means of producing steam engines were becoming familiar in the city. By the 1820s and 1830s they were being used regularly in 'manufactories, collieries, stone quarries, and steam boats', according to James Cleland, a Glasgow statistician, in *The Annals of Glasgow*. In 1825, he estimated that there were 242 land engines operating in the Glasgow district and 68 engines in steam boats, compared with 75 and 28 respectively in 1819. There were 290 land engines in the London area in 1827. At the Muirkirk Ironworks, a medium-sized concern for the 1830s and 1840s, there were in 1834 fifteen engines ranging from $3\frac{1}{2}$ to 90 horsepower; of these eight were of the Watt-type, with separate condensers, the remainder being atmospheric.

The Manufacture of Sugar Machinery

Although the expansion of coal mining and iron smelting in the central belt of Scotland during the middle years of the nineteenth century created a market for blowing engines, winding engines, and pumps, the biggest markets for locally-made steam engines were sugar factories and ship yards. The manufacture of sugar machinery grew out of the strong trading ties between Glasgow merchants and sugar planters in the West Indies. James Cook, founder of the industry in Glasgow, was a Fife millwright. He moved to Glasgow in 1788 and continued in the same business. It is likely that it was he who bought a steam engine from Boulton & Watt in 1800 for a flax mill in Glasgow, and he may well have used this as a pattern for the steam-powered sugar mills he began building in his new works, which opened in 1805. At first he was a general engineer, making spinning machinery, and mill engines, and, from 1816, twenty early marine engines, but 'the demand for sugar machinery became so pressing that he gradually dropped all other work and confined himself solely to this speciality'[2]. His engines, all of the Watt type, drove three-roller mills which extracted about 50 per cent of the juice from the sugar cane. The juice was then evaporated in open cast-iron pans of the type made by Carron Co. until the late nineteenth century (see Figure 2.1, on page 11). The firm of Neilson & Co., better known as locomotive builders, began to make sugar machinery in 1845 with an order secured from 'a friend . . . in the Isle of Cuba'[2].

More significant for the growth of the sugar-machinery industry in Glasgow was the formation in 1840 of the firm of P. and W. McOnie. Peter McOnie had been foreman in the general engineering firm of Stark & Fulton in Anderston and

Figure 3.3 A steam-driven six-roller sugar cane mill made by A. & W. Smith & Co. Ltd, at their Eglinton Engine Works, Glasgow, in 1912, The simple single-cylinder slide-valve engine is typical of the products of the firm at this period.

when that firm was bankrupted in 1840, 'he wrote to a friend who was engineer of a number of sugar estates in the Island of Trinidad'[3] seeking work there. The friend suggested that McOnie would do better to set up a workshop in Glasgow to repair sugar machinery and supply spares. He rapidly built up a repair business in partnership with his brother, undercutting David Cook & Co. (successors to James Cook), before starting on new construction with an order for a mill for Stirling & Gordon, West India merchants. By 1848, P. and W. McOnie had turned out fifty engines and fifty mills. The firm then changed its name to McOnie & Mirrlees, which itself became the parent of a number of firms. In 1851, W. and A. McOnie was formed by Andrew McOnie, younger brother of Peter, disappointed in his aim of becoming a partner in McOnie & Mirrlees, and William, Peter's former partner. W. & A. McOnie, between 1851 and 1876, built 820 steam engines, 1650 sugar mills (Figure 3.3 and see also Figure 8.12, on page 166), 1200 steam boilers, 117 waterwheels, and 169 evaporating pans (Figure 3.4) mainly for Mauritius, Brazil, and Java. The great number of mills produced reflects the multiplicity of sugar plantations—in the mid-1860s, there were 1600 in Cuba alone. The value of the Glasgow sugar machinery trade was estimated in 1876 as 'upwards of £400 000 per annum'[4]. By that time demand from the traditional West Indian markets was declining, and that from the developing sugar growing areas in the Far East and Southern Africa was rising. The expertise gained by West of Scotland makers, through long experience, was a significant factor in selling: 'As a rule, where the competitors meet on equal terms, speaking in a general sense, the race of competition is almost certain to terminate in favour of the Glasgow engineers'[5]. Robert Mallet, commenting on the sugar mills and engines displayed in the 1862 International Exhibition by Mirrlees & Tait and W. & A. McOnie, hinted at another reason for success: 'Metal has not been spared either in engine or sugar mill . . . The natural profusion of coal and of cheap but weak cast-iron in the Scottish coal fields have

produced generally two unfortunate results in the works of Scotland's engine builders – inattention to the best means of economizing fuel, and a lavish introduction of quantity rather than attention to quality of their cast-iron framing, though we excepted these exhibits from these strictures'[6]. By 1876 these criticisms had been taken to heart by Mirrlees, Tait & Watson (as the firm had become); they had then been making engines with Corliss valve gear for eight years, and an engine and mill made by the firm on view at the Philadelphia Centennial Exhibition was attracting attention 'on account of the improved details of construction, and more especially on account of the manner in which the heavy spur-wheels and flywheels are made in segments, all by machine tools, and without any hand fitting'[4].

As can be seen from Figure 3.5, most of the sugar machinery-making firms were related in some respect. There were other linkages between firms, however, which are not shown in this diagram. A. & W. Smith & Co. (Figure 3.6),

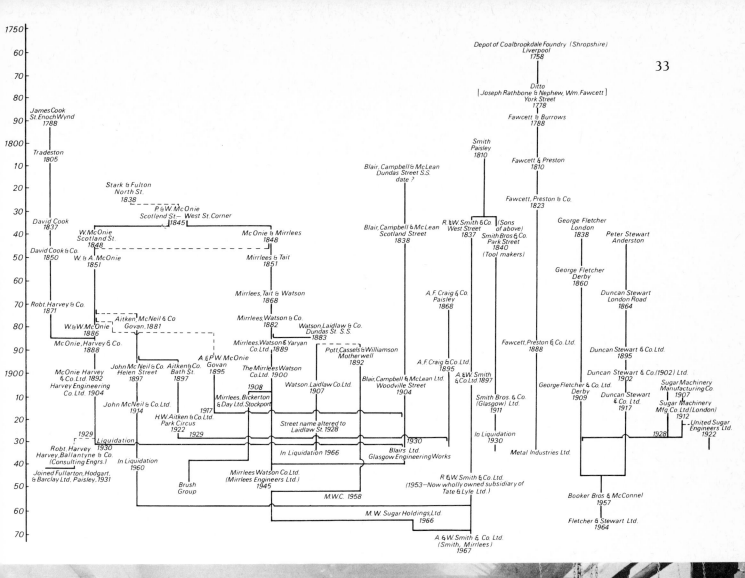

Left time axis:
1750 · 60 · 70 · 80 · 90 · 1800 · 10 · 20 · 30 · 40 · 50 · 60 · 70 · 80 · 90 · 1900 · 10 · 20 · 30 · 40 · 50 · 60 · 70

James Cook
St. Enoch Wynd
1788

Tradeston
1805

David Cook
1837

David Cook & Co.
1850

Robt. Harvey & Co.
1871

Stark & Fulton
North St.
1838

P & W. McOnie
Scotland St— West St. Corner
1845

W. McOnie
Scotland St.
1848

W. & A. McOnie
1851

W. & W. McOnie
1886

McOnie, Harvey & Co.
1888

McOnie Harvey
& Co. Ltd. 1892
Harvey Engineering
Co. Ltd. 1904

Aitken, McNeil & Co
Govan, 1881

John McNeil & Co.
Helen Street
1897

John McNeil & Co. Ltd.
1914

1929

Robt. Harvey
Harvey, Ballantyne & Co.
(Consulting Engrs.)

Joined Fullarton, Hodgart,
& Barclay Ltd. Paisley, 1931

In Liquidation
1960

Liquidation
1930

Aitken & Co.
Bath St.
1897

H.W. Aitken & Co. Ltd.
Park Circus
1922

1929

Brush
Group

McOnie & Mirrlees
1848

Mirrlees & Tait
1851

Mirrlees, Tait & Watson
1868

Mirrlees, Watson & Co.
1882

Mirrlees, Watson & Yaryan
Co. Ltd. 1889

A & P W. McOnie
Govan
1895

The Mirrlees Watson
Co. Ltd. 1900

1908

Mirrlees, Bickerton
& Day Ltd. Stockport
1917

Watson, Laidlaw & Co.
Dundas St. S.S.
1883

Watson, Laidlaw Co. Ltd.
1907

Street name altered to
Laidlaw St. 1928

In Liquidation 1966

Mirrlees Watson Co. Ltd.
(Mirrlees Engineers Ltd.)
1945

M.W.C. 1958

M.W. Sugar Holdings, Ltd.
1966

Pott, Cassels & Williamson
Motherwell
1892

Blair, Campbell & McLean
Dundas Street S.S.
date?

Blair, Campbell & McLean
Scotland Street
1838

Blair, Campbell & McLean Ltd.
Woodville Street
1904

1930

Blairs Ltd.
Glasgow Engineering Works

A.F. Craig & Co.
Paisley
1868

A.F. Craig & Co. Ltd.
1895

R. & W. Smith & Co.
West Street
1837

Smith Bros & Co.
Park Street
1840
(Tool makers)

A. & W. Smith
& Co. Ltd. 1897

Smith Bros. & Co.
(Glasgow) Ltd.
1911

In Liquidation
1930

Metal Industries Ltd.

R & W. Smith & Co. Ltd.
(1953—Now wholly owned subsidiary of
Tate & Lyle Ltd.)

A. & W. Smith & Co. Ltd.
(Smith, Mirrlees)
1967

Depot of Coalbrookdale Foundry (Shropshire)
Liverpool
1758

Ditto
[Joseph Rathbone & Nephew, Wm. Fawcett]
York Street
1778

Fawcett & Burrows
1788

Smith
Paisley
1810

Fawcett & Preston
1810

R. & W. Smith & Co. (Sons
of above)

Fawcett, Preston & Co.
1823

George Fletcher
London
1838

Peter Stewart
Anderston

George Fletcher
Derby
1860

Duncan Stewart
London Road
1864

Fawcett, Preston & Co. Ltd.
1888

Duncan Stewart & Co. Ltd.
1895

Duncan Stewart & Co. (1902) Ltd.
1902

George Fletcher & Co. Ltd.
Derby
1909

Duncan Stewart
& Co. Ltd.
1917

Sugar Machinery
Manufacturing Co.
1907

Sugar Machinery
Mfg. Co. Ltd (London)
1912

United Sugar
Engineers Ltd.
1922

1928

Booker Bros & McConnel
1957

Fletcher & Stewart Ltd.
1964

A. & W. SMITH & Co. Ltd.
ENGINEERS
GLASGOW.

now the only sugar machinery makers in Scotland, were introduced to the trade by W. & A. McOnie, who subcontracted cattle-driven sugar mills to them. Despite the growing specialization of sugar-machinery makers during the later decades of the nineteenth century, most firms retained links with the general heavy engineering industries of the region. A few firms, noted for sugar machinery, remained essentially general engineers. Duncan Stewart, after serving an apprenticeship as a calico printer's engineer, went to the West Indies as engineer on the sugar estates of the calico printer, returning in 1844 to set up a works in the east end of Glasgow. Though the firm was well-known for its sugar machinery, it was really a general engineering concern making land and marine engines, pumping machinery, dyeing and bleaching apparatus, hydraulic appliances, and, from the 1890s, steel works plant, especially rolling mill engines (see Figure 8.20, on page 171). This relationship with general engineering allowed firms to form links with subspecialists, to subcontract in times of heavy demand, and to take in work during slack periods. In 1883, the partners in Mirrlees, Watson & Co., formed Watson, Laidlaw & Co., to build centrifugal separators. During the 1860s, W. & A. McOnie subcontracted items like boilers, stills, and specialized brass castings required in the execution of sugar factory contracts. Similarly, in the depression in the mid-1880s, Mirrlees, Watson & Co., were making components for several Glasgow sugar-machinery manufacturers and general engineers. With the increasing size of sugar factories towards the end of the nineteenth century, subcontract links became stronger. Earlier factories had been circumscribed by the size of individual plantations, themselves limited by the problems of the transport of cane to the mill for crushing, and the difficulty of producing mills capable of crushing on a large scale. (Cane has to be crushed quickly after cutting, otherwise sugar is lost by fermentation.) Once these problems had been overcome by the building of light railways and technical innovations in mill construction, the large central factory, serving a whole district, became standard. A. & W. Smith & Co. Ltd, were contracting for factories at about £90–100 000 each just before the First World War. Orders on this scale were managed in much the same way as shipbuilding contracts, with extensive subcontracting, progress payments, and payment on occasion in shares of the sugar company.

The development of sugar-machinery manufacture can be characterized by the initial perception of demand, the creation of manufacturing and repairing capacity, and the growth of the market, channelled at first by ties of friendship and kinship to Glasgow firms. These ties resulted in the efficient transmission of ideas on improvement from users to makers, helping to create that expertise which was one of the keys to success. The ascendancy of Glasgow makers in overseas markets in the second half of the nineteenth century, when about 80 per cent of the world production of sugar machines was made in the West of Scotland, depended on the low cost of iron and coal in the region, as sugar mills and their driving engines contain large quantities of iron. The author of the 1876 British Association handbook could confidently state that in sugar machinery manufacture 'Glasgow is certainly far ahead of any other British manufacturing city'[5] and in 1896 the magazine *Engineering* commented: 'Probably no colonial industry, not even excepting mining, and certainly none concerned with a food product, has called for so great a weight of machinery as the manufacture of cane sugar; and it is safe to say that no manufacturing centre has provided so large a proportion of that weight of machinery as the commercial capital of Scotland'[7]. The same correspondent noted that Mirrlees, Watson & Yaryan's share of the 1878–84 boom, when trade advanced by 'leaps and bounds', was 45 000 tons of machinery, worth about £1 500 000.

In the face of competition from other British manufacturing centres, and from abroad, the maintenance of this lead was not easy. Firms held on by regularly modernizing and extending their premises. In 1876, Mirrlees, Tait & Watson's Scotland Street Ironworks was described: 'as one of the most splendid and completely equipped engineering establishments in the kingdom, giving employment when in full work to about 800 workmen'[8]. By 1896, the firm had added a foundry, capable of casting 100 tons per day, and several large new machine tools, and had recently erected, 'a large experimental house, intended for the practical testing of their evaporating apparatus before shipment, and for general experimental work'[9]. The leading firms quickly adopted improvements. Inventions introduced from Europe and America included Corliss valve gear for mill engines, Bour and Wetzell evaporating pans, the Weston centrifugal separator (for which Mirrlees, Tait & Watson held the sole rights for the United Kingdom and the principal sugar-cane countries), the Yaryan evaporator (which proved unsuccessful in sugar manufacture, though most successful for desalination of sea water and for glue manufacture), and the Diesel engine, for which Mirrlees, Watson & Yaryan took out an exclusive licence in 1897. Difficulties encountered in manufacturing Diesel engines under this licence led to its sale back to Maschinenfabrik Augsburg Nuremburg in 1899, though the firm retained a non-exclusive licence. Meanwhile in Glasgow, Duncan Stewart patented hydraulic attachments for sugar mills which were widely adopted. A spring toggle designed as a 'safety valve' for crushing mills was patented by J. G. Hudson, a partner in Mirrlees, Watson & Yaryan. In 1890, and again in 1909, the board of A. & W. Smith & Co. Ltd, agreed to pay 50 per cent of the royalty on his patent sugar-mill roller to their works manager, Mr Mackie. The cumulative effects of such relatively minor improvements could be considerable. In 1816, James Cook's mills had extracted about 50 per cent of the juice from the cane, while by 1916 the extraction rate had risen to between 92 and 96 per cent.

In the inter-war period the sugar machinery industry shared in the general depression of the world economy. Most of the sugar-producing areas were equipped with relatively new machinery with a long expectation of life (rates of depreciation were between 2 and 5 per cent a year for factory buildings and 5 and $7\frac{1}{2}$ per cent for machinery in the late nineteenth century), so that stable demand for sugar meant little work for machinery builders. Most of the West of Scotland firms survived, though with some it was on a hand-to-mouth basis.

A. & W. Smith & Co. Ltd, for example, bought the power hammer business of R.G. Ross & Co., in the early 1930s, made Loudon planes for Russia, and took out a licence for sandslingers for foundry use. The final collapse of the industry came in the 1950s and 60s, as will be seen from Figure 3.5. The surviving Glasgow firm A. & W. Smith & Co. Ltd has taken over the goodwill of most of its former rivals.

Marine Engineering

Marine engine building, like the manufacture of sugar machinery, was grafted on to the existing general engineering tradition in Glasgow. The engine of the *Comet* was a land engine of the small side-lever type (see Figures 8.5 (a) – (c), on page 161) developed by Boulton & Watt for customers who did not want a house engine which required an expensive supporting structure. James Cook made about twenty engines of this type from 1812 to *c.* 1822, including the first true marine engine built on the Clyde for the P.S. *Elizabeth,* in 1812. David Napier and his cousin Robert were, however, primarily responsible for the large-scale development of marine engineering on the river. In 1831-32, of the fifty-nine 'steam vessels plying on the river' listed by James Cleland, sixteen had been engined by David Napier and eleven by Robert, and ten by the short-lived Greenhead Foundry of D. McArthur. David Napier, an engineer of great originality, had begun making marine engines in 1816 and from then, until his move to London in 1837, made significant improvements in their reliability. John Scott Russell claimed in 1841 that: 'It is to Mr David Napier that Great Britain owes the establishment of deep-sea communication by steam vessels and of Post Office Steam packets . . . we believe that from the year 1818 until about 1830 David Napier effected more for the improvements of steam navigation than any other man[10]. Among his improvements were the use of surface condensation (P.S. *Post Boy,* 1822), not generally used until after 1850, and the 'steeple' engine (P.S. *Clyde,* 1832) frequently used until the 1840s in paddle steamers.

In 1823-24, after a period as a millwright and land-engine builder, Robert Napier began building marine engines with David Elder as his work's manager. Between then and 1841 Napier-built engines of increasing power were installed in hulls built mostly on the lower Clyde (see page 87). The combination of Robert Napier's ability as a businessman and David Elder's sound design and construction made the reputation of the Clyde as a centre of marine engineering. In the first engine built by the firm in 1823-24 for the P.S. *Leven,* David Elder introduced 'his improvements in the air-pump, condenser, and slide-valve'[11] giving greater efficiency and economy in operation, and a longer life expectancy. In the engines of the *Berenice* (1836) he used expansion valves in a marine engine for the first time. Unlike those of his competitors, all his engines were self-supporting and not dependent for their rigidity on the structural strength of the hull, so that an accident to the hull would not necessarily result in damage to the engine. To make these engines, of growing size, he designed and developed his own machine tools (see Figure 3.1, on page 28), especially 'the parent of all paring machines', or the 'devil' as it was nicknamed by his employees[11]. In answer to a Parliamentary question in 1843, the Admiralty revealed that Napier/Elder-engined ships spent less time under repair, and cost less in repairs than vessels made by Seaward and Maudslay, the English contractors for the Admiralty.

Robert Napier's reputation as the leading British marine engineer and iron shipbuilder attracted some able men into his employment and his 'dynasty' dominated marine engineering on the Clyde until the early years of this century (see page 88). Marine engineering in Greenock, however, retained a separate tradition. In 1825 John Scott purchased the works of William Brownlie for £5000 to make engines for his own hulls under the name of Scott, Sinclair & Co. The following year Caird & Co., ironfounders since 1809, began general and marine engineering. By 1829 Scott, Sinclair & Co. were building 'the largest engines ever made, which is to consist of 200 horsepower and is intended for a vessel building at Bristol'[12]. In the 1830s Caird & Co. were considered as being 'honourable rivals' of Robert Napier as the leading marine engineers. With the move of the Upper Clyde engineers into shipbuilding in the 1840s the significance of marine engineering in Greenock diminished.

Until the mid-1840s marine engineers were particularly concerned with the establishment of steam propulsion on new trade routes. From then until the end of the century their main interests were to improve the speed and efficiency of steamships on established routes and to extend their range of usefulness. The pattern of demand for ships on the Clyde created ideal conditions for improvements in design and manufacture which were to some extent self-reinforcing. The production of a succession of 'largest', 'best', and 'fastest' ships gave scope to a series of gifted designers of marine engines. The inverted vertical direct acting engine (see Figure 6.6, on page 121) which became standard for screw steamers in the late nineteenth century, was introduced by Caird & Co. in 1846 and developed by J. & G. Thomson (see page 114). Tod & MacGregor, of whom it was claimed that 'no single firm has contributed more . . . to the present extended and extending use of the screw as a propeller for steamships'[13], invested in workshops to make the fashionable horizontal screw engines of the 1850s and early 1860s, only to find tastes changing in the mid-1860s to favour the vertical style. There had been experiments with compounding of small marine engines from the 1820s, but the successful application of the compound engine to ocean-going vessels was only effected by Randolph & Elder in 1854 (see page 114). The fuel consumption figures realized by the celebrated P.S. *Brandon* of 1854 of $3\frac{1}{4}$ lbs. of coal per indicated horsepower per hour, as opposed to 4-$4\frac{1}{2}$ lbs. in best simple engine practice had been reduced in 1862 according to the firm to $1\frac{1}{2}$-2 lbs. in screw and paddle vessels respectively. Mayer, however, in 1876 commented that the most successful result at sea was probably 1.8 lbs. By that time the Randolph & Elder patent had expired and three West of Scotland firms engaged in building compound engines and converting simple engines were claiming 30-50 per cent economy by the use of compounding 'in coals alone', with space saved in the engine and boiler room[14].

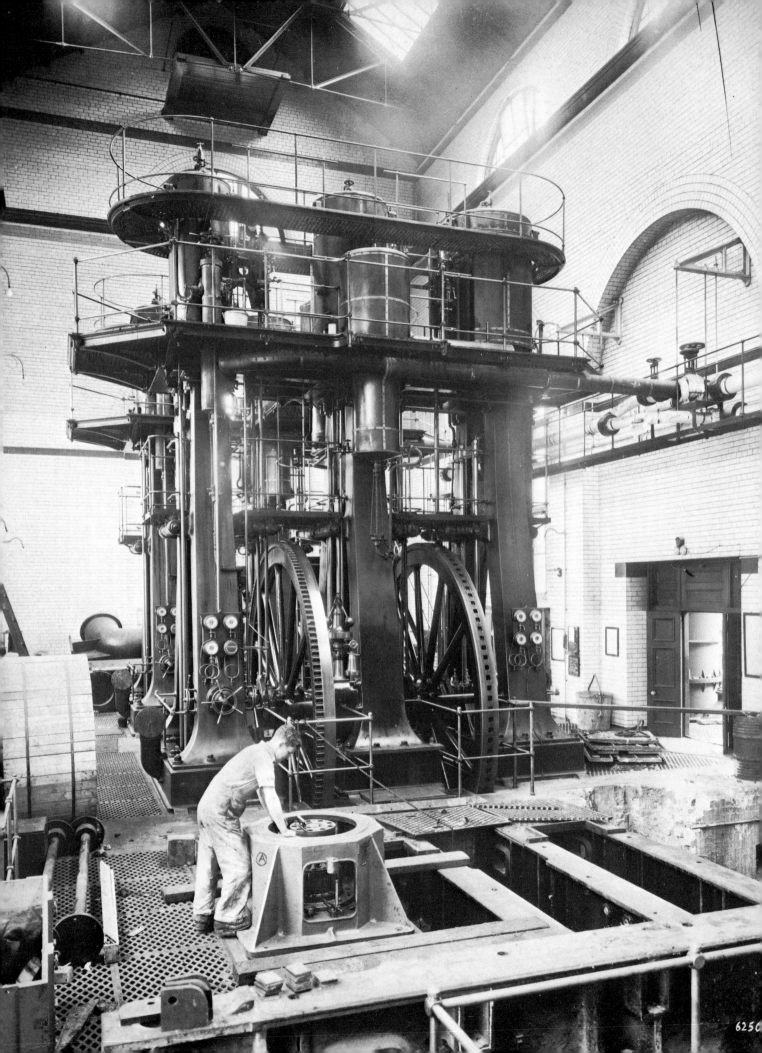

6250

The two commercially significant modifications of the compound engine were also made by Clyde engineers. Both consisted of flanking the high-pressure cylinder with two low-pressure cylinders. In the 1870s, J.M. Rowan of David Rowan & Co., introduced his modified tandem engine which was commonly used until the 1890s for medium-range passenger vessels. In 1881, F.C. Marshall described the engines of John Elder & Co.'s *Arizona* of 1879: 'The most recent form of compound engine introduced into our transatlantic steamships has three cylinders, one high-pressure between two low-pressure, having an intermediate receiver and working into one crank'[15]. Such was the success of the *Arizona* that similar engines were installed in most transatlantic passenger ships until the general application of the triple-expansion engine in the late 1880s. Although John Elder & Co., had been experimenting with triple-expansion (a modification of his three-cylinder compound engine) from the mid-1860s and had built the first successful marine triple-expansion engine for the *Propontis* in 1874 (see page 119), it was not until the building of a redesigned triple-expansion engine by A.C. Kirk (designer of the engines of the *Propontis*) of Robert Napier & Sons in 1886, that it became sufficiently reliable for general use (Figure 3.7). The perfection of the triple-expansion engine after 1886 and its further development in the quadruple-expansion engine, patented by Randolph & Elder in the 1860s and brought into use by Denny & Co. (Figure 3.8) in the 1890s, was the death-knell for long-distance sail. In the early 1900s, this expertise in reciprocating steam-engine technology attracted more orders to the Clyde industry than the developing skill in building marine turbines (see page 99).

Apart from modifications to the engines themselves, there were other ways of

improving efficiency and/or saving space. The use of superheating, from the 1860s; high-pressure steam, with smaller boilers for a given horsepower; the development of multitubular boilers of fire-tube and later of water-tube type [Babcock & Wilcox (1889), Yarrow & Co. (1887)]; feedwater heating [James Weir (1880)]; improvements in condenser design, all contributed. One of the most interesting and successful innovations in the latter part of the nineteenth century was the use of forced or induced draught to increase the output of steam from a boiler of given size. In forced-draught development, James Howden, a Glasgow marine engineer, was the most successful pioneer. His system was based on experiments carried out between 1883 and 1884. The first ship trials were made in the *New York City* in 1884, when a single boiler, replacing two of the same size produced steam sufficient to increase the effective horsepower of the main engine by 3 per cent, and reduced fuel consumption from 2.1 to 1.36 lbs. coal per indicated horsepower per hour. In the period 1884-96, more than 1000 boilers were built or converted to Howden's system, which was employed on the *Campania* and *Lucania* and later on the *Lusitania* and *Mauretania*. The high-speed engines developed for fan-driving later evolved into high-speed generating engines, while the fans themselves, and associated heat-exchanging equipment are still the prime products of James Howden & Co. Ltd.

From the 1850s, the rapidly extending market for marine engines in the West of Scotland was served by a number of firms (about twenty by 1895), doubling as engineers and shipbuilders, mostly building engines for passenger and Admiralty vessels or machinery for specialist craft like dredgers, and by a group of marine engineers *per se* (about ten by 1895). The most powerful and often the most technically advanced engines were built mainly by the great liner builders, John Elder & Co. (later the Fairfield Shipbuilding and Engineering Co.), J. & G. Thomson (later John Brown Shipbuilding and Engineering Co.), and until the early 1860s Robert Napier & Sons. In the 1890s, Fairfield and Thomson regularly headed the list of marine engines built on the Clyde expressed in terms of their indicated horsepower. Engines for ocean liners of medium size were produced by those second-rank shipbuilders who had their own engine works, like Barclay Curle & Co., Scotts Shipbuilding and Engineering Co., Caird & Co., Smith & Rodger, and after 1872 Alexander Stephen & Sons. Denny & Co., the engine building associate of William Denny & Bros, and A. & J. Inglis were particularly noted for their high-performance engines for short-distance, fast, passenger ships. Fairfield's and J. & G. Thomson's technical expertise allowed them to compete with Denny & Co. and A. & J. Inglis in this market.

Below the level where technology was being extended to its limits in the search for efficiency, power, or compactness, there were builders of smallish engines for the smaller and slower tramp ships, fishing boats, and coasters. Some were shipbuilders with engine works, like Blackwood & Gordon, and Bow & McLachlan, but most were marine or general engineers. The principal firms – Muir & Houston, David Rowan & Co., Dunsmuir & Jackson, Ross & Duncan, Mackie & Baxter, Rankin & Blackmore – were producing more engines than the engineer/shipbuilders in the 1890s, and their output expressed in terms of indicated horsepower placed them amongst the second-rank engineer/shipbuilders. There do not seem to have been very strong links between most of these firms and individual shipyards. From 1887–1908 the Ailsa Shipbuilding Co. of Troon built one hundred and fifty-six ships and bought their engines from nineteen marine engineering firms. Not all the output of the marine engineers was for the local market. In 1894, when the *Engineer* commented on the growing number of steam vessels built on the Clyde, Ross and Duncan 'sent eight sets aggregating 2930 indicated horsepower to Tyne and other English builders, and seven sets of 1395 indicated horsepower were shipped abroad'[16] out of an output of 8025 indicated horsepower. Some general engineers, like Hanna, Donald and Wilson, W. & A. McOnie, Duncan Stewart, Alley & MacLellan, and even Andrew Barclay Sons & Co. (see Chapter 4), whose main work lay in other fields, built the occasional marine engine. By 1900, Clyde marine engineers were producing over 35 per cent of the total indicated horsepower of marine engines made annually in Britain. After 1920 the pattern of decline in the marine engineering industry was similar to that in shipbuilding. Most of the independent specialist firms closed in the inter-war period, with the principal exception of David Rowan & Co., J.G. Kincaid & Co., and Rankine & Blackmore & Co. Those engine works associated with shipyards have, in some cases, outlived the yards and developed new specialities.

As the marine engineering industry on the river grew, ancillary industries developed, especially independent and specialist ironfoundries (see Chapter 2), heavy forges, coppersmiths and brassfoundries, and specialist machine tool makers (see page 53). In 1876, John Mayer reckoned that 'in no seat of the iron manufacture or of the engineering and shipbuilding industries, either at home or abroad, can we point to such a number of large forges as there are upon the Clyde, at least two of which have acquired considerable fame in many other parts of the world'. He continued: 'It would be difficult to overestimate the influence which the immense productive resources of the Lancefield forge have exerted in the creation of the gigantic ships of war and of the mercantile navies of the various nations of the world'[17]. The Lancefield forge supplied the large forgings (crankshaft, propeller, and stern frame), for the *Great Eastern* (launched 1858) and thereafter, for about 20 years, most of the heavy forgings for the Clyde shipbuilding industry. In 1876, when in addition to ten steam hammers producing rough forgings (Figure 3.9) and large slotting machines, and crank turning and other lathes were used to finish the forgings, the annual output of nearly 3000 tons of finished forgings was worth roughly £300 000. With the replacement of wrought iron by steel in the 1880s, the Lancefield forge waned in importance and was overtaken by the Parkhead forge of William Beardmore & Co. By 1914, the Parkhead forge, equipped with hydraulic presses rather than steam hammers for the biggest forgings (Figure 3.10), was the largest forge in Scotland and produced a range of products similar to that of Vickers and Armstrongs on the Tyne, and John Brown in Sheffield. In 1900, the firm

acquired the shipyard of Robert Napier & Sons to provide a ready outlet for its armour plate (see page 63). Of the other supporting industries, coppersmithing and brassfounding were the most significant. From the 1850s, numerous specialist firms were established and by 1876 there were 'two or three scores'[18] in Glasgow alone. All the marine coppersmithing at that time was subcontracted to these firms together with much of the brassfounding. The most important firm of coppersmiths was Blair, Campbell & McLean, who also supplied the sugar-machinery industry (see Figure 3.5, on page 33). The firm survives as Blairs Ltd. Mayer estimated that for the period 1872–76 the annual value of the marine work carried out by brassfounders and coppersmiths was about £200 000.

Figure 3.9 *The forge at the Queen's Park works of the North British Locomotive Co. Ltd in the 1920s. The two steam hammers in the foreground are of the twin column type, and the rest are single column, all of Rigby's patent type, built by Glen & Ross (later R.G. Ross) at their Greenhead Engine Works, Glasgow. Note the coupling-rod forgings in the foreground.*

Locomotive Building

The construction of railways in the West of Scotland from the 1820s might have been expected to stimulate locomotive-building in the region. Although the first successful locomotives to work in Scotland were made in Glasgow by Murdoch & Aitken, in 1831, locomotive-building was slow to develop in the region. Between 1839 and 1857, of the 115 locomotives built for the Glasgow, Paisley,

Kilmarnock & Ayr Railway, and its successor, the Glasgow & South Western Railway, only twenty-five came from Glasgow builders, seventy-one from English manufacturers, and nineteen from Dundee, a significant rival to Glasgow as a centre of railway engineering in the 1830s and 1840s. Similarly, the first locomotives of the Edinburgh & Glasgow railway (built in 1842) were bought from the established English firms of Edward Bury and R. & W. Hawthorn. The North British Railway (built in 1846) also relied on Hawthorns for their first locomotives. Hawthorns considered their long-term prospects so good that they purchased a works to assemble locomotives in Leith. West of Scotland engineering concerns tried to break into the locomotive market, in the 1830s and 1840s. Several firms, including John M. Rowan of the Atlas Works, Stark & Fulton, and Thomas Edington & Sons of the Phoenix Foundry, in Glasgow, and Scott, Sinclair & Co., and Caird & Co., of Greenock, built small numbers of locomotives mostly for Scottish companies during this period. In the 1840s, some of the local railway companies (Figure 3.11) began to make their own locomotives

Figure 3.10 *Forging a hollow propeller shaft at William Beardmore & Co.'s Parkhead Forge just before the First World War. The reason why the firm was able to move so easily into gun manufacture is self-evident. The hydraulic forging press in the left background is one of Beardmore's smaller specimens. Note the power manipulator for rotating the forging under the press. A shaft such as this would have to transmit several thousand horsepower.*

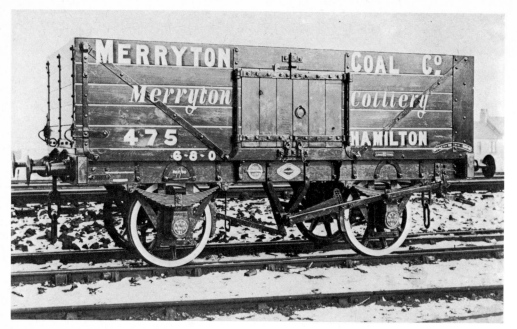

Figure 3.11 *A wood-framed side-and-end door coal wagon, built in 1900 by R.Y. Pickering Co. Ltd, of Wishaw. Wishaw and Motherwell, Lanarkshire, were the main centres of rolling stock building in Scotland, apart from the railway company workshops in Glasgow and Ayrshire. The forged iron wheel were probably made by the Glasgow Railway Engineering Co., or by William Beardmore & Co.*

– notably the Edinburgh & Glasgow Railway Co., at Cowlairs, Glasgow, the Glasgow, Paisley, Kilmarnock & Ayr Railway Co., at Cook Street, Glasgow (which moved to Kilmarnock in 1857), and the Caledonian Railway Co., at Greenock (which moved to St Rollox, Glasgow in 1856-57). Only the railway companies continued to build locomotives, the private firms, with one exception, 'were obliged to retire from the field in consequence of their inability to compete successfully with makers in the South'[19]. Some firms like Stark & Fulton went out of business, and others developed different specialities. Thomas Edington & Sons became pipe founders (see page 19) and the two Greenock firms concentrated on marine engineering, while J.M. Rowan became one of the first licensees of the Bessemer process for steel manufacture.

Mitchell & Neilson of Glasgow, which was founded *c*. 1836, was exceptional. The firm became Kerr, Neilson & Co. in 1840, Neilson, Mitchell & Co. in 1844, and Neilson & Co., in 1848. Walter Montgomerie Neilson, one of the original partners, was a son of John Beaumont Neilson, inventor of the hot-blast furnace (see page 13) and nephew of John Neilson whose Oakbank Foundry made the *Fairy Queen*, the first iron steamship built on the Clyde, launched in 1831. Before they began making locomotives in 1845, the firm made land and marine steam engines and sugar machinery at their Hydepark Foundry and continued to build marine engines until the late 1850s. Their early experience as locomotive builders helps to explain the failure of their local competitors. They found 'that the details of locomotive engines differed very much from those of the other kinds of engines which they constructed'[20]; but in the 1840s instead of abandoning locomotive building, they began to specialize in it. Initially they found it hard to recruit engineers with locomotive-engineering experience, and difficult to break into the established British markets, being forced in the 1850s to build industrial rather than main-line locomotives. By the late 1850s, despite these problems, W.M. Neilson, with his competent managing partner, Henry Dübs had developed their business so much that the lack of a rail connection at their Hydepark Works at Finnieston was a serious disadvantage. Accordingly, in 1860 a new Hydepark Works was built at Springburn (Figure 3.12) on the fringe of the built-up area of Glasgow, with a connection to the Edinburgh & Glasgow Railway. Following on the success of Neilson & Co., other general engineering firms began building industrial locomotives in the late 1850s – especially Andrew Barclay & Co., of Kilmarnock, who had emerged as the most important firm by the end of the century. Kilmarnock and Airdrie became the centres of this industry in the West of Scotland.

The growing confidence in the market for locomotives and the experience gained by Henry Dübs during the move to Springburn, led him to set up a works of his own, opened in 1865, at Polmadie to the south-east of the city. As a new works, equipped with the latest types of machine tools from Whitworth & Co., Manchester, it was well placed to compete with the Hydepark Works. The commercial acumen of James Reid, Dübs' successor at Hydepark and rapidly growing domestic and overseas markets, allowed the older firm to retain its position.

By 1876, when Glasgow-made locomotives were being exported to Italy, Spain, Russia, Sweden, India, and South America, Neilson & Co. had made 1780 locomotives and were producing about 130 a year, while Dübs & Co. had made nearly 1000 locomotives and were producing about 100 a year. The Glasgow firms had broken convincingly into the Scottish market and were making inroads into the English and overseas markets. Of the 750 locomotives built for the Caledonian Railway up to 1876, about 61 per cent had been built by Scottish firms, 16.5 per cent by English firms, and the remainder in the company's own workshops. Before 1884, all the outside orders from the London & South Western

Figure 3.12   The Hydepark Locomotive Works, Springburn, of Neilson & Co. in the early 1860s, shortly after the move from Finnieston, with the main workshops on the right. Locomotives appear to have been moved laterally on a traverser, the carriage of which is in the background. The main range of buildings survived until the closure of the works in 1963.

Figure 3.13 *A locomotive built, according to the maker's plate, by the Glasgow Railway Engineering Co. Ltd of Govan, Glasgow, c. 1900. Such was the extent of subcontracting in the locomotive-building industry, however, that its exact origin is in doubt. The locomotive appears to be of 2 feet or 2 feet 6 inches gauge, for the colonial market.*

Railway Co., went to English builders, particularly Beyer, Peacock & Co., of Manchester. Thereafter until outside ordering stopped in 1901, all the contracts, amounting to 201 locomotives, went to Neilson & Co. In comparison to overseas sales, (Figure 3.13) the British market was limited. Between 1873 and 1910 the Cape Government Railways in South Africa bought 567 locomotives from Glasgow and only 118 from other builders, mainly English but a few American. The Indian market was the largest. By 1909 the Indian railways had 7024 locomotives, of which over half had been made in Scotland. Of the 16 000 locomotives built by the Neilson & Co., Dübs & Co., and Sharp, Stewart & Co. up to 1903, India had purchased over 3500, South Africa over 1000, the Midland Railway over 1000, the Scottish railways about 1000, Japan 327, Australia 537, and South America about 700. (These totals include locomotives built by Sharp, Stewart & Co. in Manchester between 1834 and 1888.)

This pattern of growing overseas demand in the later years of the nineteenth century encouraged Walter Montgomerie Neilson to set up the Clyde Locomotive Works in 1884. Neilson, who had been a sleeping partner in Neilson & Co., since before the move to Springburn, had been ousted from participation in that firm in 1876. The promise of the early 1880s was not fulfilled in the depression of the second half of the decade, and the Clyde Works was purchased in 1888 by Sharp, Stewart & Co., whose competitive position had been eroded because of the smallness of their Manchester works and because of higher labour and raw material costs. In 1903, in the face of foreign competition and following the fashion for combination, the three firms amalgamated as the North British Locomotive Company. The *Economist* was cautiously optimistic about the merger, noting that for the four years up to 1901 Sharp, Stewart & Co., the only public company in the new group, had paid a steady dividend of 15 per cent and that in 1902 the British locomotive builders had been 'well employed', with American and German competition waning. There was praise for Neilson Reid & Co., 'the largest producers in Europe, and their works are reputedly up to the highest perfection of American "methods" combined with British efficiency'[21]. The new concern effectively rationalized production and design (Figure 3.14),

Figure 3.14 *(Opposite) Lady tracers at work in the drawing office of the Administration Building of the North British Locomotive Co. Ltd, Springburn c. 1910. The practice of employing women as tracers was started in the 1860s by Henry Dübs at his Glasgow Locomotive Works, Polmadie, Glasgow, and became general in the West of Scotland. The columns carrying arc lights with reflectors provide indirect lighting of high intensity. After the formation of the North British Locomotive Co. Ltd in 1903, the design department was centralized at Springburn.*

increasing capacity and modernizing plant. The peak years were 1905, when 573 locomotives valued at £1 543 330 were completed, and 1914, when 488 rather heavier locomotives worth £2 249 525 were turned out. The average annual production for 1904-14 was 447 which compares with the annual average of 414 for the three companies in the period 1895-99. Though the annual output of locomotives in the years 1915-18 was down to between 200 and 300, the company produced in addition over a million shell forgings, thousands of sea mines, aeroplanes (Figure 3.15), torpedo tubes (82 sets), tanks of two different types, and lathes and other machine tools. The value of war-time output was about £16 million (computed on the years 1914-19); over the same period the locomotives produced accounted for just over £12 million.

1919 was the peak year of the inter-war period, the brief post-war boom ending abruptly in 1920 (Figure 3.16). Competition in traditional markets became exceptionally severe. Rationalization of British railways in 1923, following on war-time state control, reduced the demand for locomotives. Competition from road transport and general economic depression reinforced this decline. Overseas, the South African market was increasingly satisfied by Canadian, American, and German makers. Of 1186 locomotives supplied to the South African Railways between 1919 and 1939, only 25 per cent were made in Glasgow, as compared with 60 per cent from foreign builders, 45 per cent from Germany. By 1922, production had dropped to 74 locomotives, from three works with a nominal capacity of 800 locomotives a year. Thereafter, in no year were more than 200 locomotives produced until 1943. The Atlas Works was closed in June 1929, and in 1932-33 Queens Park (formerly the Glasgow Locomotive Works) was effectively closed. In 1932 no complete locomotives were built,

Figure 3.15 *A Bristol BE2C fighter aircraft built at William Denny & Bros. yard during the First World War. Over 60 per cent of aircraft engines produced during the War were made by William Beardmore & Co., and several other West of Scotland firms, including G. & J. Weir Ltd, Alexander Stephens and Sons, and the North British Locomotive Co. Ltd, made planes of various types.*

Figure 3.16   A Whitelegg
'Baltic' locomotive ordered during
the short-lived post-war boom,
built for the Glasgow & South
Western Railway by the North
British Locomotive Co. Ltd at
their Hyde Park Works, in 1922.
This view shows the locomotive
painted in works grey with the
boiler covered with planished
steel.

though spares were made on a small scale. When revival came it was at first in a low key. Queens Park Works was producing shells in 1937 and 1938, and was then tooled up for light tank and other war-time production. A total of 762 tanks was produced. By 1943, however, the need for locomotives on the invasion fronts was so great that Queens Park was again turned over to locomotive building. Altogether 1153 locomotives were produced in the years 1939-45. The post-war boom was more prolonged than that after the First World War. The home and some foreign railways had gone into the Second World War with an ageing locomotive stock, and wartime wear and tear had made replacement an urgent necessity. As a result, between 1945 and 1956, with the absence of any significant foreign competition, large numbers of steam locomotives were built for the British, South African (Figure 3.17), Indian, Australian, and Spanish railways. At the same time the firm began to make diesel locomotives, starting in 1946 with underground-mine locomotives. The firm decided to adopt hydraulic transmission, using the German Voith patents. When the large scale dieselization of British Railways began in 1955, diesel-hydraulic locomotives proved far less reliable than diesel-electrics. The North British Locomotive Co.'s diesel-hydraulics were particularly poor (Figure 3.18) and their diesel-electric designs

were unsuccessful. In the 1960s the firm suffered from rapidly shrinking world demand and renewed foreign competition. This was reinforced by the failure of its new products, including dragline excavators and metal-cutting machines, leading to the firm's bankruptcy.

The pattern of production within this closely-knit group of companies was increasingly characterized by 'batches' – two or three in the early days, 'twenty, thirty or even fifty at a time'[22] in the 1870s, rising to lots of over 100 after the amalgamation of the firms. During the First World War, more than 300 Standard Royal Ordnance Department locomotives and 215 to a standard French design of 2-8-0s were built, and during the Second World War 545 'Austerity' 2-8-0 locomotives and 150 2-10-0s, though interchangeability in batches was normal by the 1880s. Customers' individual requirements could not be met by

Figure 3.17 *Class 15F 4–8–2 locomotive under construction for the South African Railways in Queen's Park Locomotive Works Glasgow, in 1944. The 15F was one of the most successful designs in South Africa, and many locomotives of this class are still in use.*

50

Figure 3.18 *Diesel hydraulic A1A–A1A locomotive D600 on trial for the North British Locomotive Co. Ltd, before delivery to British Railways in 1957. Later named* Active, *this was the first express passenger diesel locomotive built by NBL for British Railways. Unfortunately for the company, the design proved unsuccessful and was superseded by a German-based design before hydraulic transmission was finally abandoned by the British Railways Board in the late 1960s.*

absolute standardization. The initial cost of a steam locomotive with a life expectancy of at least twenty years was a fraction of its running cost, and any improvement in reliability or reduction in fuel consumption was likely to outweigh marginal differences in price resulting from standardization. Unlike locomotives built in the United States for the homogeneous standard gauge railway system, which lent themselves to standardization, those built in Glasgow for a multi-gauge world system, with different loading gauges, axle-loadings, and traffics, could only be partially standardized. There were few major innovations in locomotive design in the second half of the nineteenth century; but there were small improvements. These were commonly the responsibility of the customer's engineers or consulting engineers; but in many cases the details of the outline specification were filled in by the manufacturers. The North British Locomotive Co. tried unsuccessfully to develop turbo-electric and turbo-mechanical locomotives from 1909, the modified-Fairlie (Figure 3.19) locomotive from 1924, and after 1945, in conjunction with C.A. Parsons & Co., a coal-fired gas-turbine locomotive.

Machine-tool Manufacture

As elsewhere in Britain, the early engineers in the West of Scotland built their own machine tools. The degree of precision required in making the simple lathes and cylinder-boring machines used by early engine builders was not high. Gear-cutting was confined to small precision work in brass using clockmakers' techniques. Larger gear wheels were moulded in sand from one-piece patterns. Several West of Scotland foundries, including Fyfe Donald & Co., Johnstone, advertised their possession of such patterns. Little is known of the earliest machine tools used in the region. In 1821, the Camlachie Foundry, at the time one of the best equipped shops in the West of Scotland, had 'a few 10 inch and 12 inch lathes, a rude horizontal boring-mill, a vertical machine *(sic)*, and the

51

necessary appliances for making castings'. 'In those days [1838] all machine work was done by hand, there being no planing machines; all work was lined off on the castings and chipped and filed fair and straight by the hand, using the hand hammer and chisel, and similarly in iron turning no self-acting lathes then existed, all work being done by the hand, and the tool used was called the ''heel tool'', the lathe consisting of the driving head and the dead centre placed upon wooden shears, the top of which was covered by iron plates'[23]. (Planing machines were in use in the Manchester area from about 1820.)

David Elder, while in Robert Napier's employment, devised several new machines and modifications of machines for making marine engines. In the early 1840s, Randolph & Elliot, to complement their millwright business, produced a range of tools that included a double-screwing machine, a vertical drilling and boring machine, and a rolling machine for straightening and rounding iron bars for shafting. At the same time Mr Hastie of Scott, Sinclair & Co., Greenock, designed a superior self-acting lathe and a 'shaping machine' – in fact an end milling machine.

Although machine types and details were adopted from outside, advances in machine tool design in the region were conditioned by local needs until well into the nineteenth century and the character of the industry remained quite distinct from that of other areas. By the middle of the century the chief feature of locally

Figure 3.19 *A modified-Fairlie locomotive for the South African Railways under construction in the Hydepark Locomotive Works, Springburn, of the North British Locomotive Co. Ltd, in 1925. This type of locomotive was intended to compete in overseas markets with the Beyer-Garratt articulated locomotive very successfully introduced by Beyer, Peacock & Co. Ltd of Manchester, but was not a success. Of 197 articulated locomotives of Beyer-Garratt and related types supplied to the South African Railways in the inter-war period only four, all of the modified-Fairlie type, were made by NBL.*

Figure 3.20 *The whole of the work force of Thomas Shanks & Co., posing on an enormous lathe built by the company probably during the First World War. It was possibly used for turning naval gun barrels.*

made machines was their size. In 1876, some of the machine tools in the Lancefield Forge were described as 'of extra-ordinary size, weight, and power'[24]. They included a crank-turning machine made by Thomas Shanks & Co., of Johnstone, to designs by Penn of Greenwich, and a 'gigantic' slotting machine by the same makers which weighed 104 tons. 'In very few . . . cases do the engineering firms and other "workers in iron" require to go out of the district for such machine tools as are necessary to carry on their manufacturing operations'[25]. Thomas Shanks & Co., were the most important local machine tool builders. The firm was established to make spinning machines in 1824 by William Shanks, a native of Fife, after a period as a cotton spinner. On his death in 1845 his son, Thomas, became sole partner, and began making machine tools, specializing in the heavy end of the trade in the 1850s. By 1876, the firm had made the 'very largest and heaviest machine tools . . . for marine engineering'[26] (Figure 3.20) as well as shipyard tools, and its markets included 'all the leading . . . firms on the Clyde, the Mersey, and the Tyne . . . H.M. Dockyards, the engineering establishments of the Dutch, German, Italian, Danish, and Russian Governments, together with those of China, and the still more distant Japan'[27]. The other major heavy-tool firm was G. & A. Harvey, who made a wide range of heavy lathes, slotting, planing, boring, and screwing machines. Some of their machines were very large – a vertical planing machine to take work up to sixteen

Figure 3.21 *A heavy steam-driven combined guillotine and open-ended shearing machine built by Murray & Paterson Ltd of Coatbridge, being installed in Coatbridge wrought-iron works, c. 1905. Note the puddling furnace and waste-heat boiler in the left background.*

feet long by twelve feet high and a vertical boring mill to bore ten feet in diameter by seven feet six inches deep. Robert Harvey & Co. also made heavy machine tools and later Murray & Paterson of Coatbridge made heavy roll-turning lathes and other tools (Figure 3.21). Loudon Brothers of Johnstone made lathes of various sizes and radial drilling machines; but the extent of their output is difficult to determine as they acted as agents, ordering machines from many local firms. Similarly, Dempster Moore & Co., a firm of the same type that had a factory in Bonnybridge, supplied a far larger range of products than they manufactured. Both these companies specified that their name be cast on the machines ordered through them.

There were several other firms active as machine tool-builders in the West of Scotland during the second half of the nineteenth century. Crawhall & Campbell made lathes, planing and shaping machines, and drills. Dron & Lawson, Glasgow, who had a reputation for making screwing tackle, also made lathes, planing, and slotting machines. The most successful firm was John Lang & Sons, founded in 1874 by a foreman in Thomas Shanks & Co.'s works and his two sons, John and Robert. John Junior built up the firm to make small and medium-sized lathes on the interchangeable principle, imitating American designs. The Company was the first in Europe to market machine tools with cut gears, and was esteemed for quality and original design. The other significant machine-tool builders were the handful of firms specializing in plate-working tools for shipyards, boilermakers, and iron and steel works. Craig & Donald, founded in 1836, were, according to a local account, the original makers 'of the class of tools for punching, shearing, straightening and otherwise operating on the iron plates used in constructing the new type of ship'[28]. By the 1870s, they were turning out large numbers of punching and shearing machines, bending rolls, and plate-edge planers, and output continued to rise until the early years of this century.

54

Shipbuilders and boilermakers re-equipping to use steel instead of iron plates provided a substantial market in the 1880s and 1890s. James Bennie & Co. specialized in cold bending machines for angle iron in the 1870s, but became particularly noted during the 1880s and 1890s for their punching and shearing machines and heavy bending rolls (Figure 3.22). Between 1905-10 the firm turned out 278 tools, of which 54 per cent were punching and shearing or punching machines. About 53 per cent of output went overseas, mainly to European countries; of the remainder 34 per cent went to English, Welsh, and Irish customers and only 13 per cent to Scottish firms. Smith Brothers of Kinning Park and Hugh Smith & Co. of Possil were also engaged in the manufacture of plateworking tools, though the latter specialized in hydraulic machines, including powerful keel-plate benders. All these firms had substantial export markets, and supplied tools to most British shipyards. The decline in the number of shipbuilding yards, the replacement of shearing by flame cutting, and of riveting by electric-arc welding reduced demand. In 1937, Bennie and Craig & Donald amalgamated with G. & A. Harvey, Loudon Brothers, and James Allan Senior & Sons Ltd, ironfounders, to form the Scottish Machine Tool Corporation, which ceased manufacturing on any scale in the early 1960s. Hugh Smith & Co., by replacing water-hydraulic with oil-hydraulic systems, has successfully adapted to changing market conditions and still make shipyard tools.

The West of Scotland machine-tool industry has remained part of the general engineering tradition. Most of the large workshops made their own tools from time to time. Hugh Smith & Co., re-equipping a new bay in the 1890s, made four lathes and a slotting machine for their own use, while Sir William Arrol & Co., in the late 1890s, made plate-edge planers and riveting machines for themselves. The Singer Sewing Machine Co., between 1870 and 1914, built more than three-quarters of their own machine tools in Bridgeton and Clydebank.

55

Special-purpose tools were also made by firms for their own purposes. Andrew Barclay Sons & Co. Ltd built their own boiler flanging press in 1900 and Fullerton, Hodgart, Barclay & Co. made faceplate lathes for turning winding engine drum cheeks and flywheels. After their move to Springburn, Sharp, Stewart & Co., who had been active tool-builders since the 1820s as Sharp, Roberts & Co., continued to make their machine tools, particularly lathes, planers, and boring machines for themselves and for sale. More common perhaps has been the manufacture by subcontract, or to special order, of relatively small numbers of machine tools by general engineers or by firms with other specialities. A.F. Craig & Co., of Paisley and A. & W. Smith of Glasgow made Loudon planers, Andrew Barclay Sons & Co. Ltd, made Hugh Smith shipyard tools, J. & T. Boyd, textile engineers, made drilling machines, while D. & J. Tullis of Clydebank made horizontal boring machines to their own design. During the Second World War the North British Locomotive Co. Ltd and D. & J. Tullis made lathes on quite a large scale.

Woodworking machine tools were also made with success in the West of Scotland. By far the most important firm in the nineteenth century was John McDowall & Sons of Johnstone. The firm, founded in 1823, was at first general engineers, but in 1834 John McDowall developed and patented a saw frame and a wood-planing machine which were the basis for specialization in a wide range of woodworking machinery, much of which was exported. The annual output in 1876 was roughly two hundred machines, worth about £30 000. Other firms making woodworking machinery included several general engineers, such as Forrest & Barr, A. & W. Smith, and Smith Brothers; and a surviving catalogue of Hugh Smith & Co. suggests that they originally planned to specialize in that branch of manufacture. The Auchengree Foundry, Glengarnock, made furniture-making machinery in the late nineteenth century on a small scale. More recently Thomas White & Sons of Paisley have carried on the tradition, but were forced to close in 1975.

Structural Engineering

As with so many other branches of engineering in the West of Scotland, structural engineering grew out of ironfounding, with links with blacksmithing. Iron-framed buildings were introduced from England with the Houldsworths' Anderston Cotton Works in 1804-05, although in April 1803 Girdwood & Pinkerton, Gorbals, Glasgow had advertised in the *Glasgow Herald* that 'The shell of a cotton mill, with a patent cast-iron roof, and a steam engine complete, will be erected for any Company, or Gentleman of respectability, desirous of engaging in that Trade'[29]. Iron-framed cotton mills did not, however, become common in the region until the 1830s and 1840s, and even then they were greatly outnumbered by mills of composite wood and iron construction. Early iron bridges were also rare in Scotland. The first cast-iron examples were probably Thomas Telford's bridges at Bonar Bridge and Craigellachie, both cast at Plas Kynaston in North Wales. The oldest dated cast-iron bridge of Scottish manufacture may well be a little one in London Road, Glasgow, over the now-culverted course of the Molendinar Burn, made in 1826. Another early West of Scotland cast-iron bridge is in the Linn Park, Glasgow (built 1836) while the major aqueducts on the Union Canal (built 1818-22) have cast-iron troughs for the water-course in the style of Telford. Cast-iron bridges were sometimes used in early main-line railway construction, both for minor crossings, as on the North British Railway and its branches, and for the major crossings on the Caledonian Railway, the last of which survives at Uddingston on the outskirts of Glasgow. Some of the bridges on the Perth-Aberdeen route, which were originally wooden, were replaced in cast-iron before again being renewed in steel in the 1880s and 1890s. Cast-iron bridges continued to be built for road crossings until the end of the century. Hanna, Donald & Wilson of Paisley made the Albert Bridge, Glasgow in 1870-71, and Sir William Arrol & Co. Ltd were contractors for the Great Western Road Bridge over the River Kelvin in 1891. Cast-iron was also used for decorative effect in steel and wrought-iron bridges, for example, in the North Bridge, Edinburgh, another Arrol contract.

Though cast-iron remained in use for so long, by the 1890s it had been displaced by wrought-iron and steel for most bridges. The use of wrought-iron in bridge construction had begun in Scotland with the first suspension bridges, *c.* 1815. The material had been used for tiebars in iron-framed buildings from 1804. Riveted wrought-iron construction was introduced into bridge-building by Robert Stephenson and Brunel, but did not become common until the 1860s and 1870s. Bridges of the lattice-and-plate girder-type were used on the Inverness & Perth Junction Railway in the early 1860s, though masonry viaducts were used where possible. The techniques of riveted bridge construction were similar to those of boilermaking and of gas-holder building, and it is not surprizing to find that R. Laidlaw & Son (late Laidlaw, Sons & Caine), who were gas-holder specialists, were the leading Glasgow firm in bridge and pier construction in the mid-1870s. The premier company of the period 1875-1914, William Arrol & Co. (later Sir William Arrol & Co. Ltd.) was founded in 1868 by William Arrol, an experienced blacksmith, who had been a foreman for five years with R. Laidlaw & Sons. He specialized in boilers at first, but quickly moved into bridge construction. He made his reputation in this field in 1875 with the construction of a 700 feet, seven span, lattice girder bridge over the Clyde, in which he used the technique of finishing the erection at the side of the bridge, and rolling out completed spans cantilever-fashion. He followed this up by building the first bridge carrying the Caledonian Railway across the Clyde to Central Station, Glasgow, and in the 1880s was contractor for the reconstruction of the Tay Bridge and for the building of the Forth Bridge, the greatest of all nineteenth century bridges. The ironworks for the Tay Bridge was made in Arrol's Dalmarnock Ironworks, Glasgow but the great bulk of the steelwork for

Figure 3.23 *The Forth Bridge. (a) Central girder on drill road, July 1889. Most of the steel work for the Forth Bridge was prepared in a special works built by Tancred, Arrol & Co., the contractors, at South Queensferry. The central girder, or internal viaduct, carries the railway through the cantilever supporting structure. Note the wooden derrick cranes, of the type introduced by Forrest & Barr in about 1850, and the 'swan-neck' steam crane Jumbo made by Fullerton, Hodgart & Barclay Ltd of Paisley. (b) Queensferry Main Pier, 3 September 1888, showing the cantilevers complete with the central span bridge on the left under construction. To test their structural strength, Sir William Arrol had replicas built of the central span on Sir John Fowler's estate at Braemore in Ross-shire*

the Forth Bridge was prepared in a yard specially constructed at the south end of the bridge (Figures 3.23 (a) and (b)). In both bridges Arrol's own ingenuity solved many of the problems that arose. His firm developed close links with the Paisley firm of Fullerton, Hodgart & Barclay, with which he had ties of blood, reinforced later when he married Miss Jessie Hodgart, his cousin, as his second wife. Fullerton, Hodgart & Barclay supplied many of the special-purpose hydraulic machines used in the construction of the Forth Bridge, together with steam cranes, hydraulic pumps (Figure 3.24), air compressors, and driving engines for drills and airlocks, and continued to do subcontract work for the firm, mainly hydraulic pumps and air compressors for many years. In return, Arrol did riveted fabrication work for some Fullerton contracts (Figure 3.25).

Figure 3.24 A duplex hydraulic pumping engine made for John Marshall & Sons by Fullerton, Hodgart & Barclay Ltd of Paisley, in 1891. The beautiful finish is noteworthy, such details as the mahogany lagging and the fluted columns supporting the water tank are particularly pleasing. In the left background is part of a horizontal and vertical planing machine by Thomas Shanks & Co., of Johnstone.

Figure 3.25 A group of mobile hydraulic cranes built by Fullerton, Hodgart & Barclay Ltd for the Clyde Navigation Trust's Princes Dock, Glasgow, in 1894. The riveted bases were subcontracted to Sir William Arrol & Co. Ltd.

Sir William Arrol & Co. Ltd did not export widely before 1909, though the firm built bridges in Egypt and Sudan. They did a good deal of work in the London area, building Tower Bridge (1886-90), widening Blackfriars Bridge (1907-10), and constructing a number of engineering workshops and other steel buildings, from 1900. The firm built no fewer than sixteen bridges of over 500 feet span between 1875 and 1909, the longest the Tay Bridge (10 711 feet long) and the heaviest, the Forth Bridge (51 000 tons of steel). In comparison other West of Scotland firms were less significant, but Smith & Naysmith, A. & W. Smith & Co., P. & W. MacLellan of Glasgow, the Motherwell Bridge & Engineering Co., Alexander Finlay & Co., and the Brandon Bridge Building Co. of Motherwell, were all well-known bridge builders of the late nineteenth century.

Structural engineering is not confined to bridge building and includes constructional work for piers, cranes (Figure 3.26), and buildings. After the early flowering of pier construction in the 1860s and 1870s, when Laidlaw and Sons built about a dozen large piers, including one in Spain and several in South America, and A. & W. Smith built one in Spain and three in Central America, building construction became more significant. Although the great overall roof of St Enoch Station, Glasgow was built by Handyside of Derby in 1877, P. & W. MacLellan, two years later, successfully tendered for the smaller but not dissimilar roof of Queen Street Station, Glasgow. The growing scale of their products, and the need to improve productivity led most engineering and shipbuilding firms to enlarge their works at fairly frequent intervals throughout the period, *c.* 1860-1914. At the beginning, construction was normally of wood and cast-iron, the constraints inherent in these materials being immediately apparent in Randolph & Elder's engine works (1858-60) where the crane rails were supported on laminated pine beams 90 inches deep by 18 inches wide. Wrought-iron riveted girders and cast-iron columns were standard from *c.* 1860 to *c.* 1880, and cast-iron columns were not unusual as late as the 1890s. By that time, however, Sir William Arrol & Co. Ltd and other firms had introduced a recognizably modern design of workshop, with all-glazed roof, lattice columns, and girders. These workshops were framed structures in which the walls of brick or corrugated iron were not load-bearing. The earliest buildings of this basic type were the roofs of railway stations. Central Station, Glasgow had an all-glazed roof from 1879 and Carlisle Citadel from 1880, both built by companies with whom Sir William Arrol & Co. were associated. From 1895 this type of industrial building became common. Between 1880 and 1909, Arrol alone executed more than one hundred and sixty contracts for steel framed buildings of various types, many of which are still in use. The firm's private cost book for the period 1895-1900 indicates that seventy contracts in this field had an invoiced value of £224 095, with an average profit of 19 per cent. In the same period, only one major bridge contract was executed, for the North Bridge, Edinburgh. On a contract price of £87 938 this yielded 8 per cent profit. Sir William Arrol and Co. dominated the market for the largest workshops, but Arrol Brothers, the Motherwell Bridge & Engineering Co., Clyde Structural Steel

Figure 3.26 (*Opposite*) *The 180-ton hammer-head crane under construction in the fitting out basin at John Brown's Clydebank yard, c. 1906. This crane was built by Sir William Arrol & Co. Ltd, Dalmarnock, Glasgow and is one of the bigges[t] cranes the firm ever made. Larg[e] cranes of this type were introduced in the early years of the century to handle boilers, low-speed steam turbines, and parts of reciprocating engines, which could weigh upwards of 100 tons.*

Co., and the Glasgow Steel Roofing Co., were also engaged in heavy work. Other firms, like A. & J. Main, Frederick Braby & Co., and P. & R. Fleming, specialized in lighter structures, such as agricultural buildings. The incorporation of steel frames in commercial buildings in the West of Scotland, was in its infancy before the First World War.

The analysis of the private cost book of Sir William Arrol & Co., for 1895-1900 indicates that work to the value of £579 750 was executed in that period with an average profit of 16.4 per cent. Building and roof construction accounted for 39 per cent of the output by value, general girder work for 36 per cent, the remainder being mechanical engineering, mainly hydraulics. The highest rate of profit was on gasworks machinery, which yielded an average of 26 per cent, and the lowest, on general girder work, was 10 per cent. As Arrol's was the largest firm of its kind in Glasgow these figures indicate that in comparison with the locomotive building firms and the larger ship yards, structural engineering was comparatively small in scale. The output of the North British Locomotive Co. in 1904 was worth £1.7 million, while Fairfield alone built ships to the value of nearly £6 million between 1895 and 1900.

The Experience of William Beardmore & Co. in the Twentieth Century

The history of the heavy industries in the West of Scotland after 1900 can be traced in some detail by reference to the numerous reports, both private and government, and by government publications of other sorts. Recently Professor Payne has managed to disentangle the main strands of the fortunes of the Scottish steel industry between the wars in a perceptive study (to be included in his forthcoming history of Colvilles Ltd), but as the steel industry in Scotland was a supporting industry rather than a generator of economic change in its own right, the phenomena he discusses are secondary to the major manufacturing industries. It is not possible to examine the fortunes of most firms in this period owing to deficiencies in the source material available, but it seems worthwhile to look at one firm briefly, as a case study. William Beardmore & Co. Ltd is a fine example of the creation of a manufacturing empire by an exceptionally able businessman, and its dissipation by the same man in changed economic circumstances.

William Beardmore & Co. Ltd grew out of the Parkhead Forge established *c.* 1837 by Reoch Bros & Co. who made forgings out of scrap iron. About 1842 it was bought by Robert Napier to make marine forgings for his new iron ship building yard. Napier introduced his son-in-law, William Rigby, as manager, *c.* 1853, and in 1862 Rigby assumed William Beardmore as a partner in the firm, which began making wrought-iron armour plate – unsuccessfully – so they turned to making boiler and ship plates. Rigby died in 1863 and his widow and Beardmore continued the firm until 1872. William Beardmore and his brother, Isaac, then took over the firm, taking in William's son, also William, as a manager. William Junior assumed control in 1886, when the firm became William Beardmore & Co. The new managing partner, who had been educated at Anderson's College, Glasgow and at the School of Mines, London, built upon Parkhead's reputation as a heavy forge. In 1879 he had introduced three 10-ton open-hearth furnaces to make mild-steel ship plates, and in the ensuing years added to that capacity. He developed a patent armour plate, laying down a cogging and armour plate mill at Parkhead in 1899, but found his market limited by the control exercised by the existing armour firms. Accordingly, in 1900, the firm bought the business of Robert Napier and Sons, with a yard at Govan and engine-works at Lancefield, and in 1902 purchased 90 acres of ground at Dalmuir, where a naval construction works was laid out, with berths designed for building capital ships, one served by an overall gantry (see Figure 5.21, on page 103). The engine and boiler works, erected by Sir William Arrol & Co. Ltd, covered nearly five and a half acres, and was described in 1909 as 'probably one of the finest yet constructed'[30]. To back up the Dalmuir works, plant (for making large naval guns) was laid down at Parkhead, including a 12 000 ton hydraulic press and a gun tempering shop (1905) that was at the time one of the tallest buildings in Scotland. Altogether £244 600 was spent on buildings alone at Parkhead between 1884 and 1914. This massive expansion was financed partly out of profits, but also by the issue of shares in 1902 of which £749 997 were taken by Vickers, and by the issue of debentures in 1904-05 amounting to £1.5 million. In 1906, the firm bought Mossend Steelworks for £50 000 to expand plate and section capacity for Dalmuir. Beardmore took over the Mo-Car syndicate, makers of the Arrol-Johnston motor car, in 1903, and encouraged that firm to move from Paisley to Dumfries in 1912-13. Beardmore also took out a licence to build Austro-Daimler aero-engines in 1913.

By 1909, Vickers were far from happy with William Beardmore's handling of the company and sought his replacement as chairman. The new yard at Dalmuir did not prove profitable, a loss of £25 000 having been made on H.M.S. *Agamemnon*, the first battleship built there. The firm again came under pressure in 1913, when another £1 million in preference shares was issued. It seems likely that the outbreak of the First World War saved the company. Government contracts for ships, guns, and, from 1915, shells, poured in to the firm, which had the third-highest output of warships on the Clyde during the war years. From 1914 to 1918 the company built two first-class battleships, one seaplane carrier, three light cruisers, fifteen destroyers, nine submarines (including one K-class flotilla-leader), and thirty-nine smaller vessels (see page 131). Additional capacity was created at Parkhead and Dalmuir for gunmaking, the former Arrol-Johnston factory in Paisley was turned over to shell manufacture, the new Arrol-Johnston factory in Dumfries made aero-engines (2500), and new factories were set up at Tongland for aero-engine construction, Anniesland, and, in 1916, at Inchinnan for airship-building. Mossend was extended in 1917 with Government finance (£875 000) to make bar steel for shells and ship plates, and in the closing months of the war the firm bought the

Sentinel Works of Alley & MacLellan and the Scottish Ice Rink at Crossmyloof, the latter for the assembly of ABC 'Dragon Fly' aero engines, a contract for 1500 having been secured.

This feverish activity, at least partly under Government control, ceased abruptly with the Armistice. Contracts to the value of about £9 million were cancelled, and the firm was left to adjust to peace-time conditions. The war-time euphoria of a great armaments firm was not extinguished. Beardmore, by then Sir William, saw the need to take advantage of the new capacity created for light and medium engineering, and introduced motor-car manufacture at Anniesland and Tongland, revived motor-car manufacture at Dumfries, and continued the aeroplane development work started during the war. Diesel engines were also developed, under the Tosi patents for marine use, and by Beardmore's own engineers for vehicles, airships, and locomotives. More traditional branches of engineering were not neglected. A locomotive works was set up at Dalmuir and new berths were built there, Mossend was further improved, and a half-share in the Glasgow Iron & Steel Co. purchased. All these investments – to cost nearly £4 million, including working capital – were to be financed by a £5 million share issue. The whole project was designed 'to share in the general expansion of trade consequent on the victorious termination of the war'[31]. This 'general expansion' did not materialize, and Beardmore's entered the 1920s heavily committed, with an ageing chairman holding an expansionist philosophy, and with a scattered and varied empire, over which central control seems to have been largely ineffective.

On the surface, however, the company's prospects seemed bright. Gross profits for the five years December 1915 to December 1920 were just over £4 million, though after deduction of depreciation, management commissions, and dividends, this was reduced to under £2 million, of which £1.1 million was put to reserve. This annual gross profit of £800 000 could not, however, be sustained. Profits fell to £218 000 in 1921, to £96 000 in 1922, and a loss of £218 000 was made in 1923. Such reverses were no new phenomenon and reserves had been provided for such a contingency. The position deteriorated in 1924 when a loss of £503 000 was registered reducing the balance in the profit and loss account to £59 000. Things were little better in 1925 (£252 000 loss) and worse in 1926 (£761 000 loss), wiping out the reserves and leaving a deficit of £254 000, though Treasury guarantees for taxicabs and ships had been forthcoming under the Trade Facilities Act (1921) and a warship contract – for H.M.S. *Shropshire* – came to Dalmuir in 1926. In January 1927, however, the company was unable to pay wages and pressing creditors, and the banks would not advance any further money. A committee of four, headed by F.A. Szarvasy, was appointed to look into the affairs of the company, and a period of reconstruction began. The problem was to contain losses and, in June 1927, Lewis Craven Ord was brought in as joint managing director, with the specific aim of effecting economies. He was able to stem the tide, and in 1927 an operating profit of £88 000 was realized, though after allowing for interest payments and accumulated losses, a net deficit of £532 000 was recorded. At this point the Inland Revenue came to the rescue, with repayment of wartime excess profits duty, which after allowances for income tax due by the company and its subsidiaries amounted to £125 000. The deficit fell in 1928, but in 1929 rose again. The Bank of England intervened, taking or placing £725 000 of mortgage debenture stock. This was followed by a Treasury loan of £128 000 and by the replacement of Lord Invernairn (as Sir William Beardmore became in 1922) by Ord as chairman of the company.

Under the guidance of Montagu Norman, Governor of the Bank of England, a policy of retrenchment started. Mossend was closed in January 1930, and the Dalmuir yard was sold to National Shipbuilders Securities for £207 000 later that year. The Parkhead cogging and plate mills were closed and the plate, section, and rail business was sold to David Colville & Co., on the understanding that Colvilles would supply steel at preferential rates. Locomotive-building at Dalmuir was stopped in 1931, after orders for the Indian State Railways (presumably directed by the Treasury) had been built at a loss of £50 000. The Tongland factory had closed in 1922 and Dumfries followed in 1929, while aircraft development and construction based on Dalmuir also ceased in that year. The commercial vehicle section was closed in 1932. Despite these measures, losses continued and, in July 1932, Sir James Lithgow was brought in at the request of Sir Andrew Duncan, chairman of the British Iron and Steel Federation. In the ensuing reconstruction of the Scottish steel industry (see page 109), Parkhead was left out, largely because, having parted with the Mossend Works, it constituted so small a part of the industry. Government contracts began to flow in 1932, when two orders for cruiser engines were placed by the Admiralty, and by January 1933, Admiralty orders on hand amounted to £574 000 and were expected to rise. This in itself posed the problem of finding working capital for material and wages which was exacerbated by War Office unwillingness to renew a loan of £150 000 made for housing at Dalmuir in 1915. Eventually an overdraft facility of £100 000 was arranged with Lloyd's Bank.

This respite was, however, temporary. The deficiency on the profit and loss account in 1931 was £391 000, in 1932 £568 922, and in 1933, when the deficit was approaching £750 000, the Bank of England insisted on rationalization, with 'the closing down of departments at present incurring losses, the sale of surplus plant in those and other departments, in order that the chances might be increased of preserving Parkhead as a profit-earning unit'[32]. The first stages in the run-down were the closure of the Dalmuir engine works – for which the remaining group of Admiralty marine manufacturers paid £200 000 – and the sale of Mossend to Colvilles for £100 000. Nonetheless, in December 1934, the deficit had risen to £797 756, and the need for further capital reconstruction became urgent. One possibility was amalgamation with the Steel Company of Scotland, but this was discounted by Sir James Lithgow, who felt that progress at Parkhead was too slow. By the end of the year, however, the prospects of rearmament encouraged the board, under the chairmanship of H.A. Reincke to authorize the installation of a new press, the first substantial capital investment at Parkhead for more than ten years, 'having regard to the serious position in which the company would find itself in the event of the presses at present in use breaking down or otherwise proving unable to cope with the increasing volume of work'[33]. Early in 1936, the first positive steps were taken to prepare for rearmament, and in the light of the prospects for improved results, Sir James Lithgow bought the majority of the first debenture stock from the Bank of England, becoming Chairman of the company. Explaining the move at a board meeting on 26 February 1936, Montagu Norman said that the Bank of England 'reluctantly and under great pressure' had taken up most of the issue of first debenture stock 'for the purpose of saving the company from bankruptcy at a time when such an event would have been a catastrophe to the West of Scotland, entailing loss of employment to several thousands of men'[34]. Lithgow proceeded to co-ordinate Beardmore's activities with Colvilles by a whole range of informal understandings.

From then until the outbreak of the Second World War, the pace of re-equipment quickened. New tools were bought for small gun manufacture, agreement was reached with the other two armour producers on sharing Admiralty orders (Beardmore's share was a quarter), new open-hearth furnaces were built, and, in May 1936, it was decided to display the firm's name more prominently on the works. By the end of the year expenditure amounting to £419 148 had been authorized and by March 1937 this had risen to nearly £1.5 million. When war came, Parkhead Forge was, therefore, in an excellent position to supply armour plate and small guns on a large scale. After the war, however, the firm again had to face declining peace-time demand, this time compounded by the replacement in shipbuilding and heavy engineering practice of heavy forgings and steel castings by welded fabrications which could be made without expensive plant. The firm has for some years now specialized in melting and rolling alloy steel and in making work-rolls for cold rolling strip steel, for which it has built up a world-wide reputation.

Several morals can be drawn from this tale of brilliant success alternating with chronic failure. Firstly, it illustrates the point that investment is not a panacea for economic ills, for from *c.* 1900 to *c.* 1922 some millions of pounds were invested in the Beardmore empire. Secondly, research-and-development cannot of themselves solve problems, for few firms can have invested so much in applied science in the 1920s. Beardmore engineers worked on high-speed diesels for a wide range of purposes, including airship and aeroplane propulsion, and were technically successful. They also developed the *Inflexible* (built in 1928), the largest aeroplane built until the Bristol *Brabazon,* in 1949, with the aim of demonstrating the advantages of all-metal stressed-skin construction. Built to Rohrbach's patents, the construction of this craft was not unlike that of modern airliners. Thirdly, it demonstrates the dangers of relying too heavily on outside capital. Quite apart from their bankers, major shareholders from outside the company and holders of notes and debentures issued from time to time to relieve liquidity problems were in a strong position to force economies on the firm at a time when these might well have been detrimental to its long-term prospects. The ever-growing burden of debt was a massive disincentive to continuation of that far-sighted innovation which characterized Beardmores in the 1920s and early 1930s. Finally, it suggests that one of the reasons for the severity of the 1931-33 depression was a general lack of opportunity to reap the expected benefit from immediate post-war investment during the period 1920-30.

While it would certainly be misleading to draw general conclusions from the experience of Beardmores, it seems likely from what can be gathered about other West of Scotland firms that many of the company's problems were shared ones. The firms which continued were, in general, those firms engaged in heavy industry which survived the inter-war period with enough liquid capital to tide them over, or those who were sufficiently sound as to enjoy the forebearance of creditors and shareholders, but many works closed. One aspect of the inter-war economy hinted at but not explicit in the Beardmore records is clarified in the Fairfield Shipbuilding and Engineering Co.'s Valuation Book for the period 1926-34. This shows that the depreciated value of the engine works fluctuated during this period between £109 000 and £124 000, but a note shows that the value had dropped to £7600 in 1942. Similarly, the value of the yard fell from £148 000 to £114 000 between 1927 and 1932, but had slumped to £21 000 in 1941. Though book values are not particularly reliable, these figures illustrate the lack of investment in new plant in the late 1920s and in the 1930s in this particular yard. As much of the machinery in the yard and engine works remained usable, the reduced values gave a better basis for profitability in the abnormally buoyant conditions of the late 1930s and 1940s.

This brief survey of engineering in the West of Scotland has been highly selective, concentrating on some of the more important sectors, either in value of output (marine engineering, locomotive building), in links with other branches of the industry (machine-tool making, structural engineering), or in dominating world markets (sugar-machinery manufacture). Equally significant examples could have been chosen, such as sewing-machine manufacture, where the American-owned Singer Factory at Dalmuir was the largest in the world, or boilermaking where Scotland produced 52 per cent of the total United Kingdom output in 1907, mostly in the West. The aim has been, however, to suggest the significance of engineering in the West of Scotland economy, to sketch in outline the way it has developed, and to indicate the ways, though not the extent, to which its different sectors were interlinked, rather than to present a detailed analysis of this fascinating group of industries.

CHAPTER FOUR

Andrew Barclay Sons & Co. Ltd., Locomotive Manufacturers and Engineers

In Kilmarnock, as elsewhere in the West of Scotland, the late eighteenth century rise of a textile industry stimulated the development of local ironfounding and engineering. Andrew Barclay, Senior, the father of the founder of the firm, leased in the early 1800s the Biggart's woollen mill at Dalry, a small town in north Ayrshire, where 'he made and maintained his own machinery'[1]. In 1817, during the post Napoleonic war depression, he was forced to sell out to Gregory Thomson & Co. of Kilmarnock. He became their millwright, improving the barrel carpet loom invented by Thomas Morton, a local engineer, and pioneering the three-ply carpet loom.

Despite an early interest in engineering, Andrew Barclay, the founder of the company, began work in 1826, at the age of 13, as a weaver in Gregory Thomson's mill. In 1828, he was apprenticed to Lawson & Co., plumbers, tinsmiths, and coppersmiths in Kilmarnock. He left Lawsons in 1840 and went into partnership with a Thomas McCulloch in small premises near the centre of Kilmarnock, 'to make shaftings for mill works, and printers machinery generally'[1]. The partnership was dissolved in 1842 and the present firm established, with Andrew Barclay as sole partner.

Andrew Barclay would seem to have begun business as a mill engineer making a variety of products, especially driving engines and shaftings. He was immediately successful, constructing his first engine under the supervision of David Stirling, the manager of the Dundee engine works, and quickly penetrating the English market by building a large beam engine for Messrs Betts & Co., spirit rectifiers, London. Barclay was not without competition. There were already two engineering concerns in Kilmarnock, exercising a virtual monopoly of the textile trade, Bryce Blairs and Thomas Mortons. From the mid-1840s with the development of the Ayrshire coal and mineral field, John McDowall and William Ure, two notable West of Scotland engineers, showed interest in the opportunities of the Kilmarnock market and established two short-lived works, the Portland and Titchfield Foundries, in Forge Street. Thomas McCulloch continued in business at the Vulcan Foundry in the same street and began making winding engines.

In 1847, Andrew Barclay moved his works to its present site at the Caledonia Foundry on the south side of West Langlands Street (off Forge Street), feued [perpetually leased] from the Marquis of Titchfield, 'with power to erect a steam engine . . . and such other buildings . . . necessary for . . . carrying on the business or trade of engineering in all its departments'[2]. With the move to larger and better-equipped premises, Barclay 'began to supply machinery for collieries'[1]

Figure 4.1 *A horizontal winding engine with Cornish drop valve gear built in 1900-01 for the Wearmouth Coal Co. The cylinders were each 34 inches in diameter and 6 feet in stroke. Cornish drop valves, a speciality of Barclay designs, were relatively uncommon. Note the unusual method of suspending the brake gear.*

making his first winding engine, 18 inches × 3 feet stroke with 40 horsepower for Mr Howie, Senior, of Hurlford, a suburb of Kilmarnock. The *Kilmarnock Standard* commented on the quality of these early products in 1874: 'Mr Barclay about 18 years ago fitted up [for the Nitshill and Lesmahagow Coal Co.] a pair of 21 inch cylinder engines, which from that time till now have never cost the company anything for repairs'[3]. The reliable construction of Barclay's products was supplemented by his ingenuity and skill as an engineer. He patented many inventions for use on winding engines to prevent overwinding, especially a link-motion hand-gear, in 1853, and a link-motion and expansive arrangement for Cornish valves, in 1874. By 1892, he was able to claim, with some justification: 'that there is not a winding engine now made in the country but is to my design'[4] (Figure 4.1).

With the growth of his business, Andrew Barclay extended the Caledonia foundry at first on the original site and later, in 1855, to the north of West Langlands Street by the purchase of the Titchfield Foundry. This allowed him to increase the range and size of his products. The following year he built his first pumping engine, 8 inch × 12 feet stoke, for the Coltness Coal Co. Although he

Figure 4.2 *0–4–0ST (works no. 52) built for the Harbour Master, Sunderland in 1866, see here in the ownership of the Riv Wear Commissioners, c. 1913. This 'basic Barclay' is a typical Scottish industrial locomotive of its period. The cab is a later addition.*

began to build industrial locomotives in 1858, producing ten in 1862 (Figure 4.2), it was not until a further extension and reorganization of the works which doubled its capacity between 1863 and 1865 (Figure 4.3), that he was able consistently to achieve this number annually. Locomotive building was a natural adjunct of Barclay's mining engineering business. The majority of locomotives produced before 1890 were for mineral mines. Between 1858 and 1864, locomotives were sold only in the West of Scotland market, mostly to established customers, but thereafter Barclay was able to penetrate the rest of the Scottish and the English and Welsh markets, building from the early 1890s roughly equal numbers for each area.

Financial Difficulties

In July 1870, Andrew Barclay was described as the largest employer in Kilmarnock, with a workforce of 420 and an annual turnover of £70 000[5]. But the investment in his works in the mid-1860s had caused him to over-reach himself, and in 1871 he was faced with a serious liquidity crisis arising from growing competition in the mining sector and a sudden downturn in the market. In 1869, already aware of his vulnerability, he had transferred part of his locomotive and general engineering business to a new firm, Barclays & Co. consisting of his five sons, with premises at the Riverbank works, Kilmarnock. So that it would be protected in any future crisis, Andrew Barclay was not a partner in the new company. Just such a crisis occurred in 1871, and in the event, Barclay was able to make a composition with his creditors, provided that he took on David Hoey, a Glasgow accountant, as his financial manager.

NO-785

Figure 4.3 *No. 2 shop in 1909, showing a selection of lathes. The large pit lathe in the background was used for machining the cheeks of winding-engine drums. Note the connecting rods for a large winding engine on the right, with locomotive coupling rods beside them. The wooden 'foundry' cranes were characteristic of mid-nineteenth century engineering works' practice.*

To solve his financial problems, Andrew Barclay tried, improvidently, to secure a tied market for his products. In September 1872, he set up (with David Hoey) the North British Iron Hematite Co., later the Lowther Iron Hematite Co., at Workington in the potentially-rich Cumberland iron field. The works cost £109 525 and the first blast furnace was in operation by April 1873. Andrew Barclay became works manager and 'the iron work and machinery were mainly supplied by the [his] firm at Kilmarnock for which the company [Lowther Co.] paid by our acceptances to that firm'[6]. To finance its manufacture Barclay raised two securities of £15 000 and £35 000 over his own works from the Heritable Securities Investment Association. Although the Lowther Co. made profits of £17 000 in 1873, the company's financial position deteriorated rapidly in 1874 'in consequence of the depressed state of the iron trade'[6]. It was forced to borrow £35 000 from the Heritable Securities Investment Association and £44 000 secured against the works from Thomas Steven, a partner in the Glasgow ironfounding company of McDowall and Steven. At the same time James Wilson Barclay, Andrew's eldest son, became a partner in the Kilmarnock firm with responsibility for the business, as his father had been 'engaged exclusively at Workington'[7]. Andrew Barclay, despite Hoey's advice, refused to consider bringing new partners into the Lowther Co. to provide the much wanted capital. Nothing could therefore prevent the bankruptcy of both concerns. Andrew Barclay Son & Co. was sequestrated in September 1874 for debts of over £13 000 and the Lowther Co. in the following December for debts of over £80 000, and both firms were placed in the hands of trustees.

On 26 February 1875, the trustees of Andrew Barclay Son & Co. reported that: 'although business generally was dull, a fair amount of orders were being obtained'[7]. Profits were estimated at between £300 and £400 a month. In late 1875, Thomas Steven acquired the two securities of £15 000 and £35 000 over the Kilmarnock works. He agreed to reinstate Andrew and James Wilson Barclay, providing new controls were introduced in the financial and technical management of the company. This was reflected in the introduction of a new series of business records, especially: day books, detailing work done and the cost of each job; and the systematic arrangements of technical drawings (see Figure 8.6, on page 162). The first day book of 1876 provides, as Steven intended, the earliest opportunity of analysing the firm's output. Out of a total turnover of £33 536, £12 651 was for general engineering products (largely mining machinery) and £5487 for locomotives. The difference was made up in repair and jobbing work. At the same time Thomas Steven, the preferred creditor of the Lowther Co., together with seven partners, re-established the firm as a private limited company, capitalized at £250 000 compared with the original £10 000.

Meanwhile, Andrew Barclay, faced with strong competition in the market for mining machinery, began, unsuccessfully, to develop new product lines suited to expanding markets, especially steam navvies (Figure 4.4), tramway rolling

Figure 4.4   *A steam navvy of classic type, in the Barclay works yard, c. 1875. Scottish engineers made repeatedly unsuccessful efforts to break into the market for heavy earth-moving equipment, building on existing links with civil engineering contractors.*

Figure 4.5   A handsome example of a 'piano tank' – so called from the shape of the saddle tank – built in 1877 for the Callendar Coal Co., Falkirk.

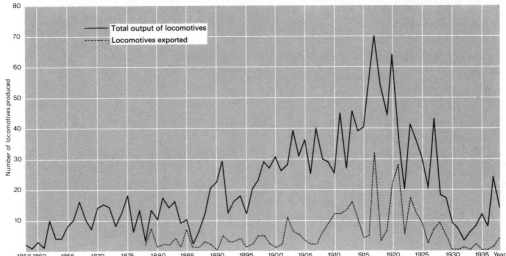

Figure 4.6   Locomotive production by Andrew Barclay Sons & Co. between 1858 and 1938.

stock, and locomobiles (traction engines). Unfortunately, in March 1876, 'two-thirds of the works were burned'[8]. Production was severely disrupted, with locomotive output falling from eighteen in 1875 to six in 1876 (Figure 4.5). Although Andrew Barclay claimed in 1882 that, 'since 1877 I have carried on my business at Kilmarnock balancing every year'[8], the combined effects of the fire and the late 1870s depression (Figure 4.6) resulted in his second sequestration in 1882. In the following year, John Waddell, an Edinburgh contractor and one of the firm's customers, and Thomas Steven arranged credit of £6000 for Barclay to allow him to make a composition of $17\frac{1}{2}$ pence in the pound with his creditors. They insisted that the management should be strengthened by the appointment of Henry Ker as the firm's London agent, Mr Bairnsfather as financial manager, and Major Royce as sub-cashier.

Although the profits of the firm in 1882–83 were £1925 on a turnover of £30 697 and £5543 on £33 784 in the boom year 1883–84, the company was running into serious difficulties, due partly to a violent clash of personalities between the Barclays and Waddell and Steven's nominees, and partly to the mid-1880s recession. Andrew Barclay decried Ker's appointment: 'We did not get any new orders through him'[9]. He attacked Royce's book-keeping: 'I am not aware that our books were ever brought to a regular balance'[9]; and complained bitterly at the tight control maintained by Bairnsfather and Waddell over the management of the company, especially their refusal to allow him to tender on a small profit margin: 'We did not make tenders which were likely to be accepted because . . . we would not be permitted to take [the] contracts'[9]. With the depressed market for engineering products in the mid-1880s and the resulting fierce competition for orders, it was natural for Steven, through Bairnsfather and Waddell, to insist on adequate profit margins. Sensibly, they tried to protect their investment in the company by taking on small orders and avoiding big commitments. By 1886, the number of workers employed by the firm had fallen to between 25 and 30 men. Andrew Barclay protested that, 'it would not pay to keep the works open'[9]. Steven and Waddell, by now exasperated, decided to remove Barclay and his son from the management of the company. Barclay learnt of this and himself petitioned for bankruptcy with liabilities in excess of £60 000 rather than lose control of his firm. The turnover for 1887 was a meagre £8472, with only £2855 for new locomotives and £953 for a set of plunger pumps and a coal crushing machine.

From 1869 until 1886 Barclay & Co., although owing Andrew Barclay & Son £10 572, had continued in business at the Riverbank works independently. But in 1886 Thomas Steven had sequestrated the partners for debts of £4618 and taken possession of the works which he had bought in 1874. In 1889, Andrew Barclay and his sons agreed to purchase both the Caledonia, Titchfield, and Riverbank works from Thomas Steven for £20 000, payable in six annual instalments of £1000, with the balance, plus 5 per cent interest, due in 1898. In 1892, Barclay was unable to fulfil the agreement as the profits for the ten months May 1891 to February 1892 were only £682 despite a turnover of £40 688. Thomas Steven commissioned John Mann, a Glasgow accountant, to examine the future of the two works at Kilmarnock. His report suggested that Andrew Barclay, now nearly 80, was becoming too old to manage the firm effectively; there was, according to Mann, 'ample evidence that the business had been not only drained by private expenditure; but is leaking at every point'[4].

A Fresh Start

As the company required between £2000 and £5000 of fresh capital to meet its liabilities and remain in business, Mann recommended that the business be formed into a limited company. He advised that Andrew Barclay should sell his interest in the firm to the new company and be retained as managing director at a salary of £500; but with an independent cashier to control cash flows. Mann's report was accepted and the principal creditors – Thomas Steven and Joseph Reid, a Glasgow iron merchant – became directors of the new company. Andrew Barclay remained as managing director, with three of his sons John Galileo, Andrew D., and Andrew Junior, as senior managers. Immediately the board began to bring pressure on the Barclays to increase the efficiency of their management, resolving in October to close the Riverbank works unless some improvement took place. The weaknesses in the Barclays' management was exacerbated by the 'exceptionally severe depression of trade'[4] with turnover falling to £26 735 in 1892-93. In January 1893, John Galileo was forced to take on a contract for a winding engine 'at what was understood to be a low figure in order to keep the works going', but his costings were 'altogether unreliable . . . resulting in a loss to the company of £557 785'[4]. Early in 1893 Andrew Junior was suspended by the board, to be followed in July by John Galileo, then works manager, after he had tendered for a vertical pumping engine for Chester Corporation on his own account.

On 2 August 1893, F.G. Allan, an experienced engineer, was appointed works manager with assurances that the board 'will support you in everything that will make the business sound and profitable'[4]. Although turnover fell to £24 887 for the year, in the half year to March 1894 the directors were able to report a small profit of £1026 compared with a loss of £1241 in the previous half year, 'due in part to change of management, in part to work of routine character, largely locomotive building and repairing'[4]. In May 1894, Allan recommended with the board's concurrence, the closure of the Riverbank works, which had been shut since November. He also suggested that, as the market for winding and stationary engines showed little sign of recovery, it was advisable to introduce new specialities, such as coal cleaning plant and duplex pumps, and to change the emphasis of the production: 'the locomotive trade should be cultivated much more than it is, and engines should be built for stock'[4]. The board agreed and authorized Allan to go ahead.

Meanwhile the directors were becoming increasingly dissatisfied with Andrew Barclay. In April 1894 in a final attempt to retain control of his firm, he tried to raise enough capital to buy off Thomas Steven and Joseph Reid, offering them £11 000. Reid accepted and left the board in October to be replaced by Thomas Steven, Junior. In late August relations between Barclay and the rest of the board reached a crisis with Barclay refusing either to explain the sharp fall in profits to £505 or to sign bills on behalf of the company. At their November meeting the board expressed 'grave dissatisfaction . . . with the conduct of the managing director'[4]. An extraordinary general meeting was called to consider the matter on 5 December, when it was resolved to remove Andrew Barclay and appoint a successor.

With the appointment of Thomas Turner of Shelton, Stoke-on-Trent, as managing director in April 1895, the prospects for the company slowly began to improve. By February 1896, the firm was employing 345 men with a projected

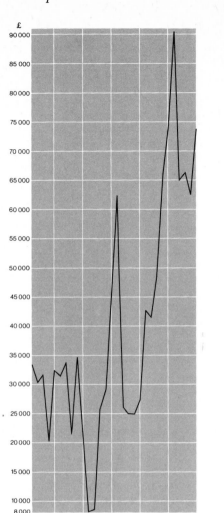

Figure 4.7 *Turnover of Andrew Barclay Sons & Co. between 1876 and 1905.*

turnover of £32 000. The company, though, was still precariously short of cash with a book loss of £4906, and depending for its working capital on constant financial assistance from its creditors. To ease the financial situation, the directors, Hugh and Thomas Steven, Junior (Thomas Senior having died in December 1895), reduced the fixed capital from £15 000 to £10 243 in July 1897, and began to consider ways of re-organizing the works in accordance with Allan's suggestions of August 1893. Already locomotive production, which had reached a low of twelve in 1895, was beginning to increase steadily (see Figure 4.5, on page 73). By 1898, together with locomotive repair work, it accounted for nearly 60 per cent of the firm's turnover, and more significantly bore on average profits of 13.2 per cent, whereas stationary engine building and general engineering yielded only 6.5 per cent. The figures for 1898 and 1899, which showed a widening in the profitability and turnover gap (Figure 4.7), confirmed the board in its decision to reconstruct the works for locomotive manufacture and repair, with some general engineering business to take up surplus capacity.

Thomas Turner was requested to examine how this might best be achieved

Figure 4.8 *The new boiler shop in 1903, with boilers at various stages of construction. On the left a horizontal drilling machine is working on a boiler barrel, and in the foreground are inner and outer fireboxes. The relatively small size of industrial locomotive boilers is clearly illustrated here (compare with Figure 3.17, on page 50).*

and reported on 20 December 1899 that there were three options open to the board:

'1.   To build a boiler works (only) elsewhere, with a view of adding machinery and other shops later, to make a complete locomotive works.

2.   To commence locomotive works entirely at once elsewhere.

3.   To build boiler works only on Titchfield ground'[10].

(Previously most locomotive boiler shells had been bought in.) The directors felt unable to recommend the second alternative, 'because of the high cost of equipping a complete new works'[10]. Instead, they chose the third and decided that, 'the boiler shops should be proceeded with at once, and be made capable of turning out 75 boilers per annum, 25 of which would represent renewals or repairs and the other 50 would be for new locomotives'[10] (Figure 4.8). In the long term they decided on 'the arrangement of a locomotive works on the area of the Titchfield ground . . . to turn out 40 tank locomotives per annum'[10]. In an expansive mood, with a record turnover of £55 417 and profits of £9785, they authorized the extension of the erecting shop at a cost of £4000 (Figure 4.9).

By 1903, when the production target was almost attained, (with an output of 50 new boilers, 20 repairs, 4 fireboxes, and 39 locomotives (Figure 4.10), £32 000 had been spent on capital projects, including new offices. Despite the record output profits fell from £11 916 in 1902 to £9988 in 1903, and future demand was uncertain. Capital expenditure was restricted to machines that would do away with hand-finishing work and raise productivity so that the costly night-shift could be abandoned. Simultaneously, to improve output, piecework and bonus

systems were introduced. In April 1904, the board authorized Turner 'to make certain locomotives at cost price with the view of keeping the works fully employed'[10] (Figure 4.11). With a slight improvement in the market early in 1905 the board's confidence in its expansionist policy returned. A further £3257 was spent on two milling machines and an extension to the machine shop. But by the autumn the outlook was once more depressed and Turner was again authorized to reduce locomotive prices 'as this department was the most profitable and could be run at a lower ration of expense'[10] (Figure 4.12). In January, in an effort to reduce oncosts, the board urged that 'every effort should be made to get on to lines of standardizing products especially locomotives'[10].

The market improved rapidly in 1907. Turner was able to report in May 'that the order book was at present well filled with locomotive orders and that there were a number of engines'[10] (Figure 4.13). The board, though, was cautious of becoming too involved in the general market and agreed 'to try to secure new locomotive and locomotive-repair orders in preference to general engine work'[10]. Consequently, locomotive output in 1907 reached 40 for the first time. Production fell back in the following three years (Figures 4.14 and 4.15)

Figure 4.9 *A classic erecting shop scene, with the four 3 foot gauge 4–6–0 tank locomotives (works nos. 933-6) built for the Letterkenny & Burtonport Extension Railway, in 1902, and the 2–4–0T Lady Margaret (works no. 976) for the Liskeard & Caradon Railway. In the right foreground a standard 0–4–0 saddle tank is under construction. This view shows the then new extension to the erecting shop. Note the arc lighting.*

Figure 4.10 *A sparkling new standard Barclay 0–4–0ST (works no. 974) of 1903, in a typical colliery scene. This locomotive exemplifies the results of the modernization programme begun in 1899.*

Figure 4.11 *Three compound engines built to drive centrifugal pumps for a graving dock at Belfast Harbour, in 1907. The directors considered in 1904, when the order was placed, the possibility of having these engines built outside as prices were very low owing to the depression of that year.*

dropping to 25 in 1910, but revived in the run up to the First World War, with the construction of 158 locomotives in the years 1911–14. By 1913, the output of the company was firmly geared to locomotive production, which accounted for £51 248 of the turnover of £129 300 in that year, with only £14 960 for colliery machinery. Moreover, the difference was made up largely of locomotive repairs, mostly the supply of new boilers. During the war the firm passed under Government control. Further capital improvements were made to meet wartime demand and the expected post-war boom. Between 1914 and 1919 a prodigious 261 locomotives were turned out (Figures 4.16 and 4.17), 86 for Government departments. Profits increased to £22 091 in 1919, rising to a record of £42 842 in 1920.

The sudden downturn in the market after 1920 (Figure 4.18) resulted in losses of £19 705 in 1922 and an output of only 20 locomotives. The board's reaction characteristically was to try to reduce competition by negotiating with other industrial locomotive manufacturers, and to consider work-pooling arrangements proposed by the Locomotive Manufacturers' Assocation. In 1925, the board recognized 'that the capacity of the locomotive builders far exceeds

Figure 4.12 *(a) Crane locomotives were a minor Barclay speciality. They made 38 between 1881 and 1947. This one (works no. 880) built in 1899 for Glenfield & Kennedy Ltd, the Kilmarnock hydraulic engineers, is seen here outside their foundry. The works plate is dated 1902.*
(b) Before a rail link was installed in 1902-03, locomotives were moved from the works by road, normally on their own wheels. A gang of men was sometimes used, but here a Burrell single-crank compound traction engine belonging to David Proctor, a local contractor, is hauling no. 923 built for J.R. Wood & Co., Southampton, in 1902.

(a)

(b)

Figure 4.13 *The erecting shop in 1907, with the engines shown in Figure 4.11 on the right, and the casings of their centrifugal pumps beyond. The largest of the three winding engines in the centre bay was built for the Weardale Coal Co., Thornley Colliery and had cylinders 32 inches by 5 feet, with Corliss valve gear. Beyond it is a 20 inch by 3 feet 6 inch engine for the Stella Coal Co., Blaydon-on-Tyne and beyond that a crab engine for Duncan McNeil & Co. ($8\frac{1}{2}$ inch by $6\frac{1}{2}$ inch). In the foreground is a 16 inch by 36 inch hauling engine for the Burrakur Coal Co. Ltd. In the next bay is a 22 inch by 48 inch Corliss valve winding engine for Buruyeat Brown & Co. Ltd, Cardiff. One locomotive is visible.*

Figure 4.14 *A contrast between Alexandra Docks & Harbour Co.'s 0–6–2 saddle tank no. 31 (works no. 1155), in shop grey, and Ashington Coal Co.'s, no. 8 (works no. 1162), a 2 feet gauge 0–4–2T, in 1908. Locomotives were occasionally painted grey for photography, as this colour shows details clearly.*

Figure 4.15 *Four standard locomotives built for stock in 1909 in works grey livery. Standard locomotives were built to spec' from 1905 and were stockpiled during depressions.*

Figure 4.16 *A group of 0–6–well tank locomotives, constructed for the War Office for use on light supply railways behind the trenches on the Western Front during the First World War. Barclay built 25 of these, ROD 601-25 (works nos. 1518-42) in 1917-18.*

Figure 4.17 *Fireless locomotive (works no. 1496) built in 1917 for the Imperial Paper Mills Ltd, Gravesend. Numerous engines of this type were built during the First World War and later for use in works with a high risk of fire. They drew steam intermittently from stationary boilers and could operate for about 4 hours at a time. The locomotive is seen here in service.*

Figure 4.18 *Six of the standard class E2-foot gauge 0–4–0 well tank locomotives built in 1921 (works nos. 1727-33) most of which went to India. More than twenty of this type were built. 'Series production' was introduced during the First World War. Its development was checked by the collapse of the post-war boom.*

Figure 4.19 *Barclay's unprofitable essay during 1925-27 in main-line locomotive construction is little known. Here LMS 4359 (works no. 1903) poses in a curious works livery on an appropriately dull day. These locomotives went into service painted black.*

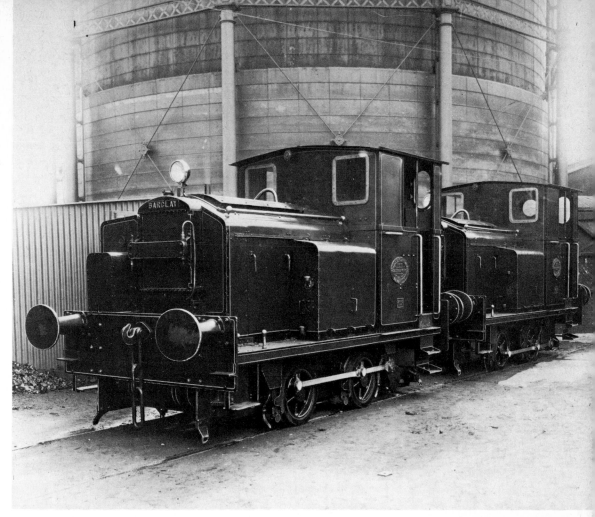

Figure 4.20 *Two diesel locomotives built for the Admiralty in 1940 (works nos. 339 and 340). The wisdom of the company's decision to build industrial diesel locomotives was fully justified during and after the Second World War. By the 1950s diesels dominated the order book.*

present requirements and any likely to arise for some considerable time to come'[11]. Nevertheless, the company managed to secure a large order for 25 express freight tender locomotives for the London, Midland, and Scottish Railways Co. (Figure 4.19). Unfortunately, the coal strike and 'the advance in prices of fuel, power and material, and also the increased cost of production resulting from inevitable delays in obtaining necessary parts'[11] made the contract unprofitable, with a loss of £15 811 in 1927.

A Policy for Survival

In the realization that there was overcapacity in the locomotive market due to wartime investment, the board far-sightedly attempted to introduce new product lines, including diesel locomotives in 1928 (Figure 4.20), that might provide a basis for recovery. In 1928, the goodwill of John Cochrane (Barrhead) & Co., specialists in 'power hammers, pumps, ... driving engines of smaller size, and water filtering and softening plant'[11] was bought for £700 and in 1929 the manufacturing rights to H.S. and W. Moore's gas generators. However, the depression worsened and locomotive output fell to single figures in 1930, dropping to 3 in 1932. Although the gas generators were an eventual failure, the policy of diversification within general engineering partially offset the decline in

84

locomotive output. In September 1930 the board reported that 'the works have been kept occupied to the extent of about 60 per cent output by the addition of the Cochrane specialties (Figure 4.21) and the Moore patent gas engines'[11].

By 1933, with total losses of nearly £29 000, it 'was impossible even to maintain the same volume of output secured in the previous year'[11]. The order book was sustained by the spares business, which enjoyed a mild boom, mirroring the lack of investment in new products. 1934, though, was a turning point. Orders and enquiries for both locomotive and general engineering products (including Cochrane specialities) increased and the company made its first profit since 1930. Output and profits gradually improved with the approach of the Second World War. By 1939, the board was sufficiently confident in the future to negotiate a loan of £10 000 from the Special Areas Reconstruction Association Ltd, and £35 000 from the Nuffield Trustees 'for the purpose of re-equipping and reorganizing its works for the better and more economic operation thereof'[2]. After the war, as a result of this judicious investment, the firm moved with success into the diesel market. It is now the only surviving locomotive manufacturer in Scotland.

Shipbuilding

CHAPTER FIVE

Shipbuilding

Until the American War of Independence (1776-83) few ships had been built in the West of Scotland; but between then and about 1840 a flourishing wooden-shipbuilding industry grew up in Greenock, Port Glasgow, and Dunbarton (Figures 5.1 (a) and (b)). With the combination, locally, of cheap coal and iron, engineering expertise, and the Lower Clyde skill in wooden shipbuilding, the West of Scotland became, in the early nineteenth century, a significant shipbuilding centre. It was, however, only after Henry Bell's *Comet* (launched in 1812) had shown the potential commercial possibilities of steamships that the Clyde's output became anything other than of local interest. With its hull built in Port Glasgow by John and Charles Wood, its engine by John Robertson of Glasgow, and its boiler by David Napier at the Lancefield Works, Glasgow, the *Comet* set a pattern that was to be followed for the next three decades (Figure 5.2). Even such celebrated engineers as Robert Napier continued, until the 1840s, to sub-contract the building of his hulls to Lower Clyde yards. John and Charles Wood pioneered hull designs suitable for steam propulsion. In the *James Watt* of 1820 they abandoned the 'cod's head' and 'mackerel tail', common in sailing-vessel design, to compensate for the depression of the bow by the masts and sails. Instead, Charles Wood designed the hull to be symmetrical about the midships, 'for the first time an even balancing body was introduced . . . a wonderful and enormous stride in naval architecture and which in itself formed for ten or fifteen years, the pattern steam ship'[1]. By the 1840s, the initiative in the industry rested firmly with the engineers. Owners placed contracts with them on the basis of the reliability and performance of their engines rather than their skill as hull builders.

Engineers turn to Shipbuilding

The engineers, familiar with the method of working wrought iron, were ideally placed to introduce, in the 1840s, the new cost-saving technique of iron shipbuilding, which had been pioneered in England. Tod and MacGregor, who had begun business as engineers in 1834, opened the first iron shipyard on the river in 1836 (Figure 5.3). It was, though, the entrepreneurial skill of Robert Napier that made the Clyde's reputation for iron shipbuilding. In 1841, Napier opened his own iron shipyard at Govan, launching his first ship, the *Vanguard*, in 1843 (Figure 5.4). At the same time he bought the Parkhead Forge from his cousin to supply forgings for his engines and hulls. Despite the misgivings of Lloyds and the Admiralty, iron ships were an immediate success in the passenger market as, although the price was higher, running costs were about 25 per cent

Figure 5.1 *Not at all the traditional view of Clyde shipbuilding, these two paintings are of wooden ships about to be launched from Scotts' West Burn yard in Greenock (Figure (a)), and Barclay Curle's yard at Stobcross, in c. 1830, (Figure (b)). Then, as now, a launch attracted crowds of sightseers. The Christian, (Figure 5.1 (a)), built for Messrs Stirling Gordon & Co. for the West Indies trade. On the left are the masts of vessels in the drydock, which is still in use. Barclay Curle & Co., who started as ship-repairers, in 1818, were the only important wooden shipbuilders on the upper river. The painting (Figure (b)) is one of the few illustrations of a Clyde shipyard of the period, and shows an unknown vessel. On the left a small steamship is under construction.*

Figure 5.2 *P.S. Margery, launched in June 1814 by William Denny & Bros of Dumbarton, had its engines built by James Cook of Tradeston, Glasgow, one of the most celebrated engineers of his day. The Margery was the first steamer on the Thames. There were numerous small shipyards on the estuary of the Leven in the early nineteenth century. Most firms were short-lived, for example, Scott & Linton, who went bankrupt during the building of the* Cutty Sark, *in 1869. The amounts of fixed capital involved in wooden shipbuilding were so small as to encourage many shipwrights to set up on their own account.*

less than for wooden hulls. Initially, Robert Napier sold his iron ships to those firms with whom he already had special relations, either as an engineer or financier, but by the 1860s he had penetrated nearly every passenger market and had built ships for many different owners, including several foreign firms and navies.

Robert Napier's firm was the kindergarten of Clyde shipbuilders. The majority of the Clyde marine-engine works and iron shipyards, established in the mid-nineteenth century, were set up by former employees; notably Tod and MacGregor, in 1834 by David Tod and John MacGregor, formerly engine works managers; William Denny & Bros, Dunbarton, in 1844 by William Denny, formerly ship designer and chief draughtsman; J. & G. Thomson (later John Brown Shipbuilding and Engineering Co. Ltd), in 1847 by James and George Thomson, formerly engine works managers; and Randolph & Elder (later the Fairfield Shipbuilding and Engineering Co. Ltd), in 1852 by John Elder, formerly chief draughtsman (see page 113). In managing their own yards these men borrowed many of Napier's engineering and entrepreneurial techniques, particularly the acquisition of capital both by accident and design, in shipping companies; the building of loss leaders to encourage custom; the insistence on consistently high quality products; and the introduction of new equipment only after adequate testing and of proven cost-efficiency to owners.

Shipbuilding and Shipowning

In 1840, Robert Napier helped to finance Samuel Cunard's North American Royal Mail Steam Navigation Company, as a way into the potentially lucrative Atlantic market. He even suggested improvements in the design of the first three

Cunarders, and added a fourth to the projected order, so that they would have a greater impact. His investment was rewarded by the acquisition of the majority of the Cunard contracts until the 1860s. In 1866, Barclay Curle & Co. became partners in the newly formed Liverpool-Hamburg Steamship Company and three years later were offered a stake in Donaldson Brothers' proposed new steamship company to trade between the Clyde and the River Plate[2]. In 1887, Sir William Pearce, John Elder's successor at Fairfield and formerly Robert Napier's general manager, together with G.E. Dodwell, founded the Canadian Pacific Steam Ship Line, which amalgamated in 1891 with Canadian Pacific Line. Fairfield continued to have a large equity stake in the company until the 1930s and built sixteen ships for the firm between 1891 and 1931 (Figure 5.5).

Interest in shipowning companies was not only acquired by the purchase of shares, but also by agreeing to accept part payment of a contract price in stock. In 1867, Barclay Curle built the *Caernarvon Castle* on joint account with Donald Currie in return for a 50 per cent stake in the vessel. In this way William Denny &

Figure 5.3 *An engraving of ...od and MacGregor's second ...ard at Meadowside, built in ...844, showing the new graving ...ock opened in 1858. The open ...ountry on the opposite side of the ...iver was to be occupied by the ...airfield and Linthouse shipyards ...y 1870.*

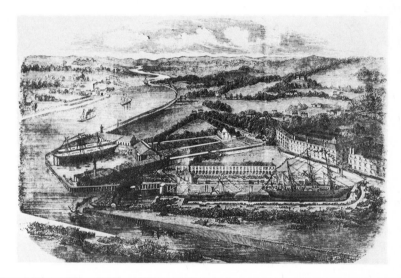

Figure 5.4 *P.S.* Persia, *the ...rst iron ship built for Cunard, ...n the stocks at Robert Napier's ...ovan yard, in 1855. This is one ...f the earliest photographs of a ...lyde shipyard known to exist. ...n the right of the* Persia *are the ...rames of another large iron ship. ...n wrought iron vessels these ...ere far more closely spaced than ...n comparable steel vessels built ...fter 1880. The narrowness of ...lates of the hull of the* Persia *is ...haracteristic of wrought iron ...onstruction. The* Persia *was the ...argest vessel in the world when ...aunched, with a speed of over 13 ...nots.*

Figure 5.5 *The* Empress of Scotland *on trials in 1950. This ship was built originally as the* Empress of Japan *by Fairfield in 1930, and re-fitted as the* Empress of Scotland *in 1950. She has been described as the finest and fastest Pacific liner ever built and was the last of the classic three-funnel Canadian Pacific liners in service. Although the financial ties between Fairfield and the line were broken in the 1930s, the relationship was renewed with the building of the third* Empress of Britain, *in 1956.*

Bros built up, during the second half of the century, large shareholdings in several railway and estuarial navigation companies, in particular the Irrawaddy Flotilla Co., and so were able to secure a continuous supply of contracts for ferries and fast packet boats in an otherwise competitive market. Between 1865 and 1914, William Denny & Bros built 250 special river vessels for the Irrawaddy Flotilla Co., yielding profits of 17.99 per cent compared with 2.71 per cent for larger vessels for general markets with which the firm had special relations. When Charles Connell, founder of Charles Connell & Co., shipbuilders, of Scotstoun, died in 1884, he left shares in twelve ships built by the company, and in three shipping companies for whom he had built ships. Likewise, Anthony Inglis of A. & J. Inglis, who died in the same year, left shareholdings of £17 270 in the British India Steam Navigation Co. Beardmore's shareholding in the Italian Lloyd Saubado line was necessary for the continued existence of their yard after 1920. Shares were often accepted in lieu of cash, particularly during depressions. To quantify these relationships is difficult as they were usually covert and interest was often acquired either through nominees or by extending credit facilities.

Loss Leaders

In 1834, Rober Napier built the *Dundee* and the *Perth* for the Dundee, Perth & London Shipping Co., deliberately at a loss so as to gain further orders. He justified this in a letter to Patrick Wallace in 1833: 'in getting up the first of these vessels great care and attention would be necessary to gain the different objects in view and in doing this an extra expense may be incurred, but which may be avoided in all the other vessels'[3]. This practice, which was, perhaps, sensible when firms built ten or twelve similar vessels annually, spelt disaster when used

Figure 5.6 *The* City of New York *and* City of Paris *were the finest passenger liners of their day and the first to have twin screws. In Figure 5.6 (a) the* City of Paris *is awaiting trials in the fitting out basin in J. & G. Thomson's Clydebank yard, in 1889. The large curved structure beneath the bridge is the roof of the dining room. Arched roofs became a feature of large Atlantic liners built at Clydebank. The other three vessels are the second class cruisers, H.M.S. Terpsichore, Thetis, and Tribune. The first class saloon of the* City of New York *(Figure 5.6(b)), illustrates the lengths to which the builders went to produce a vessel of unparalleled magnificence.*

later in the century in estimating for large complex one-off ships and engines that occupied the greater part of a firm's production capacity.

J. & G. Thomson, in contracting to build the Inman liners *City of New York* and *City of Paris* (Figures 5.6 (a) and (b)) in 1887, and Fairfield Shipbuilding & Engineering Co. Ltd, the Cunarder's *Campania* and *Lucania* in 1893, adopted Napier's maxim and incurred large losses on the contracts which severely weakened their liquidity. In explaining the loss of £10 250 on the *City of New York* and *City of Paris* the directors of J. & G. Thomson, echoing Napier, reported: 'We had to do with work of a magnitude hitherto unattempted and with details of construction in a great measure novel and without precedent of cost, we were also exceedingly desirous to meet as far as we possibly could the wishes of owners in prospect of a continuance of a connection likely to be very beneficial'[4]. Typically these contracts were signed during trade depressions as vehicles for the introduction of technical advances which would give customers either a cost or speed advantage over their competitors[5].

The expansion of Clyde shipbuilding between 1820 and 1850 was a reflection of the growing expertise of the marine engineer rather than of any superiority in hull design and construction, or of a raw material cost advantage. The Napiers and their contemporaries on the Clyde developed the passenger steamship, with emphasis on high speed and reliability, whereas the parallel shipbuilding industries of the Thames, Mersey, and the North-east of England specialized respectively in naval craft, North Atlantic merchant ships, and coasters. By the 1860s the cost advantage in labour and raw materials of the Clyde and, to a lesser extent, the North-east of England, was outweighing any supposed superiority of Thames workmanship in the construction even of naval vessels. Indeed, a correspondent in the *Engineer* wrote in 1867: '. . . the alleged superiority of London over Glasgow workmanship is now more fanciful than real'[6].

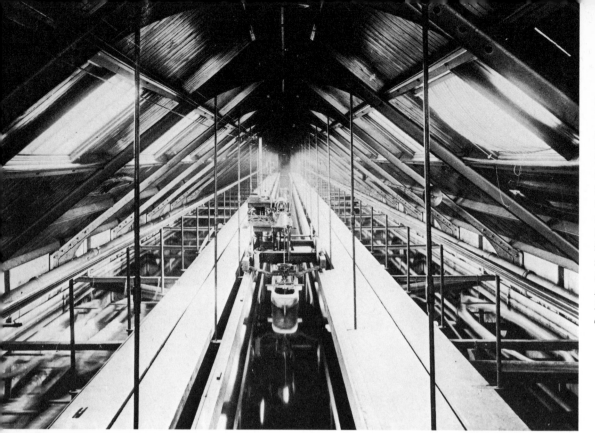

Figure 5.7 *The test-tank at William Denny & Bros, Dumbarton, modelled on William Froude's experimental tank at Torquay (1871), was, when built in 1884, the first commercial test-tank in the world. The moving carriage, in the centre of the picture, pulls the wax model through the water and the instruments on the carriage measure the resistance of the hull to movement through the water. At this time William Denny & Bros were the leading innovators on the Clyde.*

Improvements in Hull Design

Improved standards of hull construction were accompanied by a more scientific approach to hull design. The work of such engineers as William Fairbairn and William MacQuorn Rankine on the structural strength of hulls, and of William Froude and William Denny on hull forms, reduced costs of construction and increased operating efficiency (Figure 5.7). In 1879, William Denny first used steel in the building of an ocean-going passenger vessel – the *Rotomahana*. Until about 1885 there were problems associated with the use of steel, owing partly to the adoption of the wrong qualities of steel, and partly to inadequate supplies and consequent high prices. In 1881, steel plates were reported as costing £10.50 a ton as opposed to iron plates at £6.25 a ton. Although it had been realized that the only satisfactory plates were those made by the Siemens (open-hearth) process, it was not until 1885 that Sir John Biles announced to the Iron and Steel Institute that for a given size of ship, iron was equal in cost to steel and steel gave an advantage in carrying capacity, owing to a reduction in weight of between 13-14 per cent. By that date, steel had completely replaced iron in construction.

The Heyday

Between about 1850 and 1890, through the absence of any significant foreign competition, the intense rivalry between the various shipowners, and continuing technical advances in marine engineering, the Clyde shipbuilding industry became abnormally large. The successful introduction of the compound engine by John Elder in 1854 and the redesigned triple-expansion engine by A.C. Kirk in 1886, required most owners to re-equip to meet competition both in price and speed. As these inventions were made on the Clyde, it was natural for owners to come to the West of Scotland for new tonnage. Moreover, within each phase of development, from single cylinder to quadruple-expansion engines, minor improvements were made by individual firms, often only reducing running costs by a fraction; but in a highly competitive market such improvements attracted customers. In March 1867, the directors of Barclay Curle decided to build 'a pair of high- and low-pressure engines of a description which Messrs Blackwood and Gordon are now making, as any improvement that will save fuel is of so much importance'[7]. This development of more sophisticated propulsive and auxiliary machinery, coupled with improvements in hull design made Clyde-built vessels cheaper to operate in a variety of markets.

The Lower Clyde

When iron shipbuilding began on the Upper Clyde in the 1840s, the Lower Clyde yards with the exception of Caird & Co., and Scott's Shipbuilding & Engineering Co., both at Greenock, continued to build wooden sailing vessels for the merchant trade. Steam propulsion and metal hulls were not viable on many trade routes until later in the century, as both the initial investment and the running costs were higher than for sailing ships. Although iron and steel replaced wood as a hull material in the 1870s and 1880s (Figure 5.8), steam propulsion was not

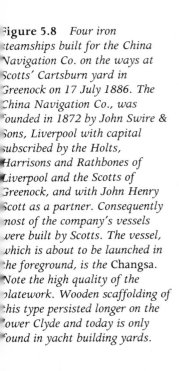

Figure 5.8 *Four iron steamships built for the China Navigation Co. on the ways at Scotts' Cartsburn yard in Greenock on 17 July 1886. The China Navigation Co., was founded in 1872 by John Swire & Sons, Liverpool with capital subscribed by the Holts, Harrisons and Rathbones of Liverpool and the Scotts of Greenock, and with John Henry Scott as a partner. Consequently most of the company's vessels were built by Scotts. The vessel, which is about to be launched in the foreground, is the* Changsa. *Note the high quality of the platework. Wooden scaffolding of this type persisted longer on the Lower Clyde and today is only found in yacht building yards.*

Figure 5.9 *S.S.* Devonshire *on the measured mile at Skelmorlie, Ayrshire, in 1897. This typical tramp steamer was built by Russell & Co. of Port Glasgow in that year for the Helmsdale Steamship Co. and was fitted with triple-expansion engines made by Rankin & Blackmore of Greenock.*

Figure 5.10 *The* Clan Galbraith, *a standard four-masted barque, built by Russell & Co. in 1894. These vessels were designed to carry grain, nitrates, oil, and other bulk cargoes, where economy of operation was more desirable than speed of delivery. Because profit margins on such cargoes were low owners required cheap vessels that were easily managed. Lithgow's standard ships were fitted with steam winches to operate the sails and other labour saving devices. In 1891, Lithgow built the auxiliary barque,* Maria Rickmers, *the largest sailing ship ever built in Britain, in a vain attempt to combine sail and steam. The high risk of the sails catching fire meant that such ships were never a viable proposition, and in the 1890s Lithgow began to build standard steam ships (see Figure 5.9 above).*

adopted until the general introduction of the triple-expansion engine in the 1890s (Figure 5.9). The division between the builders of tramp and other tonnage was a reflection of the different markets in which they operated. Historically, tramp tonnage cost much less than liner tonnage and consequently was written off over a shorter period. Moreover, tramp companies, unlike liner companies, were organized either to manage a particular vessel or as extendable partnerships. Russell & Co., of Port Glasgow were the most successful of the tramp builders. Under the control of W.T. Lithgow from 1874, the firm introduced standard sailing ships – the bulk carriers of their day – to reduce their price (Figure 5.10); and to ensure continuity of production during depressions Lithgow would often take shares in a ship, to be repaid in boom periods. At his death in 1908, W.T. Lithgow left shares in eighty-one ships or shipping companies. During the last two decades of the century the firm frequently built a larger annual tonnage than any other Clyde yard, and increased their capital value from £52 621 in 1879 to £703 839 in 1906, never making a trading loss.

Figure 5.11 *Between 1905 and 1966, Barclay Curle & Co. built sixty ships for the British India Steam Navigation Co. Figure 5.11 (a) shows the launch of the motor passenger troopship* Dunera *from the Barclay Curle yard in 1937, and Figure 5.11 (b) the* Dunera *on trials in the Clyde the following year. This ship is typical of the many smaller passenger ships built by the lesser yards on the river. These vessels with their chunky appearance were designed to carry large numbers of passengers cheaply.*

Specialization

In the 1840s, it was possible for every iron shipbuilding yard to tender successfully for any contract. Between 1840 and 1885 Cunard ships were built in five Clyde yards, thereafter only in two, John Brown and Scott of Greenock, with the exception of the *Tyrrhenia*, taken over from the Anchor Line while building at Beardmores in 1920. By the end of the nineteenth century most of the Clyde yards building liner tonnage had developed special relationships with individual markets and companies. This was partly a consequence of financial or familial links between shipowners and shipbuilders, and partly of increasing specialization. The large Atlantic liners built by J. & G. Thomson, later John Brown, would have been quite unsuited to the Indian or Australian trade, where fuel economy was more important than speed (Figure 5.11). Some firms, originally general shipbuilders, later concentrated on highly specialized markets. In the 1870s, William Simons of Renfrew, who had started as general shipbuilders in Greenock in 1818, were producing mainly dredgers and ancillary craft (Figure 5.12). The physical limitations of the sites was one of the principal

Figure 5.12 *From the 1860s several Clyde yards began specializing in craft for harbour construction and improvement, including dredgers of various types, hopper barges to remove spoil, and rock breakers. By the end of the century Clyde firms dominated the world market, notably William Simons & Co., Lobnitz & Co, and Fleming & Ferguson & Co. The* André Rebouças, *a stern-well bucket dredger, is a typical product of Lobnitz's yard at Renfrew. It was built in 1909 and is seen here in the fitting out basin. The sheerlegs in the background, used for lifting heavy machinery, still stand, the last of their type on the Clyde.*

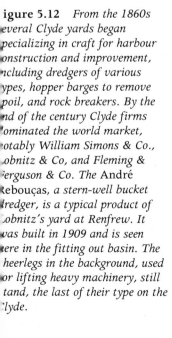

Figure 5.13 *'In order to accommodate the Aquitania with the minimum of disorganization of the other large berths it was decided to embrace in the one berth the width formerly occupied by two berths' (*Engineering, 1914). This photograph shows the berth, yet further extended, after the launching of the Queen Mary at Clydebank, in 1934. The derricks are those installed for the building of the Aquitania, in 1911, and were replaced, in 1936, by tower cranes for the building of the Queen Elizabeth 1. The launching ways are unusually wide to take the weight of this very large vessel. Note that the berth is aligned so that the ship is launched towards the mouth of the River Cart.*

reasons for specialization. Yards on the upper reaches, like Alexander Stephen & Sons, Barclay Curle & Co., and Charles Connell & Co., which were capable of building the largest ships of the 1880s, could not increase their capacity without either removal or extensive re-equipment. John Elder's new shipyard at Fairfield, laid out in 1864, designed for the largest passenger liners of the period was, by 1905, unable to build the giant Atlantic liners demanded by international competition. On the other hand, J. & G. Thomson, who had moved from Govan to a green-field site at Clydebank in 1871, though perhaps less technically advanced than Fairfield, could construct new berths facing the mouth of the Cart to build such vessels and so secured the major Cunard contracts after 1905 (Figure 5.13).

Cost Advantages

The cost advantage in labour and raw materials persisted on the Clyde from 1850 until the outbreak of the Second World War, and attracted established shipbuilders and other industrialists to move to the river or invest in the industry. In 1851, Alexander Stephen & Sons, wooden shipbuilders in Dundee, opened an iron shipyard at Kelvinhaugh in Glasgow (Figure 5.14). John Brown & Co., the Sheffield steelmakers, bought the Clydebank yard in 1899, and the Glasgow steelmaker, William Beardmore, acquired Robert Napier & Sons' Govan yard in 1900. Yarrow & Co. moved from Poplar on the Thames to Scotstoun in 1906 to build torpedo boats and destroyers (Figure 5.15), and Harland & Wolff of Belfast rebuilt three yards into one in Govan in 1912. In the same year Swan Hunter, the Tyne shipbuilders, bought Barclay Curle & Co., because their engine works' costs were significantly lower than those of the Tyne. In 1930 a twin Sulzer diesel built at the Wallsend Shipbuilding & Engineering Co. cost £72 358, and a twin Doxford engine of the same horsepower built by Barclay Curle & Co., cost £62 703 (£6000 less for labour, and £3000 less for materials).[8]

Shrinking Markets

From the turn of the century to the outbreak of the First World War, several factors emerged which were to rob the Clyde shipbuilding industry of its dominance in world markets. Although the Norddeutscher Lloyd had ceased to build its ships on the Clyde in 1890 in favour of its native Germany, it was not until the construction of the Blue Riband holder, *Kaiser Wilhelm Der Grosse* in 1897 that German shipbuilders were able to compete with the premier Clyde

(a)

(b)

Figure 5.14 *In 1869, Alexander Stephen purchased the Linthouse estate on the south bank of the Clyde, near Govan, and laid out a new iron shipyard there, abandoning the yard at Kelvinhaugh the following year. In 1872, the firm opened its own engine works at Linthouse to free it from dependence on outside producers. Figure 5.14 (a) shows Alexander Stephen inspecting the house immediately prior to its purchase, in 1869. Figure 5.14 (b) shows the old mansion house c. 1900, now converted into the firm's offices and engulfed by the shipyard. Shortly after this it was demolished to make way for new buildings.*

(a)

(b)

(c)

(d)

(e)

(f)

igure 5.15 *(Opposite) The*
ove of Yarrow's shipyard from
oplar to Scotstoun involved the
nstruction of an entirely new
ard on a (literally) green-field
te. This series of views shows
e yard in process of
nstruction and comes from a
nique album illustrating the
ilding of the yard by the
ntractors, Sir William Arrol &
o. Ltd. (a) Scotstoun West
ation from the north-west
rner of the site, 20 March
906; (b) Trench for the west
de of the wet basin looking
uth-west, 1 June 1906;
) Engineers' shop in course
erection, looking north, 3
ptember 1906; (d) Boiler shop
oking south-east, taken from
e railway embankment in (a)
) December 1906; (e) Wet
sin, looking south-west, with
e dredger Craigiehall *at the*
trance, 20 May 1907;
) Launch of the Para, *first of ten*
rpedo-boat destroyers for the
azilian Government, 14 July
08.

yards (Figure 5.16). The emergence of foreign competition was accompanied by the reduction of competition either by amalgamation or agreement between shipowning companies. In 1886, the Inman line passed under the control of the International Mercantile Marine Corporation of America, which in the next two decades acquired controlling interest in the White Star, Dominion, and Holland-America lines, becoming the largest shipping company in the world. The Union and Castle lines joined in 1900 to form the Union-Castle line, P. & O. amalgamated with the British India Steam Navigation Co. in 1914, and in 1915 the Canadian Pacific Company took over the Allan line. Between 1907 and 1928, the Royal Mail Shipping group took over twenty-six shipping companies, including the Pacific Steam Navigation Co., Lamport and Holt, Elder Dempster, Bullard King & Co., and, the Coast, Shire, Nelson, Union-Castle and Glen lines. By 1928, the group controlled 13 per cent of all British vessels. Competition for ferries and pleasure steamers – another important Clyde market – was reduced by the prohibition of racing and the amalgamation of railway companies. This contraction of the Clyde's shipbuilding market by foreign competition and the amalgamation of owners continued until the 1960s, when the demand for liners almost disappeared with the appearance of cheap and reliable air travel.

Although tonnage produced by Clyde yards continued to increase in the period prior to the First World War, these changes in the market were reflected in a fall in the number of ships built, which was accompanied by a lack of incentive to develop new methods of propulsion. After the building of the

gure 5.16 *Although the*
ajority of the ships in the
erman merchant navy were
ilt in Germany after the end of
e century, a few vessels were
dered from abroad, probably
cause German yards were
able to meet the demand. The
erst Bismarck was built in
05 by Fairfield for the
amburg-America line, part of
e International Mercantile
arine Co. The interior may well
ve been designed by Charles
nnie Mackintosh or one of his
pils. On the declaration of war
e line was the second largest
ipping company in the world.

Figure 5.17 *In 1901, the* King Edward *was built by William Denny & Bros for a consortium, including the inventor of the turbine, Charles A. Parsons. There was some difficulty in obtaining the best results from the relatively high-speed engines as the propellers were unsuited to rapid rotation. Ultimately, the steamer was successful and became the prototype for a large number of estuarial and cross-channel steamers built by the firm.*

Figure 5.18 *The world's first ocean-going motor ship was the* Selandia, *built in Copenhagen for the East Asiatic Steamship Co., in 1911. She was quickly followed by a sister ship, the* Jutlandia, *built by Barclay Curle & Co. at Scotstoun, in 1912. Both vessels were fitted with Burmeister and Wain diesel engines, and to emphasize the change in propelling machinery the exhausts were led up the masts, eliminating the traditional funnel. The success of these ships caused Barclay Curle to buy the North British Diesel Engine Works, Glasgow, in 1912 to build diesel engines.*

Lusitania in 1907, capacity rather than speed was the chief requirement of passenger ship owners. Despite the building by William Denny & Bros of the first turbine passenger ship, the *King Edward*, in 1901 (Figure 5.17) and the construction by Barclay Curle & Co., of the first motor ship in Britain, the *Jutlandia* (Figure 5.18) in 1912, these propulsion systems were developed mainly abroad or in the North-east of England. The Brown-Curtis turbine, which was designed by Professor Biles at Clydebank, was intended for specialist application in naval craft (Figure 5.19). Although licences for building diesels of established designs were taken out by several local engine builders, the Clyde failed to produce its own diesel engine through lack of capital and expertise. Moreover, Clyde marine engineers believed, with some justification, that the steam turbine, rather than the diesel, was the natural successor to reciprocating steam engines.

Figure 5.19 *(Opposite) The high speed of rotation of the steam turbine could be lowered by reduction gearing which was introduced by Sir John Biles in the* Transylvania, *built by Scott of Greenock, in 1913. Before the the normal expedient was to increase the diameter of the rotor so that the velocity of steam through the blades could be maintained while reducing the*

revolutions of the shaft. An example of a large turbine of the Brown-Curtis type is seen here in the engine shop at Clydebank, in 1916. The larger set of blades is for forward propulsion, while the smaller set on the right is for 'reversing' the vessel. Note on the left the thrust collars which, by rubbing against half collars on a block, transmit the push of the propellers to the hull.

Writing in 1925, Professor Biles, an ardent advocate of the steam turbine, argued cogently that 'in all . . . cases [for high speed passenger vessels] the steam is superior to the diesel in commercial efficiency'[9]. The implications of this loss of technical initiative did not become apparent until the 1950s, with the general replacement of triple-expansion engines by diesels and the fall off in naval orders.

These potential weaknesses in the industry were both disguised and reinforced by the increase in naval construction with the approach of the First World War. Admiralty contracts, except for specialist light craft such as minesweepers, gun boats, and torpedo-boat destroyers, were confined, until the outbreak of war, to the larger yards of John Brown, Beardmore, Fairfield, the London & Glasgow Shipbuilding & Engineering Co., and Scotts of Greenock.

Naval vessels took about twice as long to build as passenger ships of the same tonnage and usually occupied the larger berths normally reserved for quality liner tonnage (Figures 5.20 (a) and (b)). Harland & Wolff of Belfast were able to take advantage of the Clyde's preoccupation with Admiralty orders by not building naval ships and by taking orders from owners who previously had had long-standing relations with Clyde yards. More seriously for the future, yards were encouraged by the profitability and number of naval contracts extensively to re-equip for this market before and during the First World War. William Beardmore & Co., moved the old Napier yard from Govan to Dalmuir in 1905 specifically to build naval vessels (Figure 5.21). When John Brown & Co., took over the Clydebank yard in 1899, it was reconstructed to take advantage of the large passenger liner and naval market. Between 1906 and 1908, Fairfield re-equipped both their engine works and West Yard to maintain their competitive position in these markets, especially in the construction of turbine machinery (Figures 5.22 (a) and (b)).

(a)

(b)

Figure 5.20 *Admiral Lord Fisher's naval policy, which shaped the British navy that fought in the First World War, resulted in new designs for all classes of ships. The new generation of battleships, the dreadnoughts, were much faster and had greater fire power than their predecessors. As other nations acquired comparable vessels, Fisher demanded faster and better-equipped vessels and he had built a fleet of very fast, heavily armed, but lightly armoured, ships of a new type – battlecruisers. He described these as his 'new testament ships', as they fulfilled the promise of his 'old testament ships', the dreadnoughts[10]. Figure 5.20 (a) shows the battlecruiser, H.M.A.S.* Australia *ready for launching at Clydebank, in 1911 The sophisticated hull design necessary to obtain higher speeds is obvious. Note the hull was flush riveted to reduce resistance Figure 5.20 (b) illustrates the delicate operation of preparing a gun turret to receive a barrel on H.M.S.* Colossus, *a dreadnought at Scotts' yard, Greenock, in 1910.*

Figure 5.21 *The efficient handling of materials became a serious problem for shipbuilders as the size of vessels increased. One solution was to use derricks as at Clydebank (see Figure 5.13, on page 96); another, and more expensive, was to build an overall gantry as shown here at William Beardmore & Co.'s Dalmuir yard. This structure was built by Sir William Arrol & Co., in 1905–06 and was 750 feet long, 115 feet wide, and 133 feet high. The side cranes were designed for light lifts and the overhead gantry cranes of 15 tons capacity were used either by themselves or together for heavier loads. This photograph also shows H.M.S. Agamemnon, the last pre-dreadnought battleship to be built, during launching with boilers on board in June 1906. The space for the side armourplate is clearly visible. This was fitted on the ways and removed for launching. An editorial in the magazine* Engineering *(Vol. 81, page 826) was critical of the Admiralty's decision to build H.M.S. Agamemnon at a cost of £1 615 140 as compared with £1 797 497 for the far superior and more versatile H.M.S. Dreadnought.*

The Tramp Builders

Unlike the liner builders, the tramp builders were not affected by these inherent structural weaknesses of the industry. In the last two decades of the century, with the introduction of the triple-expansion engine, sail gave way to steam on nearly all trade routes, with a consequent replacement of tonnage favourable to Clyde builders. Unlike the liner yards, the tramp builders never established their own engine works, preferring to buy their engines from specialist builders, like David Rowan & Co., Rankin & Blackmore, and John Kincaid & Co. Because of the volatile and more competitive state of their market, and the lower price of their products, tramp builders had a more realistic approach to re-equipment and capitalization. The essential ingredient of success in their market was not technical superiority but financial liquidity and a high level of productivity. During the First World War, these yards, despite the initial failure of the Admiralty to recognize their significance in the replacement of merchant

Figures 5.22 (a) and
(b) *Fairfield Shipbuilding &
Engineering Co. works, c. 1909.
These two complementary
illustrations show the layout of
the yard and engine works after
reconstruction in 1906 and 1908.
The constraints on the maximum
size of ships built are obvious.*

(a)

(b)

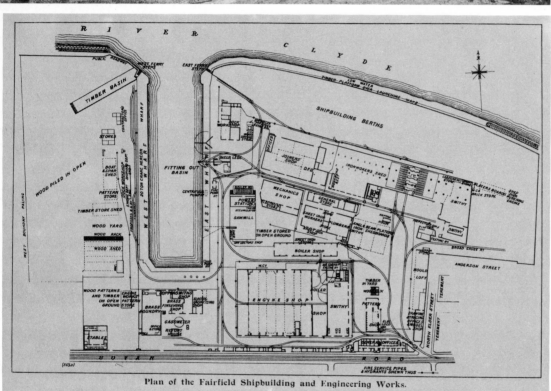

Plan of the Fairfield Shipbuilding and Engineering Works.

tonnage, built, especially after 1916, large numbers of standard ships based on designs pioneered by W.T. Lithgow of Russell & Co., Port Glasgow.

In the immediate post-war euphoria the tramp builders were not tempted into large-scale recapitalization of their plant to meet the expected boom. Rather the brothers Henry and Sir James Lithgow of Russell & Co., to become Lithgows Ltd in 1919, were the first to recognize that the industry on the Clyde had to be reconstructed and the capacity substantially reduced if it was to meet growing world competition and reduced markets. The market of the whole of the British shipbuilding industry had been severely cut back during the war when foreign yards were able to expand into traditional British markets, as British yards were prevented by wartime controls from competing for orders. However, in foreign yards labour was cheaper and was organized more effectively in shifts, a practice always resisted on the Clyde. Before and during the war the Lithgows had begun to consolidate their position with a view to rationalization by buying the Port Glasgow yards of Anderson Rodger in 1912, Robert Duncan & Co. in 1915, William Hamilton & Co. in 1919, and Dunlop Bremner in 1923. This policy of private-sector rationalization and reconstruction was pursued effectively by the Lithgow brothers throughout the inter-war period by not only buying into a wide range of West of Scotland shipbuilding and marine engineering firms, but also by initiating and supporting the setting up of National Shipbuilders Securities Ltd, and the Scottish Development Council.

Reactions to Depression

Although the inter-war slumps hit tramp builders more than liner and other specialist builders, during this period the balance of power in the industry moved permanently in their favour. All the builders who had shared in naval contracts during the war, encouraged by Admiralty grants and the prospect of a boom, invested heavily in new equipment and plant in the immediate post-war period. In January 1919, Fairfield's board authorized the expenditure of £70 000 on the development of their West Yard, which was to be closed permanently in 1933, and £30 000 on their engine works, and in May, the further spending of £27 445 on the formation of No. 6 berth to the east of the yard.[10] Between 1919 and 1921, the small dredger builders, Lobnitz & Co. of Renfrew, spent £11 400 on new plant and machinery. In 1918-19, 'as there was so much engineering work in . . . destroyers', Alexander Stephen and Sons extended their engine and boiler works so that 'they were capable of producing an output in excess of the capacity of the shipyard to produce hulls'[11]. William Beardmore & Co., as part of their post-war recapitalization programme (see page 64), built four new berths at their Dalmuir yard which was closed down in 1930. Re-equipment, coupled with the continuation of the wartime excess profits tax until 1920, severely weakened the liquidity of the liner and specialist builders. By December 1919, Alexander Stephen and Sons already found themselves short of capital and were unable to continue their expansion plans for the shipyard, estimated to cost £100 000.

This lack of liquidity was aggravated by structural changes in the industry. Although shipowners had acquired interests in shipbuilders previously, Handyside & Henderson, proprietors of the Anchor line, owned the yard of D. & W. Henderson at Meadowside from 1872, their involvement in the industry grew rapidly after the war. During 1919, the Royal Mail Shipping Group acquired Harland & Wolff, which owned the London & Glasgow Shipbuilding & Engineering Co. of Govan (acquired in 1912) (Figures 5.23 (a) and (b)) and Caird & Co. of Greenock (acquired in 1916). In 1919, the group bought the small yards of A. & J. Inglis at Pointhouse and D. & W. Henderson of Meadowside. In 1920, the

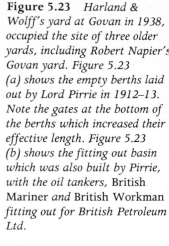

Figure 5.23 *Harland & Wolff's yard at Govan in 1938, occupied the site of three older yards, including Robert Napier's Govan yard. Figure 5.23 (a) shows the empty berths laid out by Lord Pirrie in 1912–13. Note the gates at the bottom of the berths which increased their effective length. Figure 5.23 (b) shows the fitting out basin which was also built by Pirrie, with the oil tankers,* British Mariner *and* British Workman *fitting out for British Petroleum Ltd.*

(a)

(b)

ill-starred Clarence Hatry, through his Northumberland Shipbuilding Company, acquired majority shareholdings in Fairfield and the Blythswood Shipbuilding Co. (established the previous year to build oil tankers). At the same time the Earl of Inchcape, chairman of P. & O. acquired controlling interests in Alexander Stephen & Sons. After the First World War, shipowners, like shipbuilders, clearly predicted boom conditions and reasoned that by buying into shipbuilding companies they could secure a ready supply of new tonnage at a low price in what was assumed would be an otherwise highly competitive market. In the severe post-war depression this involvement of shipowners in

Figure 5.24 This uninspiring vessel, the diesel-electric paddle ferry Robert the Bruce, was the first all welded ship built in Britain, by William Denny & Bros, in 1933. Welding was universally adopted by the mid-1960s. Investment in this new technique was characteristic of the reaction of the more progressive shipbuilders to the depression (see also Figure 8.14 (b), on page 167).

shipbuilding spelt disaster. Instead of receiving a continuous supply of new orders from the shipping companies, the shipbuilders found themselves with none, and more seriously were obliged to use such liquid capital as they had to shore up the consortiums. In 1924, Hatry went bankrupt and was imprisoned for fraud. His group was dismembered in 1927. Three years later, Lord Kylsant, by then chairman of the Royal Mail Shipping group, met the same fate: the company was dismantled in 1933.

With the collapse of the shipbuilding industry on the Clyde in the 1930s, the majority of firms either closed down for the duration of the depression or struggled on with a very few under-priced contracts taken on to maintain their labour pool. Some yards tried to diversify. Alexander Stephen and Sons began building steel houses in 1926; but had to abandon the project because the royalty fees were too high. Ability to weather the storm was a reflection of liquidity, firms flush with cash and not saddled by commitments to shipowners were able to undercut their competitors, keep their yards open and, surprisingly, attract capital for the purchase of new equipment that would reduce costs and raise productivity (Figure 5.24). In 1930, Swan Hunter on the Tyne was ideally placed with reserves of £1 290 000 and a further £276 500 at Barclay Curle & Co. on the Clyde. Nevertheless they were unable to compete with Lithgows, who in 1931 offered to build a single screw steamship for Hogarths for £55 000, £7000 under the Barclay Curle price, 'which bore only a few hundreds for charges'[12].

The 1930s depression revealed in detail the profound structural weakness of the Clyde industry. The traditional markets of the majority of Clyde yards were stagnant, with, in the liner market, no prospect of long-term recovery. Here the reduction in the market by amalgamation was reinforced by the rapid drop in emigration and the growth of state-subsidised foreign competition. Shipbuilding capacity on the Clyde and in Britain as a whole was far in excess of actual or

Figure 5.25 *Barclay Curle & Co.'s West yard, in 1921, showing four ships under construction, the vessel on the left (yard no. 583), is the Siraia for the Compagnie Générale Transatlantique. The cranes were new at the time. A sensible reaction to the depression by Barclay Curle & Co. was the extension of their ship-repairing capacity by the demolition of these berths and the construction of a new dry dock. This complemented the one purchased from Shearer & Co., in 1912, which was situated to the right of this picture.*

projected demands. With the unwillingness of the Government either to recognize the problems of the industry or to intervene in it, the only solution was rationalization by agreement. Unfortunately, in an industry which, at least on the Clyde, had always fostered the competitive spirit, the failure of any attempt to find a basis for an agreed policy of reduction of capacity and reconstruction was inevitable. The only scheme that appealed to the builders was the setting up of National Shipbuilders Security Ltd in 1930, which as the name suggests was designed to secure a base price for the building rights of any firm going into liquidation. The company was financed by shares taken up by all the builders participating in the company and by a one per cent levy on the value of all the tonnage launched. Between 1931 and 1937, the company acquired either all or part of the building rights of nine Clyde yards. Sir James and Henry Lithgow had, or acquired, interests in five of these yards and effectively used National Shipbuilders Security Ltd to extend their own process of rationalization. Of the rest, Barclay Curle & Co.'s West yard was required for major dry dock development (Figure 5.25), and the other three were so small and old fashioned as to be insignificant. The Lithgow brothers, in supporting the formation of National Shipbuilders Security Ltd, regarded it as a vehicle for either strengthening the capital structure of a shipbuilding group or company, or for providing a company with enough capital to start a new business on the same site using existing skills and manpower. Within their own group they were able to achieve both these objects, capital acquired from the sale of yards in Greenock, Port Glasgow, and Old Kilpatrick helped the firm to reconstruct on the Kingston yard, and the sale of their shipbuilding rights in 1934 allowed the Ayrshire Dockyard Company to specialize in steel rolling.

The difficulties of the Clyde shipbuilders in agreeing on a policy of rationalization and reconstruction in the inter-war years was mirrored in the Scottish steel industry. Shortly after the First World War, the shipbuilders, reasoning along the same lines as the shipowners, had acquired control of the steel industry to secure their supplies in the expected boom. In 1920, Lithgow bought the Clyde Iron Works; Barclay Curle & Co., with its parent company, Swan Hunter, and William Beardmore & Co., bought the Glasgow Iron & Steel Co.; Workman Clark & Co., of Belfast acquired part of Hatry's Northumberland Shipbuilding empire, the Lanarkshire Steel Co.; Harland & Wolff bought David Colville & Co.; and a consortium headed by F.J. Stephen of Alexander Stephen & Sons bought the Steel Company of Scotland. If boom conditions had prevailed for some time after the war this might have been a wise decision, as the constraint that had terminated the classical nineteenth century boom was invariably a short-fall in steel supplies. In the event the shipbuilders found themselves with an uncompetitive, undercapitalized, and antiquated industry, badly in need of reconstruction and re-equipment. The crisis in the steel industry came much earlier than for shipbuilding. With the sudden fall-off in orders for ships in the 1920s, the demand for steel dropped and the elaborate preparations by the shipbuilders to protect their supplies became unnecessary. The steel companies and shipbuilders had difficulty in agreeing on a policy of rationalization. The understandings reached in 1928-29 were totally undermined by the collapse of the Royal Mail Group in the prevailing world slump. In 1930, through the intervention of Sir John Craig, Colvilles Ltd, was formed by the amalgamation of David Colvilles Ltd and James Dunlop & Co. Further rationalization only took place after protracted negotiations in which the Treasury, Bank of England, and the Lithgow brothers played significant roles. The completion of the process in 1936 with the absorption of the Lanarkshire Steel Co. into Colvilles probably resulted from the impetus of re-armament.

Coming to Terms with the new Reality

The high level of demand for both naval and merchant vessels during the Second World War seriously distorted the realistic attempts to rationalize the Clyde shipbuilding industry (Figure 5.26). Some yards that would otherwise have closed in the late 1930s remained open in the expectation of war. Others that had been closed or put on a care-and-maintenance basis by National Shipbuilders Securities Ltd, like the yard of William Beardmore & Co. at Dalmuir, were re-opened either for building, or for refitting and repair work. The structural weaknesses of the industry revealed in the depression were disguised by the artificial conditions of wartime production, and the 1950s boom, characterized by the absence of significant foreign competition and the temporary revival of the liner market. In the 'never had it so good' mood of the 1950s the lessons of the depression were forgotten. The pressure of orders in the seller's market of the

Figure 5.26 *The pressure on Clyde yards during the war is clearly indicated in this view (probably taken in 1943) of the Fairfield fitting out basin, with three destroyers, two tank landing craft, and an aircraft carrier. The empty ground beyond the aircraft carrier is the site of the West yard, sterilized by agreement with National Shipbuilders Security in 1933.*

1950s mitigated against the extensive re-equipment and reconstruction of the yards, because of the disruptive effect on production.

When the yards began to re-equip in the late 1950s and early 1960s, several seriously misjudged the market in believing that demand for their traditional products would remain buoyant. The staple diet of the Clyde, passenger ships of all varieties, only proved such a satisfactory main course after the war through wartime sinkings and the technical difficulties that delayed the introduction of cheap, reliable air transport (Figure 5.27). Barclay Curle & Co., Alexander Stephen & Sons, and Fairfield extensively re-equipped in the early 1960s, largely to meet markets that were to disappear within a few years. As a result the firms failed, Barclay Curle closed its shipyard in 1965, Fairfield went into liquidation in 1965, and Alexander Stephen & Sons hived off their yard in 1968 to Upper Clyde Shipbuilders Ltd. The demise of the passenger ship market in the 1960s was accompanied by a change in world shipping practice. Up-river harbours were closed in favour of ports at river mouths, and consequently the demand fell for dredgers, in which four West of Scotland Clyde yards specialized. At the same time new roads and bridges replaced ferries, which had been built by the smaller Clyde yards since the 1840s. In 1958 the dredger building firms of William Simons & Co. and Lobnitz & Co., neighbours in Renfrew, amalgamated and were taken over in 1959 by G. & J. Weir, the pump manufacturers, who in turn sold the goodwill to Alexander Stephen & Sons in 1964 and closed the yards. William Denny & Bros of Dumbarton, specialists in ferries, went into liquidation in 1962, after an abortive attempt to reconstruct as hovercraft builders.

Although closures were inevitable, neither the builders nor the Government were prepared for the crisis on the upper river in the mid-1960s. Desultory attempts had been made by the shipbuilders throughout the 1950s to find a solution by amalgamation. John Brown had made occasional overtures to Fairfield, and Lithgow had tried in turn to sell Fairfield to shipowning companies.

110

By 1962, the situation had become impossible, the majority of the yards on the upper Clyde were incurring substantial losses through fixed-price contracts, poor productivity, and rising material costs. On the liquidation of Fairfield Shipbuilding & Engineering Co. in 1965, Fairfield (Glasgow) Ltd was formed to manage the shipyard, with government backing and under the control of Sir Iain Stewart. Sir Iain was convinced that the shipbuilding industry was not managerially equipped to remain competitive, principally through bad labour relations, reinforced by lack of communication, and a failure to introduce the production techniques being evolved in the engineering industry. In Fairfield (Glasgow) Ltd he tried to correct both these problems. With the first he was partially successful, but the price that had to be paid in wages was high and only aggravated the problems of other yards by pushing up the wage rates generally on the river. The introduction of production engineering was fiercely criticized by other builders in the belief that shipbuilding could not be forced into the straitjacket of work measurement and standard time. But with the vogue for standard ships it is possible that such techniques will improve productivity and make for a more efficient use of plant and machinery.

Unfortunately Sir Iain Stewart did not have time to prove his point. In 1967, the Geddes committee recommended the amalgamation of all the surviving yards on the upper reaches; John Brown, Yarrow & Co., Charles Connell & Co., Alexander Stephen & Sons, and Fairfield, into Upper Clyde Shipbuilders Ltd. The amalgamation was pushed through by the Labour Government, in the belief that Geddes and the Government knew best and without taking the specialities of the individual firms into account. The engine works were split off and remained independent. John Brown and Fairfield, as large passenger shipbuilders, themselves ill-sorted bedfellows, were quite unsuited to an amalgamation with Alexander Stephen & Sons, small passenger shipbuilders, whose yard was anyway not viable, and Charles Connell & Co., traditionally

Figure 5.27 *'Clyde built at its best', the* Ivernia, *one of the last traditional passenger liners built at Clydebank for Cunard & Co.'s Canadian service, in 1955. The advent of cheap trans-Atlantic air transport in the late 1950s caused the* Ivernia *to be withdrawn from this service. In 1963, she was refitted at Clydebank as a cruise ship and renamed* Franconia.

tramp builders. Yarrow & Co., as naval specialists, were always the odd man out. Moreover if Upper Clyde Shipbuilders Ltd was to have effected a long-term reconstruction of the industry on the Clyde it required a fresh start. Unfortunately several loss-making and very specialized contracts, like the *Queen Elizabeth 2*, the *Kungsholm*, the *Bremen*, H.M.S. *Fife*, and several dredgers, were carried forward. As a result the company was unable to implement Geddes' recommendation to build standard cargo ships on a production-line basis to meet certain specific target dates. In the event Yarrow & Co. withdrew from Upper Clyde Shipbuilders in 1971 and the company was liquidated in 1972. The Fairfield and Connell yards were reformed as Govan Shipbuilders Ltd, and the Clydebank yard sold to Marathon (UK) Ltd for building oil rigs.

By contrast the yards of the Lithgow group at Port Glasgow, Scotts Shipbuilding & Engineering Co. at Greenock, and Yarrow & Co., were able to remain competitive. Yarrow, on the formation of Yarrow Admiralty Research Department in 1948-49, effectively tied up the naval market, leaving all the other naval builders at a disadvantage. Lithgow's reconstruction by amalgamation in the 1930s bore fruit. The Kingston yard was designed to facilitate an efficient materials flow and to keep charges to a minimum. Although the group had acquired the engine works of John Kincaid & Co., Rankin & Blackmore, and David Rowan & Co. in the inter-war years, these companies had wisely been allowed to retain their autonomy. With the fall in demand the firm was able to close David Rowan and Rankin & Blackmore, without damaging the group as a whole. Kincaid's was left as the group's engine builders and maintained its competitiveness by strong management and a continuous programme of re-equipment. Scotts Shipbuilding & Engineering Co. was better placed on the lower Clyde at Greenock than up river builders and had, anyway, always effectively straddled the naval, passenger, and cargo ship markets, by specializing in submarines, second- and third-rate liners, and by building oil tankers and general cargo ships. Following the recommendations of the Geddes commission, Lithgow and Scotts were obliged to amalgamate in 1967. The Lithgow yard at Port Glasgow has now been extensively reconstructed to build large tankers and bulk carriers.

The layout and location of the majority of the surviving yards is determined by their antecedents. The yards of Yarrow and Connell (now Scotstoun Marine), in South Street, Scotstoun, are constrained by the railway lines at their rear, which leave no room for development away from the river. This handicaps any attempt to rebuild the yards with efficient flow lines. The Clydebank and Fairfield yards were laid out principally to build passenger and naval tonnage, with the building berths and platers sheds on the flanks and the fitting out and engine building facilities in the centre. This was a sensible arrangement when fitting out and engine building was elaborate, and costlier than hull construction. Now, with the cessation of passenger and naval work, and engine construction, the yards are poorly equipped for the efficient throughput of materials.

CHAPTER SIX

The Fairfield and John Brown
Shipbuilding and Engineering Companies

Of all the shipyards founded by Robert Napier's pupils, John Brown (formerly J. & G. Thomson Ltd) and Fairfield (previously Randolph, Elder & Co., later John Elder & Co.) are, perhaps, the best known and the easiest to compare. When Robert Napier leased the Lancefield Works from his cousin, David Napier, in 1835, George Thomson joined the firm as foreman at Lancefield and later became assistant to David Elder, the work's manager. His brother James Thomson, who had moved to Manchester on the completion of his apprenticeship with Graham, Wellington & Co., millwrights and engineers in Partick, returned to Glasgow in 1828 as Robert Napier's leading smith, finisher, and turner and, in 1847, the brothers began business as marine engineers at the Clyde Bank Foundry, Finnieston. John Elder, David's son, served his apprenticeship with Napiers, and then moved to England to gain experience. He returned in about 1848 to take charge of Robert Napier's drawing office, with the expectation of taking a leading part in the business. When this was denied to him he became, in 1852, a partner in the well-established millwrighting business of Randolph, Elliot & Co., the name being changed to Randolph, Elder & Co.

J. & G. Thomson and Randolph, Elder & Co., following Napier's example, began as marine engineers and only later opened their own shipyards. Both enjoyed familial and financial relationships with their customers. The Thomsons first order was for a 58 horsepower steeple engine for the *Cygnet* for G. & J. Burns. Their brother Robert had served as an engineer with this company until 1839, when he became the first superintendent engineer of the newly-formed British and North American Steam Packet Co., later Cunard & Co., in which G. & J. Burns had a large shareholding. In 1851, the Thomsons opened their own shipyard at Govan and between then and 1872 built, out of a total production of 110 vessels, 42 ships for companies or individuals connected with G. & J. Burns. When Randolph, Elder & Co. began iron shipbuilding at a small yard in Govan in 1860, they built their first vessel the *McGregor Laird* for the African Royal Mail Co., later to become part of the British and African Steam Navigation Co. Alexander, John Elder's brother, worked as a clerk for the African Royal Mail Co. and in 1868 with John Dempster, another employee, founded Elder Dempster & Co. and the British and African Steam Navigation Co., in which Charles Randolph was one of the principal shareholders[1]. From 1861 to 1874 Randolph, Elder & Co. built 16 ships for these firms, which, together with the 36 vessels built for the Pacific Steam Navigation Co. and the 10 for the Nederland Steam Navigation Co., in which the firm also had large shareholdings, accounted for nearly one-third of their whole production.

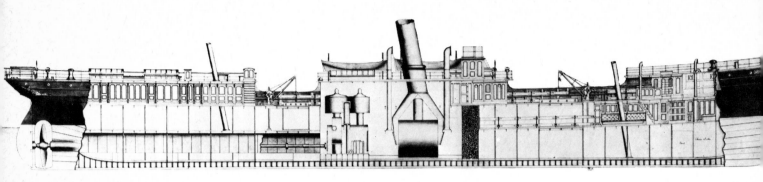

Figure 6.1 *A longitudinal section of the S.S.* Ban Righ *built by John Elder & Co. for the Aberdeen Steam Navigation Co. in 1870. The compound engines can be seen clearly.*

The initial success of both the Thomsons and Randolph and Elder was largely a reflection of their skill as marine engineers. James Bourne, in 1852, described the engines made by J. & G. Thomson for the *Frankfort* as 'among the best examples of direct-acting screw engines that we yet possess. They are simple, compact, and substantial, and upon the whole are a very eligible class of engines for merchant vessels'[2]. While the Thomsons continued to improve the inverted, direct-acting, geared, simple engines, Randolph, Elder & Co. developed the marine compound engine (Figure 6.1), building the first in 1854 for the *Brandon* of the London and Limerick Steamship Co. This engine reduced the rate of coal consumed per indicated horsepower from about $4\frac{1}{2}$ lbs to $3\frac{1}{4}$ lbs. By experimenting with James Watt's proposal for steam jacketing the cylinders, John Elder was, in the mid-1860s, able to reduce coal consumption further to between 2 lbs and $2\frac{1}{2}$ lbs. The prohibition of the use of these engines in mail boats and a suspicion of high piston speeds by owners prevented their general introduction until the 1870s. However, on the long routes to West Africa, Australia, the West Indies, and South America, especially down its coalless Pacific coast, their economical fuel consumption was attractive. Indeed the success of the Pacific Steam Navigation Co. depended largely on its introduction (Figure 6.2). In the late 1850s, Randolph, Elder & Co. installed compound engines in most of the company's ships with a startling effect on fuel consumption, which was reduced in the *Bogota* from 38 cwts of coal an hour to 19 cwts with an increase of speed from 9.75 knots to 10.47 knots. In 1863, the firm built the first naval compound engine for the *Constance* (Figure 6.3) which was tested in a race from Plymouth to Funchal in Madeira against the *Octavia* and *Arethusa* both of a similar tonnage to the *Constance,* but with simple engines. 'When the *Constance* was within thirty miles of Funchal she was 130 [nautical miles] ahead of the *Octavia* and 200 [nautical miles] from the *Arethusa*. The engines of the latter two had then to be stopped owing to the coal on board being nearly exhausted, and they finished the distance under canvas'[3]. In 1877, Chief Engineer King of the United States Navy paid tribute to John Elder's tenacity in developing the

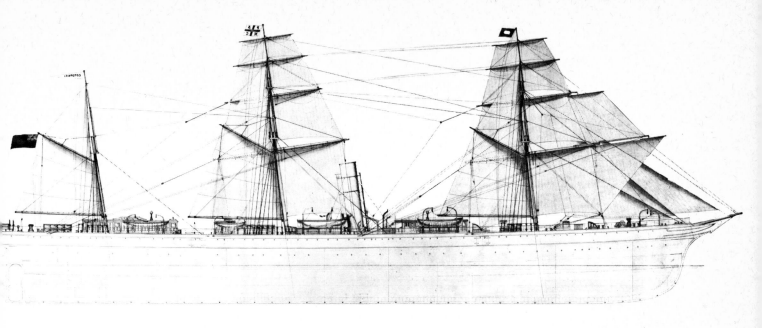

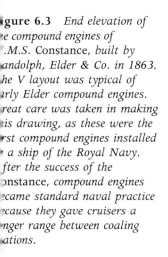

Figure 6.2 *A profile and rigging plan of the S.S. Cotopaxi which was built by John Elder & Co. for the Pacific Steam Navigation Co. in 1873, as part of an order for five vessels. This vessel was fitted with compound engines built by the firm.*

compound engine, 'designing and constructing every year several sets, each more and more improved in design and detail'[4].

The large demands of the Confederacy during the American Civil War (1861-65) for fast blockade-runners was not only an incentive to both firms to develop faster engines, but also brought them several orders. In 1864, Randolph, Elder & Co. in five months built five blockade runners, with compound engines, which achieved trial speeds of $20\frac{1}{2}$ miles per hour. Thomsons were less fortunate in their dealings with the Confederacy. Their contract for the *Pompero* attracted the attention of the Emancipation Society of Glasgow in 1863 and she was seized on her way down river. However, the firm benefited indirectly. By 1864, 111 British packet ships of a total of over 60 000 tons had been sold to the Confederacy, leaving a large demand by British owners for replacements.

Figure 6.3 *End elevation of the compound engines of H.M.S.* Constance, *built by Randolph, Elder & Co. in 1863. The V layout was typical of early Elder compound engines. Great care was taken in making this drawing, as these were the first compound engines installed in a ship of the Royal Navy. After the success of the* Constance, *compound engines became standard naval practice because they gave cruisers a longer range between coaling stations.*

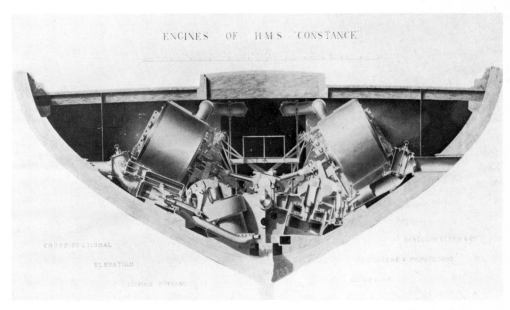

ENGINES OF H.M.S. 'CONSTANCE'

CROSS-SECTIONAL

ELEVATION

LOOKING FORWARD

115

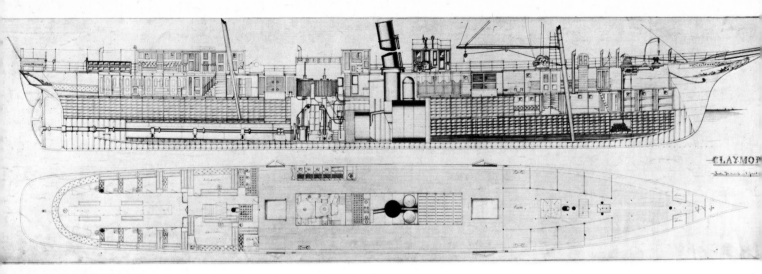

Thomsons built the *Iona* (II) in 1863 for D. Hutcheson & Co. to replace the *Iona* (I), which had been sold to the Confederacy in 1861 but sank on her way to America in a collision in the Firth of Clyde, and when the *Iona* (II) was in turn sold to the Confederacy, they built the *Iona* (III) in 1864.

The Move Down River – Fairfield in the Lead

The participation of both firms in the market for blockade runners was exceptional. Not until the mid-1870s did they begin to compete in the same markets, never building a ship for the same companies until 1880, a reflection of their differing technical expertise and relationships. By then their management and locations had changed. In 1864, Randolph, Elder & Co. abandoned their yard in the centre of Govan and moved to a new shipyard on a green-field site at Fairfield on the outskirts of the burgh. 'Having gone lower down the river than any of the other large Glasgow builders, Messrs. Randolph and Elder have at Fairfield about as complete and convenient a shipbuilding establishment as any in the world'[5]. In the same year Elder became the sole partner, the firm becoming John Elder & Co. He began to build a new engine and boiler works at Fairfield, which was not completed until 1874. Elder most ambitiously had designed these to include: 'a boiler shop, separate from and to the west of the engine works, as well as a floating dock and repair slip'[6] which were abandoned on his death in 1869. In that year the firm built fourteen steam ships and three sailing ships of a total of 25 235 tons, nearly double the production of any other Clyde yard. The firm was reconstructed with three partners, one of whom, William Pearce, became sole partner in 1878. Pearce, trained in the Royal Dockyard at Chatham, had supervised the building of the first iron naval ships and in 1863, at the age of 28, was appointed general manager of Robert Napier's shipyard. Until he assumed sole control Pearce was unable to influence the firm's market and it continued to build vessels for its established customers, building, between 1869

Figure 6.4 *A three dimensional section of the S.S. Claymore built by J. & G. Thomson for David MacBrayne & Co.'s West Highland trade in 1881. The fine quality of the draughtsmanship of this illustration and Figures 6.1-6.3 is characteristic of contemporary practice in other Clyde shipyards.*

and 1872, 22 ships for the Pacific Steam Navigation Co., 7 for the British and African Steam Navigation Co., and 8 for the Nederland Steam Navigation Co.

With the gradual decline of Robert Napier & Sons in the 1860s, it was J. & G. Thomson & Co. rather than John Elder & Co. who assumed their mentor's mantle. George Thomson became sole partner of the firm on the retirement of his brother in 1863 and died in 1866 leaving the business in the hands of trustees, but under the management of his eldest son James Rodger Thomson. The following year the company built its first Blue Riband holder, the *Russia*, for Cunard & Co., said to be: 'the most beautiful vessel that had ever been seen upon the ocean up to that time'[7]. Despite the loss of £5034 in 1869, the mood of the trustees and J.R. Thomson was towards expansion into the premier Atlantic market; previously the company had only built second rate Cunarders, leaving the premier contracts to Napier. J.R. Thomson supported this policy in a letter to his trustees in 1870 advocating a move to a larger site: 'We have the early prospect of being called upon to tender for several large vessels, mostly mail steamers of a large size, larger than anything we have hitherto built . . . we are not, however, in our present yard in a position to tender for such vessels . . . The trustees will find by reference to our balance sheets for years past that the only vessels that have been at all remunerative are the large class of screw steamers and especially those for mail services'[8]. The following year the shipyard in Govan was acquired by the Clyde Trust for the construction of a graving dock and the firm moved to a new shipyard at a remote green-field site six miles down the Clyde near Dalmuir, later named Clydebank after the firm. The Clydebank yard cost about £32 000 to build and was financed atypically by a loan of £30 000 only, granted by the Union Bank of Scotland because the firm had been long-standing customers. The engineering and boiler works remained in the Thomson's original premises at Finnieston and Kelvinhaugh until 1881-83 (Figure 6.4) when new works were built at Clydebank for the construction of large triple-expansion engines. John Grant, who had joined the firm in 1847, speaking at the opening of these works in 1884, prophesied accurately that 'he visualized the day when the great passenger liner of the future would launch into the mouth of the Cart (incredulous laughter)'[9].

Thomson's move to Clydebank was reflected in a marked increase in the tonnage of their vessels. Previously they had built only 11 ships of over 2000 gross tons and none over 3000, the majority being under 1000; thereafter most were of over 1000 tons and the *Bothnia* and *Scythia* built in 1873 and 1876 for Cunard were over 4000 tons. The firm was unfortunate as the move coincided with the onset of a severe trade depression, which forced the trustees to take on contracts for iron-hulled cargo sailing ships for a variety of new customers, such as the Lyle Shipping Co., and the General Ship Co. to be employed in the developing trade with China, Australia, and South America. By August 1874, the trustees had to ask the managers to make economies and to increase productivity: 'The trustees trust that under these circumstances every effort will be made by all in charge to push forward the work in hand, and that any little sacrifice of comfort or convenience will not be thought of for a moment in comparison with the heavy interest at stake'[10]. Between 1875 and 1878, the yard built 15 sailing ships out of a total production of 23 vessels, and only two passenger ships, the *Gallia,* for Cunard in 1878-79, and the *Columba* for D. Hutcheson & Co. in 1878. 'The *Columba's* first claim to distinction lies in the fact that she was built of steel . . . Secondly she was the largest steamer of the whole river [Clyde] fleet . . . Thirdly, her general form and lines followed closely those of *Iona* (III), i.e. a saloon steamer with ornamental curved slanting bow and square stem, two splendid funnels and single mast . . . Fourthly, the steamer's accommodation was the last word in extent, equipment, and furnishings according to the fashion of the time'[11]. Despite the quality of both the *Gallia* and *Columba,* the firm still found it difficult to obtain orders on favourable cash terms. In 1879, they agreed to build the *Servia* of 7392 gross tons for Cunard in part exchange for the *China,* the *Algeria,* and the *Abyssinia,* and for £20 000 on signing the contract and a further £25 000 in either cash instalments or debentures in Cunard stock.

John Elder & Co. had experienced the same problems as Thomsons in the mid-1870s, building 8 sailing ships between 1874 and 1876 out of a total production of 35 vessels and only 3 ships in 1877 compared with 8 the previous year. When William Pearce became sole partner in 1878, the company began to expand rapidly into new markets. In that year they completed H.M.S *Nelson* 'a new type of ocean-cruising broadside armour-plated ship'[12] and built between 1878 and 1879 six *Comus* class corvettes. The construction of the Blue Riband holder *Arizona* for the Guion line in 1879 was a turning point, bringing the firm for the first time into direct competition with J. & G. Thomson. The *Arizona,* 'the forerunner of all the Atlantic greyhounds'[13], was followed by the record breakers *Alaska*, the first ship to cross the Atlantic in less than a week (launched 1882) and the *Oregon* (launched 1883) for the Guion line, and the *Umbria* and *Etruria* (both launched 1884) for Cunard. In response to a rise in demand for passenger ships on nearly every trade route during these years, both firms increased their production and acquired new linkages.

It was John Elder & Co., under the able management of William Pearce, that was most successful, building a prodigious 108 ships between 1880 and 1888, compared with the 44 built by J. & G. Thomson. Pearce, by accepting shares as part payment for ships, acquired large stakes in several shipowning companies, including the Guion line, the New Zealand Shipping Co., the Isle of Man Steam Packet Co., and the Liverpool and Great Western Shipping Co., and so was able to influence these companies ordering policy. In 1887, he was co-founder of the Canadian Pacific Steam Ship Co. precursor of the Canadian Pacific Line (see page 89), and between 1880–85 to secure a continuous flow of work in the yard he built 11 ships on his own account of a total of 52 986 tons at an estimated cost of £1 464 000. John Elder & Co.'s success was more a reflection of Pearce's ability as a businessman than the firm's shipbuilding or engineering expertise. All three Guion liners were uncomfortable, rolling heavily, dependent for their speed on large compound engines, rather than improved hull design. Despite the development by the company of the first successful marine triple-expansion engine for the *Propontis* in 1874, the inability of existing boilers to produce steam safely at the required pressure delayed its general application until the introduction of efficient water-tube boilers in the mid-1880s. The firm built the first triple-expansion engined Atlantic mail steamers the *Aller, Trave*, and *Saale*, for the Norddeutscher Lloyd in 1886. By contrast, J. & G. Thomson & Co., under the direction of their naval architect, John Biles, reduced the number of beams in an Atlantic liner from 12 to 8 in the *Aurania* (built 1882–83) and introduced improved hull design, based on William Froude's test-tank experiments, for the first time in the Blue Riband holder *America* of the National line (built 1883–84).

Technical Success and Commercial Problems

The last years of the nineteenth century brought problems for both firms. The declining profitability of the North Atlantic route, with the consequent failure of the Guion and Inman lines, the retirement of the National line from competition for the main services, and the takeover of several companies by the International Mercantile Marine Co. (see page 99) caused the number of orders to fall. These were further reduced by the growth of foreign competition especially from Germany, and by a substantial increase in the price of Atlantic liners, after the building by Thomson in 1888 of the *City of New York* and *City of Paris* of 10 499 gross tons which were nearly twice as big as the *America*. Although neither firm relied on first-rate Atlantic liners to fill their order books, the large investment in both the yards in the 1880s to build steel ships and triple-expansion engines depended to an extent on a continuous supply of such contracts to maintain profits and cash and work flow. Building large naval craft was the only alternative. In March 1888, William MacKinnon, J. & G. Thomson's accountant, wrote to Charles Gairdner, the general manager of the Union Bank of Scotland, discussing tenders submitted by the firm for two small ships: 'This is a class of work that can be undertaken by so many firms that it will be keenly competed for and they do not expect to succeed, but they are making tenders all the same. But when the larger cruisers come out a very careful estimate will be served and an effort made to secure a part of the work'[14] (Figures 6.5 (a) and (b)). William Pearce, recognizing the significance of Admiralty contracts, made their dispersal from Royal dockyards to commercial firms a main plank of his successful parliamentary election campaign of 1885. A few days before the election John Elder & Co. was converted into a limited liability company and renamed the Fairfield Shipbuilding and Engineering Co. Ltd, 'to enable it to execute Government contracts in the event of Mr Pearce being returned to Parliament'[15]. Although Pearce was able to influence Admiralty policy, Fairfield received no contracts in 1886, while Thomson built H.M.S. *Scout* in 1888 and the whole of the unsuccessful *Archer* class of torpedo cruisers.

The building in 1888-89 of the *City of Paris* and *City of New York* (see Figures

(a)

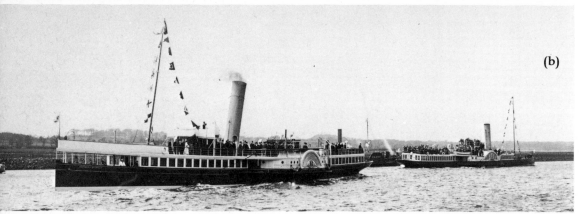

(b)

5.6 (a) and (b) on page 91), fitted with a luxury and magnificence unequalled at the time'[16] for the Inman line, not only lost J. & G. Thomson money (see page 91) but also fatally weakened the firm's liquidity. Although the firm was unlucky, the *City of New York* developed several faults on her maiden voyage and the feed pumps had to be replaced, they seriously misjudged the market in believing that the building of these ships was likely to bring enough orders to compensate for the re-equipment of the yard to build them. Recapitalization extended into August 1889 after the ships had been delivered and was defended by J.R. Thomson in a letter to William MacKinnon: 'The smaller lathes etc., are much required to enable us to overtake the work entailed by the construction of the new style of engines [triple-expansion engines] where so much auxiliary or small machinery is required: this work we are obliged to execute ourselves as the expense of getting it done outside is simply prohibitive . . . The items in list Shipyard consist of machines necessary to enable us to handle and work the large [steel] plates which are now being used in hulls of ships to economize the amount of rivetting' (Figure 6.6)[17]. The only solution was to seek Government contracts which not only justified re-equipment, but also, unlike merchant contracts, were paid for in advance instalments, which 'would help us considerably financially'[14].

Both Firms Change Hands – Clydebank Moves Ahead

The deteriorating state of the firm in 1888-90 was, in part, a reflection of management failure. David Ritchie, an accountant, wrote to Charles Gairdner in September 1888, commenting on the loss of the contract for the *Blenheim*: 'I do not very much regret the loss of the contract. Subsequent events showed there must have been a considerable amount of guesswork in the calculations on which the tender was based'[14]. In July 1889, he repeated his reservations about the management's ability, especially that of J.R. Thomson, when he wrote to Gairdner discussing the orders for the cruisers *Tauranga* and *Ringarooma*: 'I hope MacKinnon will impress upon him [J.R. Thomson] the great necessity for exercising the strictest economy in all departments of the yard connected with the construction of these ships so as to ensure the small profit at present estimated'[14]. In the event J. & G. Thomson & Co. was forced into becoming a limited liability company in 1890 to raise a debenture mortgage to pay off its debts.

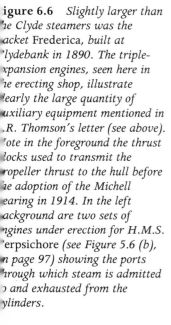

Figure 6.6   *Slightly larger than the Clyde steamers was the packet* Frederica, *built at Clydebank in 1890. The triple-expansion engines, seen here in the erecting shop, illustrate clearly the large quantity of auxiliary equipment mentioned in J.R. Thomson's letter (see above). Note in the foreground the thrust blocks used to transmit the propeller thrust to the hull before the adoption of the Michell bearing in 1914. In the left background are two sets of engines under erection for H.M.S. Terpsichore (see Figure 5.6 (b), on page 97) showing the ports through which steam is admitted to and exhausted from the cylinders.*

The new company concentrated its production on naval orders, building, between 1890 and 1896, 24 naval craft out of a total production of 48 ships. These included two battleships and five cruisers but no significant passenger liners. Originally the principal shareholders in the new company were the brothers J.R. Thomson and George P. Thomson, sons of the original George, holding 23 868 out of the 25 000 shares issued on a capital of £250 000. But by 1892, they found this commitment too great and were forced to sell their shares to C. Dunlop and Partners, the firm's Glasgow lawyers. The Thomsons retained a shareholding of 50 shares each. This arrangement did not last long for in 1895 the Glasgow iron merchant W.A. Donaldson stepped in, providing financial support and buying 7200 shares. At the same time the lawyers reduced their holdings to 1500 shares and the Thomson family acquired a further 1000 shares. In 1896 the company's name was changed to the Clydebank Engineering and Shipbuilding Co., a token of the Thomson family's gradual disassociation from the firm. At the same time J.R. Thomson was removed as managing director and John Gibb Dunlop appointed. Immediately the order book began to reflect a move away from total dependence on naval work towards a mixture of contracts with emphasis on fast, high-performance packet boats. By 1898, though, the firm was again in severe financial difficulties, with an overdraft of £22 265 on its capital account, resulting from the re-equipment of the engine works.

In 1899, it was taken over by the principal creditors, John Brown & Co., the Sheffield steelmakers, who had for some time been looking for an opportunity to diversify into shipbuilding. The firm was renamed the John Brown Shipbuilding and Engineering Co., but enjoyed little autonomy, all policy decisions being taken by the John Brown board in London or Sheffield. John Brown & Co., unlike Thomsons, had the cash resources substantially to re-equip and re-capitalize both to extend the product base of the yard in response to changes in the market and to maintain the facility to build large passenger liners and naval vessels. In 1900, the ground to the west side of the basin, acquired by Thomsons for future development, was laid out with building berths for small, high-speed passenger steamers, supplemented by new plating and light engineering shops (Figure 6.7). Further capital improvements were made regularly up to 1914, especially for the construction of large vessels and turbines. John Brown's success was reflected in a more balanced blend of contracts. Between 1899 and 1914, out of a total production of 81 ships, only 28 naval craft were built, 9 Atlantic liners, 17 cross-channel and estuarial passenger vessels, and 9 refrigerated cargo ships, in which the firm had specialized since 1898.

The death in 1888 of Sir William Pearce, with his rare combination of engineering expertise and entrepreneurial skill was a tragedy for Fairfield. He was succeeded as chairman by his son, Sir William G. Pearce, a barrister. In 1889, the firm became a public limited company with Sir William McOnie, an eminent Glasgow engineer (see page 34) as one of the directors. Despite his appointment, by 1890 the board was already finding it difficult to prevent disputes between the engine and shipbuilding departments, and especially to control the

shipbuilding department. Richard Barnwell, the managing director, comment-ing on the loss of money in that department in 1890 wrote: 'it is imperative we get two men of the highest commercial standing to strengthen the board'[18]. In the event nothing was done and in 1893 substantial sums were lost by the department on the *Campania* and *Lucania* for Cunard & Co. (Figure 6.8) resulting in the dismissal of R. Saxton White, the shipyard manager. By the autumn the situation in the yard was serious with no contract profits and only two sailing barques under construction. In September Sir William Arrol (see page 57) was appointed a director and Edmund Sharer, an able shipbuilder from North-east England was brought in as shipyard manager. Bickering between the departments seems to have continued; but was firmly put down by the board under the guidance of Sir William Arrol. This problem, though, was not solved and continued to concern the directors. In 1899, George Strachan, the company secretary, repeated the sentiments of the directors of J. & G. Thomson in explaining the loss of money on the *City of New York* and *City of Paris* (see page 91) when he wrote to Sir William G. Pearce describing the losses by the shipbuilding department on the *Omrah* for the Orient line: 'No-one except those directly in charge of the construction of the ship could have any idea of the vast amount of work'[18]. In 1914, after the trading loss of £21 373 in 1912, the shipyard manager was again sacked. The problem re-emerged after the war. During the 1919 recapitalization the shipyard manager was dismissed for order-ing new machinery without the board's approval.

123

Figure 6.8 *The loss-making* Campania, *built at Fairfield, in 1893, on trials in the Firth of Clyde. Though lacking the immediate visual appeal of the* City of New York *(see Figure 5 (a), on page 97), the* Campania, *and her sister ship the* Lucania, *set new standards for Atlantic liners and were described by Henry Fry as 'the finest and the fastest in the world'*[18]. *They had an average speed, in all weather, of 20 knots. Their engines developed 30 000 horsepower in all, and were of the 5 cylinder, 3 crank triple-expansion type. Profiting from experience with the* City of Paris, *when one of the propeller-shafts fractured at high speed, emergency governors were fitted which would stop the engines in the event of accident.*

The extensive re-equipment of the Fairfield works, begun before Sir William Pearce's death in 1888 was continued by the new management and included the building of new offices, the installation of large machine tools, 'to manipulate the heavier [steel] plates and castings demanded by modern marine practice'[19] and the reconstruction of the engine and boiler shops to build triple-expansion engines and water-tube boilers. The company, like J. & G. Thomson, misjudged the market. The heavy losses in 1893 on the *Campania* and *Lucania,* which exceeded £100 000, reflected the growing weakness of the linkages and markets built up by Sir William Pearce. Immediately after his father's death, Richard Barnwell had begun to advise Sir William G. Pearce to dismantle some linkages, in the evident realization that these would be of little further use to the company. In February 1888 he wrote to him: 'I think the disposing of the New Zealand Shipping Company's interest will be a splendid business and lighten your responsibility considerably'[18] and in November 1890 he advised perspicaciously the sale of the company's interest in the Guion line to the Inman International line: 'I certainly favour the idea of selling as it is natural that at times the interests of the shipowner and shipbuilder will clash'[18]. After the appointment of Sir William Arrol and Edmund Sharer to the board in 1893, the products of the company began to mirror changes in the market, with emphasis on intermediate vessels for the Canadian Pacific and Castle lines, passenger ferries, and especially naval vessels with the building of 25 naval ships, including one battleship and 12 cruisers (Figure 6.9) between 1894 and 1908.

Figure 6.9 *A deck view of H.M.S.* Good Hope, *a Drake-class armoured cruiser built by Fairfield in 1901 and fitted out as a flagship. It was the largest armoured cruiser built up to that date. She fought in the battle of Coronel in 1914, when an officer in H.M.S. Glasgow noted: 'At 19 50 hours there was a terrible explosion between her mainmast and her after funnel, the flames reaching a height of over 200 feet, after which she lay between the [battle] lines, a black hull lighted only by a dull glow'. Admiral Cradock and all the crew were lost.*

(a)

After the takeover by John Brown & Co., of the Clydebank yard in 1899, the two companies outwardly drew closer together, with little direct competition, similar building costs, and, with the formation of the Coventry Syndicate in 1905-06, shared markets for Admiralty contracts. It is not possible readily to compare the costs of building merchant ships as even those of equivalent tonnage were fitted out to widely differing specifications; but naval ships of the same class can be compared, as except for small modifications they were built to standard designs. H.M.S. *Cressy,* an armoured cruiser, completed by Fairfield in 1900 cost £457 517, whereas her sister ship H.M.S. *Sutlej* completed by John Brown the following year cost £474 301. Similarly H.M.S. *Commonwealth,* a King Edward VII class battleship, completed by Fairfield in 1903 cost £544 274 and her sister ship H.M.S *Hindustan* built by John Brown in the same year cost £547 713. The Fairfield board, though, was faced with serious problems. To maintain its competitive position the firm needed large capital backing which the board found the Bank of Scotland increasingly less willing to provide. In particular the introduction of the turbine after 1901 caused both firms to extend their engine works and invest in new machine tools. John Brown, relying on the resources of the Atlas works at Sheffield, stole a march on Fairfield with the installation of turbines in the Cunarder *Carmania* in 1905 (Figures 6.10 (a) and (b)) when Fairfield were building the last Atlantic liners with reciprocating engines, the *Empress of Britain* and *Empress of Ireland* for the Canadian Pacific line. Despite the expenditure of over £225 000 by Fairfield on extending their wet basin and other improvements between 1902 and 1905, Alexander Gracie, the managing director, wrote with some urgency in June 1906: 'If we want to keep our position we must spend considerable sums during the next two or three years . . . first in the matter of modern appliances and second for the manufacture of turbines'[18]. He explained why the present engine works were inadequate at a board meeting the following February: 'for the same amount of horsepower to be turned out in a given time 50 per cent more area is required in the case of turbine

(b)

machinery than for reciprocating engines'[21]. In the event the firm only spent the relatively small sum of £20 000 on improvements in that year (see Figures 5.22 (a) and (b)). John Brown, however, maintained their advantage by introducing in H.M.S. *Brisk* (1910) the Brown-Curtis turbine, especially designed for naval ships (see Figure 5.19).

Although the two firms built about the same number of ships between 1900 and 1913, John Brown was dominant. After the takeover in 1902 of William Beardmore & Co., the Glasgow steelmakers, by Vickers, Fairfield could no longer rely on a local supplier of armour plate at preferential rates. The following year the company Secretary, George Strachan, had discussions about naval orders with Sir Eustace Tennyson D'Eynecourt of Vickers, an ex-Fairfield employee, and Lairds, the Birkenhead shipbuilders. No permanent arrangements were evidently made, as in 1905 William Beardmore opened a naval shipbuilding yard at Dalmuir in direct competition with both John Brown and Fairfield. In that year Fairfield reluctantly agreed to join the Coventry Syndicate to secure supplies of armament and armour plate. John Brown & Co. had 50 per cent and Cammell Laird & Co. and Fairfield each had 25 per cent shareholdings in the concern which owned the Coventry Ordnance Works with plant in Coventry and at Scotstoun, Glasgow. It was set up in an attempt to reduce the damaging effects of depression, clearly foreseen in the boom year of 1905, and allowed for joint tendering and work sharing on naval orders. Between 1905 and 1914 its achievement was striking with the acceptance of 33 naval contracts by John Brown, 26 by Fairfield, and 24 by Cammell Laird. In 1906, John Brown & Co. further extended by acquiring a majority shareholding in Harland and Wolff, the Belfast shipbuilders, thus securing control of virtually the whole of British

Figure 6.12 *Though dilution – the introduction of female labour to do men's jobs – was not so extensive in shipbuilding as in engineering, these girls and others helped to increase war-time production. They are testing condenser tubes for warships by applying hydraulic pressure and hitting them with a mallet to show up defects. Condenser trouble was always a problem for the Grand Fleet, often putting ships out of commission. The apprehensive look of the girl on the left may be explained by the chalked notice on the window 'When the boys come we are not going to keep you any longer girls'. One of the 'pin ups' shows men in the trenches.*

shipbuilding capacity for very large passenger liners. Lord Pirrie, managing director of Harland and Wolff, was appointed to the John Brown & Co. board in 1915.

Cushioned from the effects of the 1907-11 depression by naval contracts neither firm was very badly affected. Fairfield profits dropped to £46 159 in 1910, compared with £149 367 in the previous year, recovered to £119 993 in 1911 and disappeared in 1912 when the firm made a trading deficit of £21 373. This reflected losses on eight bad contracts between 1911 and 1914, including the survey ship H.M.S. *Endeavour* and the S.S. *Ermine* (Figure 6.11). Unfortunately figures are not available for John Brown. In 1913, the total horsepower of machinery produced at John Brown was 239 000, a world record, closely followed by Fairfield's 202 000. These totals, which neither firm could have expected to repeat the following year, were largely made up by machinery for the *Aquitania*, H.M.S. *Tiger*, the *Empress of Russia*, and the *Empress of Asia*, large prestige vessels. By 1914, the capacity of yards like Fairfield and John Brown could only consistently be fully employed by generously topping-up the order book with naval contracts. The large demands made on both yards during the war reinforced their future problems by encouraging investment in equipment for Admiralty work and disguised their inherent weakness. The wartime production of both companies was prodigious (Figure 6.12). Between

(a)

(b)

Figure 6.13 *By 1919, the size of the turbines had been greatly reduced by the introduction of gearing (see also Figure 6.10 (b) on page 127). These complementary views show the geared turbines (two sets) for H.M.S. Colombo, a Carlisle-class cruiser completed by Fairfield in 1919. Figure 6.13 (a) depicts one turbine with the casing removed, showing the high-pressure blading on the right and the low-pressure on the left, both geared into the large central pinion. The other view (Figure 6.13 (b)) shows the casing in position, with the condenser on the left. This was one of the last ships to be built with single-reduction gearing.*

Figure 6.14 *Building submarine engines at Clydebank in 1915, probably for submarine E35 and E36. This view shows four engines in various stages of completion. The one in the right background is being rigged for testing. In the left foreground is set of pistons. Each submarine had two of these engines. This was John Brown's first experience of building internal combustion engines. The E Class was the standard British submarine of the First World War.*

1914 and 1919, Fairfield built 54 ships (Figures 6.13 (a) and (b)) and 27 barges including H.M.S. *Valiant* and H.M.S. *Renown,* 10 submarines, and 31 torpedo boat destroyers, while John Brown built 45, including H.M.S. *Barham,* H.M.S. *Repulse,* H.M.S. *Hood* (not completed until 1920), 37 destroyers, and 5 submarines (Figure 6.14), more than any other yards in Britain.

Departed Glory

At the end of the war Fairfield's over-commitment to Admiralty work was a handicap. Fifteen wartime contracts were cancelled compared with five at John Brown. The firm was unable to return to peacetime production until 1921–22 and was prevented from taking full advantage of the post war boom (Figures 6.15 (a) and (b)). Until 1920, the firm, in common with other builders, confidently expecting the boom to be sustained, authorized the expenditure of £205 724 on improvements (see page 105), and, in 1918, entered into abortive negotiations to acquire a financial interest in Barclay Curle & Co. John Brown, in an only slightly less expansionist mood, returned to full peacetime production in 1920 (Figure 6.16) building five merchant ships in that year. In March 1919, the managing director reported to the parent company's board on the piling to No. 1 berth: 'This will complete the transformation of the East yard, making every berth suitable for modern broad-beamed vessels, and at the same time leaving ample room between each vessel'[22]. Towards the end of the year the parent company authorized the expenditure of £174 000 on the engine and boiler works, and the shipyard, 'in view of vessels now being laid down on all 8 berths in the Yard a condition of matters which has never existed before'[23]. The company's immediate post-war success largely depended on their connection with Harland and Wolff, the Belfast shipbuilders, in which the Royal Mail Shipping group (see page 105) acquired, in 1919, a majority shareholding. John Brown & Co. retained their shareholding in the company and Lord Pirrie, the managing director, continued to sit on the John Brown & Co. board. There was even talk in 1920 of amalgamating the two companies with a head office in the old Govan town hall in Glasgow. Between 1920 and Lord Pirrie's death in 1924, John Brown built 8 ships of 81 418 gross tons for lines in the Royal Mail Shipping group out of a total production of 172 284 gross tons, including the *Loch Katrine* the first motor ship for the group.

With the conversion of the Coventry Syndicate into the English Electric Company in 1919, Fairfield briefly became independent of ties with other builders. But in 1919 Lady Pearce, widow of Sir William Pearce, died and a large number of the company's shares came on to the market and were bought by Clarence Hatry's Northumberland Shipbuilding group. This gave Hatry a controlling interest in Fairfield and the company was assimilated into the group which by 1920 included the Monmouth Shipbuilding Co., William Doxford & Sons (the Wear shipbuilders and engineers), Workman Clark & Co. (the Belfast shipbuilders), the Blythswood Shipbuilding Co. (a Glasgow firm of tanker

Figure 6.15 Two views of S.S. Montrose, built by Fairfield for the Canadian Pacific Steamship Co. Figure 6.15 (a) shows the hull at an early stage of construction, in December 1919, with the tank top being completed and most of the frames in position. Figure 6.15 (b) shows the cabin-class dining room of the vessel as completed in 1922. Work was delayed by the depression of 1921–22 and by a series of industrial disputes, including rail and coal strikes.

(b)

Figure 6.16 The aftermath of the First World War. This peaceful scene shows H.M.S. Hood, the largest British capital ship ever built, with W-class destroyers, H.M.S. Venty and (alongside the merchant ship) H.M.S. Venomous; and beside the Hood, V-class destroyer H.M.S. Veteran. The merchant ship is probably the S.S. Bodnant a war-time standard ship. Note the forest of derricks on the left, gradually supplanted by tower cranes from 1932, when one was installed for the Queen Mary. Other firms, such as Charles Connell & Co., were re-equipping with tower cranes as early as 1919.

builders), the Lancashire Iron and Steel Co., the Lanarkshire Steel Co., and Globe Shipping Co. With the sudden collapse of the post-war boom in 1920, the immense apparatus of Hatry's group was to be a serious disadvantage to Fairfield. At first the group tried to tide Fairfield over the depression by arranging for the company to build three sets of triple-expansion engines for William Doxford & Sons (delivered in 1921), and four sets for the Monmouth Shipbuilding Co. (delivered in 1922), and by negotiating contracts for three tankers (two built in 1921 and one delayed until 1925). Fairfield was badly hit by the depression. A cable ship was all that was built in 1920, followed by two tankers in 1921. John Brown, partially protected by contracts from the Royal Mail Shipping group, was similarly affected. The managing director reported in April 1921, 'As regards work obtained through Lord Pirrie, I regret to state that we have been asked by the Royal Mail Steam Packet Co. to completely suspend all operations on the *Loch Katrine*'[24]. Only three ships were launched during 1921, including the *Windsor Castle* and *Loch Katrine* for the Royal Mail Shipping group and early in 1922 work was stopped on the Cunarders *Alaunia* and *Franconia*. In June the parent company was informed: 'sheds are empty, and all the machines are standing idle'[25]. By July the company was forced to tender for two cable ships, the *Mirror* and *Norseman*, 'at a price comprising solely the cost of material and labour in order to provide work for the nucleus of our best and oldest established men'[26]. The signing of the Washington Treaty in 1921, severely limiting naval shipbuilding, jeopardized the future of both companies. Both yards were designed partly for naval shipbuilding and both needed naval work to fill their order books, even in boom years. In 1922, contracts for battlecruisers, 'super-Hoods', were cancelled with both yards.

The passing in 1921 of the Trade Facilities Act, designed to maintain employment by providing guaranteed loans for a variety of capital projects, including shipbuilding, coupled with a rise in demand by liner companies for new tonnage to maintain services, resulted in an improvement in the autumn of 1922. Work was resumed on the *Franconia* and Fairfield completed more merchant tonnage by the end of the year than in any year since the war. The improvement was short lived. No ships were completed at Fairfield in 1923 and only the cruiser H.M.S. *Berwick* in 1924. The Fairfield board also found itself under pressure to lend money to shore-up the Northumberland Shipbuilding group's failing liquidity. In March 1924, they advanced money to the Northumberland Shipbuilding Co. to build a ship, 'as that yard finds it difficult under the present circumstances to finance the vessel themselves'[27] and in August the board agreed to buy the Monmouth Shipbuilding Co. for £25 000. John Brown was only slightly better placed, building four ships in 1923, including a tanker of 6921 gross tons, three passenger ships the *Oronsay, Princess Kathleen*, and *Princess Marguerite* in 1924, and completing in 1925 the *Alaunia* and three other small vessels. By May 1925, the situation at Clydebank was serious with, 'the East and West yard ironworks sheds . . . absolutely empty and like a desert'[28]. The managing director was pessimistic, unable to see any

Figure 6.17 *The Fairfield fitting-out basin in 1925, with the T.S.S.* Letitia, *built for the Anchor-Donaldson line being masted by the 200-ton fitting-out crane the largest on the Clyde. On the left is the M.V.* Aorangi, *built for the Union Steamship Co. of New Zealand, with the most powerful marine diesel engines of the day. Note the two tower cranes on the right.*

way of maintaining the existing labour pool: 'Business at present is so unsettled that it is exceedingly difficult to have even a semblance of continuity of work [after the completion of the *Alaunia*]. We . . . found ourselves at a loss how to find work for roughly 100 experienced turbine bladers and turbine workers, who had been employed by us continuously for the last 15 years . . . We cannot afford to let such skilled and experienced artisans drift out of our reach'[29]. 1925 was a better year for Fairfield with five ships completed including the liner *Aorangi* for the Union Steam Ship Co. of New Zealand equipped with Fairfield-Sulzer two-stroke single-acting air-injection engines producing 13 000 brake horsepower, the most powerful diesel engines in the world. In 1955, A.C. Hardy described the *Aorangi* 'as opening the era . . . for the big motor passenger liner', and paid tribute to the Fairfield staff 'that had had no previous diesel engine experience . . . and no precedents or examples upon which to enlarge or modify'[30] (Figure 6.17). Confirming the growing demand for motor ships between 1925 and 1939 and the success of the *Aorangi*, Fairfield built 14 sets of diesel engines under licence between 1925 and 1939, while John Brown built 12 sets. Unlike the pre-First

135

World War depression the successful introduction of new technology, although it attracted some orders, did not provide a solution as freight rates failed to rise sufficiently to justify its introduction (motor ships cost 20 per cent or 30 per cent more than steamers) and the Admiralty, unlike the German navy, did not consider it reliable for naval tonnage.

Although the Government estimated that £233 000 was lost on fifty-nine contracts completed in Britain between 1922 and 1924, neither Fairfield nor John Brown made a loss on a contract until 1924. On nine ships (ship numbers 496–504), built between 1923 and 1924, John Brown made profits of £84 700 on costs of £1 415 615 while Fairfield between 1922 and 1924 made profits of £679 942 on costs of £6 504 803 on five ships (ship numbers 526, 528, 595, 596, and 616) (including the *Empress of Scotland* and the T.S.S. *Montrose* ordered by the Canadian Pacific Line during the war). Except for four loss-making contracts in 1925–26 and three in 1928–29, John Brown continued to make contract profits throughout the depression. Significantly five of the loss-making contracts were for motor ships explained by the managing director in 1933 in a report to the board on the re-equipment of the engine works: 'For equal powers, the labour on a diesel installation is about 200 per cent greater than it is on a reciprocating steam installation'[31]. Losses only exceeded profits in 1928, when the company lost £122 889 on contracts. Fairfield were only slightly less fortunate, making losses of £48 727 on costs of £2 238 707 on the five ships built between late 1925 and 1927. The firm was, however, able to record a trading profit by carrying out repair and reconditioning work and by drawing on capital reserves. Unfortunately, these losses came at a bad time for Fairfield, Clarence Hatry went bankrupt in 1924 and the Northumberland Shipbuilding group was liquidated in 1927. The Fairfield board was forced to write off £400 000 of capital; but the company managed to survive and record profits on contracts in 1929.

Until 1930 John Brown built in excess of 20 000 gross tons each year including some tankers and motor ships; but relying on a staple diet of large passenger liners and cross-channel ferries. Unlike the market for tramp steamers, the passenger ship market was less volatile as liner companies, obliged to maintain services, needed to build new tonnage to attract customers and meet competition. Nearly all the liners built by John Brown and Fairfield between 1924 and 1930 were for the popular emigration routes to Canada, Australia, and New Zealand. As a result of a severe cash crisis in 1930, the financial structure of the John Brown parent company was reorganized and the share capital reduced. The company's steel works were rationalized by merger with those of Thomas Firth & Sons. The shipyard was left intact as, 'if any reduction in valuation of Clydebank were made, our ordinary shares would be wiped out completely, which could not be considered for a moment'[32]. The situation was serious. In March the managing director of Clydebank, envying Swan Hunter's liquidity, declared: 'the only tangible advantage Clydebank can claim is the fact that we are at present engaged on the construction of the hull and machinery of the largest vessel [the *Empress of Britain*] that has been built in Great Britain

Figure 6.18 *Ship no. 534 looming in its abandonment like a monument to the glory departed; as if shipbuilding man had tried to do too much and had been defeated by the mightiness of his own conception' (George Blake in* The Shipbuilders, *London; Pan Books, 1972, p. 31). This photograph shows the hull of what became the* Queen Mary *on 9 September 1932, after work had been suspended for nearly a year. The hull was painted continuously until work restarted in August 1934.*

since 1913'[32]. Although agreement was reached with Cunard & Co. for the building of the *Queen Mary* (ship number 534) the yard's problems grew. In order to build the ship £45 900 had to be spent on extending and strengthening the berth and installing a 10-ton hammerhead crane. By August 1930, with the launch of H.M.S. *Beagle,* there were no ships on the ways and the yard's overdraft was in excess of the limit set by the bank. Work on the *Queen Mary* began in December and, with the rapid deepening of the depression, stopped on 12 December 1931, as the London discount market refused to discount bills outstanding on the ship (Figure 6.18). The main shipyard was closed, with over

3000 redundancies, and only the West yard remained open to build five small naval vessels.

Fairfield was experiencing a similar cash crisis. At the Annual General Meeting in 1930 the chairman complained of 'the curtailment of warship and high-class passenger work and the great difficulty experienced in securing remunerative prices for the few orders'[27]. The crisis worsened, only four small ships were built in 1931, none in 1932, two destroyers in 1933, and a paddle steamer in 1934. In March 1933, the Bank of Scotland refused to advance a further £200 000 over and above the £300 000 already loaned and the Bank of England stepped in with a £150 000 loan 'stipulating that these facilities should be looked upon as a temporary advance to be repaid out of future profits'[27]. The West yard was closed permanently in June and the building rights sold to National Shipbuilders Securities Ltd for £30 000. In his annual report the chairman attacked the Government for continuing to restrict naval construction under the Washington Treaty and argued that in times of depression naval building should be increased, 'to advance our technical skill and maintain our skilled workmen in regular employment'[33]. With the beginning of the re-armament programme, the company's prospects seemed better. But when the Anchor line failed to honour a bill of £145 000 due in November 1933, it foundered and with the encouragement of the Bank of England Sir James and Henry Lithgow stepped in, paid the claim of the bill holders, and secured the whole of the Bank of Scotland overdraft. Fairfield thereby became a member of the Lithgow group.

Reawakening

After the passing of the final Trade Facilities Act in 1926, the Government, largely because of opposition from the shipping industry to state intervention, made no further finance available to the shipbuilding industry until 1935. The Government loan made in 1934 to Cunard & Co. to enable work on the *Queen Mary* to begin again was exceptional, and resulted from pressure from John Brown, Cunard, Viscount Weir, and David Kirkwood, M.P. for Clydebank, on the correct assumption that it would encourage the liner market. The fresh start on the *Queen Mary* (Figure 6.19) in April 1934 marked the beginning of a period of stability at John Brown which was to last until the 1950s. The Ottawa Agreement of 1932, which stimulated the building of refrigerated motor ships for the Australian and New Zealand routes, benefited the firm after 1934. Between then and 1939, four such vessels were built at Clydebank out of a total production of seven merchant ships, including the *Queen Mary* and *Queen Elizabeth*. Neither yard, though, could have remained viable by basing its production after 1935 solely on merchant tonnage. As the chairman of Fairfield rightly pointed out in his annual report in 1936, it was re-armament that provided the fillip to the industry: 'The revival in shipbuilding is due to the renewed confidence of shipowners in the future of shipping, as evidenced by the

activities of the home market and the placing of many contracts for new vessels assisted by the recent decision of the National Government to restore the Navy to its former high standard of efficiency'[33]. Between 1936 and 1939, Fairfield completed 9 naval contracts out of a total production of 15 and John Brown 9 out of a total production of 16 (including 2 destroyers for the Argentine navy).

During the Second World War, both yards were controlled by the Government and their output was again prodigious. Fairfield, with fewer berths after the closure of the West yard in 1934, built 30 ships between 1940 and 1945, including a battleship and 2 aircraft carriers. In addition the yard constructed 16 landing craft and maintained a continuous stock pile of replacement triple-expansion engines. John Brown's wartime production exceeded in both total tonnage and horsepower that of the First World War. The firm built 37 ships including a battleship (Figure 6.20), a monitor, 2 cruisers, an aircraft carrier, 5 landing craft, 13 sets of submarine engines, and 2 sets of destroyer engines. The Dalmuir basin of William Beardmore & Co., which had been sold to National Shipbuilders Security Ltd in 1931, was re-opened under the management of John Brown. There, and at Clydebank, 11 merchant ships were reconstructed for war service and 116 warships were repaired and reconditioned. With financial assistance from the Admiralty, both companies were encouraged to re-equip with 'modern types of machinery and plant designed to save labour and increase production'[33]. Fairfield authorized in 1942 the expenditure of £162 000 on improvements to their shipyard and engine works and in 1945 a further £142 000 on the modernization of the engine works.

139

Both companies prospered in the post-war years, through the absence of foreign competition, high freight rates stimulated by the Korean War and an increase in demand for cargo liners and oil tankers. Their order books emphasized that their traditional markets for fast passenger ships of all types were gradually declining. Immediately after the war both yards refitted passenger ships for peacetime use and built new ones to replace wartime losses. John Brown refitted the *Queen Mary* and *Queen Elizabeth* and built the *Media* and *Caronia* for Cunard. Fairfield refitted the *Empress of Japan* as the *Empress of Scotland* and built the *Princess Marguerite* and *Princess Patricia* for the Canadian Pacific Line under an agreement made with the line in 1942 to come into effect at the end of the war. Thereafter, in response to post-war demand, both yards began to build a variety of cargo liners, tankers, refrigerated ships, and ore carriers.

Figure 6.20 *The Clydebank fitting-out basin in 1941, with the main armament being installed in H.M.S.* Duke of York, *a King George V class battleship.*

Problems and Solutions

The recession of 1956-57, when four orders were cancelled with John Brown and three with Fairfield, coupled with the resurgence of foreign competition in the late 1950s, foreshadowed the eventual failure of both companies in 1968 and 1965 respectively. The Government's reaction to the depression, by placing Admiralty contracts with both yards, was as characteristic as it was anachronistic. The problem in both yards was to secure a sufficient flow of merchant contracts in their new range of products to justify substantial recapitalization. A long-term scrap-and-build policy, with substantial financial aid for capital projects, could have provided the incentive to both companies to abandon their traditional products and expertise. Although both yards modestly re-equipped after the war and Fairfield again in the 1960s, neither could afford the massive reconstruction undertaken by competitors in Japan, Germany, and elsewhere with state aid and protected markets.

Despite a brief recovery in 1959–60 the problems of both companies were rapidly overtaking them, reinforced by the increasing overcapacity in the engine works on the river. In June 1962 the managing director of John Brown warned: 'There is no indication of a revival in shipbuilding which could keep an engine works employed to capacity'[34] and suggested that the dual functions, shipbuilding and engineering, be separated by the establishment of two distinct companies. This was done by the formation of John Brown Engineering (Clydebank) Ltd in 1963, principally to build land gas turbine equipment with the occasional marine engine for the shipyard, now John Brown Shipbuilding (Clydebank) Ltd. In the same year Fairfield engine department was amalgamated with David Rowan & Co. Ltd, also controlled by the Lithgow group, in an attempt to reduce oncosts by rationalizing design work; but with no intention of abandoning marine engine building. The new company Fairfield-Rowan Ltd was a wholly owned subsidiary of the Fairfield Shipbuilding and Engineering Co. John Brown, meanwhile, was considering possible amalgamation with Fairfield and with their traditional partners Cammell-Laird and Harland and Wolff. Although Fairfield, as part of the Lithgow group, was secure so long as the group had sufficient capital reserves, it was the most vulnerable. It was not on the lower Clyde, like the rest of the Lithgow yards, it joined the group late, largely at the request of the Bank of England, and the management had never been as extensively reconstructed by Sir James and Henry Lithgow as the other companies in the group (with the exception of William Beardmore & Co.). Lithgows tried to sell the yard to P. & O. and other shipowning interests in the late 1950s and early 1960s.

Fairfield failed first. In October 1965 the board decided that the cash position was so serious and the financial forecasts so poor that liquidation was inevitable if the finances of the whole group were not to be seriously weakened. After much negotiation and the injection of Government funds, Fairfield (Glasgow) Ltd was set up, 'not merely to save a recently modernized Scottish shipyard from

extinction . . . but in addition to provide a proving-ground for new relations in the shipbuilding industry'[35] (see page 111). Fairfield-Rowan did not become part of Fairfield (Glasgow) Ltd and the engine works were closed. The financial press was hostile, reasoning that closure would be more beneficial to an industry already suffering from surplus capacity. Yet Fairfield was probably far better equipped than John Brown's shipyard, also faced with serious cash problems. The parent company was anxious to sell the yard; but could find no buyers. However, the Labour Government had already appointed in February 1965, a Shipbuilding Enquiry Committee under the chairmanship of Sir Reay Geddes which was to recommend the amalgamation of the Upper Clyde yards of John Brown, Fairfield, Connell, Stephen, and Yarrow into Upper Clyde Shipbuilders Ltd in 1968 (see page 111).

The failure of both firms was a reflection of the fall in demand for their traditional products, warships and passenger vessels (Figure 6.21) of all types, which both yards had been designed to build (see Figures 5.22 (a) and (b), page 104). The profitable construction of new products in demand, especially bulk carriers (Figure 6.22), would have required the total reconstruction of

Figure 6.21   *The* Queen Elizabeth 2 *on trials in the Firth of Clyde in 1969. This ship was built by John Brown with Government assistance, and has been a great success for the Cunard Co. It was, however, an unfortunate contract for John Brown, as no further orders of this type could realistically be expected.*

Figure 6.22 *The launch of the last ship, the* Alisa, *from the Clydebank yard in October 1972. Contrary to usual practice the vessel was not named at launching, but later, in the fitting-out basin of the former Harland & Wolff yard at Govan (see Figure 5.23 (b) and page 105). The* Alisa *was launched from the same berth as the Queens and other large vessels built at Clydebank.*

Clydebank and further major capital improvements at Fairfield, to increase throughput and reduce oncosts. Fairfield and John Brown expertise in bulk carrier construction had been built up during the post-war boom; but neither firm had the finances in the 1950s to match the new resources of foreign competitors. Unfortunately, neither political party was willing to provide the necessary capital injection until too late. Although Fairfield (Glasgow) Ltd and later Upper Clyde Shipbuilders Ltd were formed in the right spirit, the timing was not propitious.

PART THREE

Other Industries

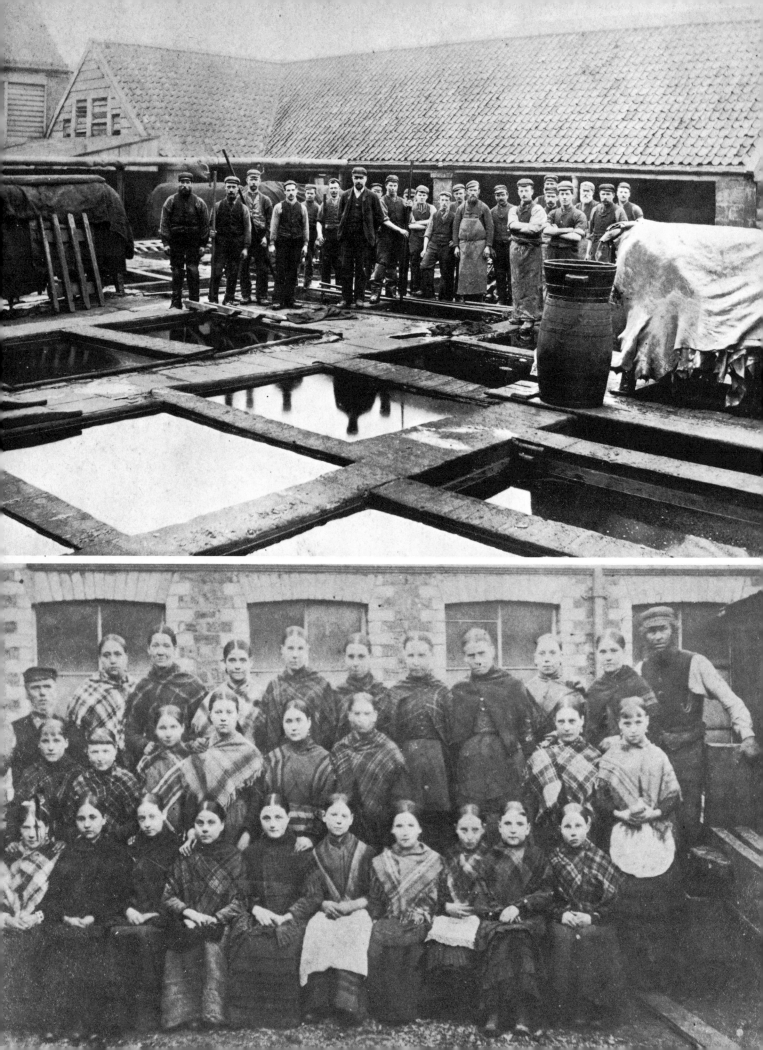

CHAPTER SEVEN

Other Industries

Figure 7.1 *W.J. & W. Lang's Seedhill Tannery, Paisley, c. 1900, with tanpits in the foreground, hides piled on trestles, and part of the drying shed on the left. The techniques of tanning had changed hardly at all since the eighteenth century. This tannery is still operating, using modern methods.*

It was inevitable that strong ties should develop between the heavy industries and other West of Scotland manufacturing concerns. The conditions which stimulated the growth of ironworking and later shipbuilding in the late eighteenth century encouraged industries like weaving, spinning, pot making, and boot making (Figure 7.1), whose markets lay mainly in plantation colonies. Export cargoes of locally-produced goods and raw materials helped to balance the inward trade in tobacco, sugar, and, later, cotton and timber. Though the main market for such goods lay in the West Indies and North America, links were forged with India and the East in the early nineteenth century. Indian fabrics set aesthetic and technical standards in the West of Scotland and their successful imitation by local spinners, weavers, dyers, and printers allowed them to exploit eastern and middle eastern markets. The large number of emigrants to the colonies from Scotland during the eighteenth and nineteenth centuries was of significance to West of Scotland manufacturers. The natural longing of the 'exile' for the comforts of home encouraged the brewing of beers, the blending of whisky for export and the making of confectionery, ready-made suits, shirts, cigarettes, clay pipes, cars, 'Camp Coffee', bootlaces (Figure 7.2), and a variety of other goods for colonial markets.

Suppliers to Shipbuilders

Industries like sawmilling, paint making, canvas and carpet weaving, rope making, furniture construction, and the supply of marine sanitary conveniences were more closely allied to shipbuilding. Ropewalks were historically a feature of British seaports, but none grew in size and importance to the same extent as the Gourock Ropework Co., which was founded in 1736. By the 1850s, this firm, as well as supplying ropes for rigging and mooring to local markets, sold them, and related products such as nets and canvas, through a world-wide network of agencies and depots. Nets and lines were a speciality of W. & J. Knox of Kilbirnie, founded in 1778, who still have extensive export markets. A number of smaller firms made lighter ropes and twines. A handful still survive, particularly James Picken & Son, Abercorn Ropeworks, Paisley, where traditional methods are still used to make cordage (Figure 7.3). Eastern Scotland was the main centre for the weaving of sailcloth, but from the eighteenth century sailcloth was made at Greenock and Port Glasgow, where the Newark Sailcloth Works and the Gourock Ropework Co. were in production until 1970. The introduction of wire-rope rigging by William Simons, the shipbuilders, in 1851

Figure 7.2 *A group of 'Paton's Angels', c. 1890. William Paton began making braided bootlaces in Johnstone, Renfrewshire in the 1840s, and built up a world-wide reputation. Though the firm faced stiff competition from Germany before the First World War, it survived, and still thrives.*

Figure 7.3 *The interior of the Abercorn Ropeworks, c. 1910, showing the twinewalk and the winch for stretching the strands after laying. The trough on the right contains finished twine. The scene is not very different to-day.*

Figure 7.4 *Weaving chenille Axminster carpets on hand-loom in James Templeton & Son's, Tullis Street Factory, in the late nineteenth century. James Templeton and an Irishman named Quiglay invented the chenille process, in 1839. This involved weaving woollen cloth, with cotton warps, cutting it into strips and steaming it into a V form, and weaving the strips of 'fur' (seen in the basket in the centre of the picture) into carpets. The loom on the right is 33 feet long.*

Figure 7.5 *An early (1870s) advertisement for Shanks' Patent Water Closets, when they were still made of cast-iron in George Smith & Co.'s Sun Foundry, Glasgow. A water-closet of this type was recently removed from a country house in Perthshire, and is now preserved by Armitage Shanks. At the bottom of the advertisement are wash-hand basins, fountains, and a 'urinal for two persons'.*

opened up a new market for wrought iron. Iron (later steel) wire ropes were made on a large scale by firms in Coatbridge, Govan, and Shettleston, for both marine and land use.

Most of the shipyards, especially Fairfield, J. & G. Thomson, William Denny Bros, and Cairds had their own cabinet-makers, but the fitting out of passenger liners with their elaborate furnishings gave employment to furniture manufacturers in Glasgow, Beith, and Lochwinnoch. These used ingenious machinery, much of it made by the Auchengree Foundry, Glengarnock, Ayrshire, to produce the floridly-carved furniture so much in vogue in the 1880s and 1890s. A number of Glasgow upholsterers supplied ship furnishings. The carpet makers of Glasgow, Ayrshire, and Renfrew found ready markets for their products in liner construction, though domestic and export demand was more significant (Figure 7.4). Less glamorous than the rich trappings of first-class public rooms were the sanitary fittings – pipes, water closets (Figure 7.5), wash-hand basins, and baths – supplied by a few sanitary earthenware makers, especially Shanks of Barrhead and Doultons of Paisley, and by a large number of plumbers and brassfounders. Several Glasgow firms made stained glass for passenger liners and steam yachts. Glasgow makers also turned out ships'

Figure 7.6 *Lord Kelvin with a compass of his design, made by his firm, Kelvin and James White Ltd, one of the most important scientific instrument makers in Britain in the late nineteenth and early twentieth centuries.*

buckets, flags, signal rockets, navigational instruments (Figure 7.6), engine packing and fire hoses, and local suppliers provisioned and plenished vessels, and purveyed launch lunches. Even games equipment for Cunard luxury liners came in the 1880s from a Glasgow firm.

Manufacturing for Export

As the nineteenth century wore on, the general trading base of the West of Scotland expanded, with the addition of new products, such as chemicals (bleaching powder, soda, superphosphate, calico-printers requisites, and sheep dip), linen and cotton thread, sugar, starch, firebricks, leather, roofing felt, commercial stationery, india-rubber goods, cotton and silk cloth, lace curtaining, moulding and veneers, drugs, 'fancy' packaging, photographic apparatus, wallpaper, and almanacks. The West of Scotland chemical industry was dominated by Charles Tennant & Co., whose St Rollox Chemical Works was, in the 1830s and 1840s, the largest in the world. Scottish firebricks and gas retorts, especially those made from the Glenboig clays, were world-renowned from the 1870s. Firebricks still enjoy a wide market, despite competition from Europe. Although the expansion of cotton spinning, which had provided the impetus to industrialization (see page 4), ceased in the West of Scotland in the 1840s, the manufacture of cotton thread and cloth continued to grow. Handloom weaving of shawls and silk handkerchiefs on a modest scale survived in Lanarkshire until the 1890s. In the 1870s, it was claimed that the largest weaving factory in the world was in Glasgow. The Paisley thread firms dominated the world market for cotton thread, even before their amalgamation as J. & P. Coats in 1893. The Linen Thread Co., formed on the same model in 1896, was strongly represented in the West of Scotland by W. & J. Knox, and Finlayson, Bousfield & Co., of Johnstone.

Textile finishing had been a significant industry in the region from the 1770s or earlier, and flowered with the introduction of the power-loom after *c*.1800. The plain product was decorated by printing in numerous 'printfields' throughout the area. By the 1890s, the industry was concentrated in the Vale of Leven, Dunbartonshire, and from 1898 was controlled by the United Turkey Red Co. Ltd, and by the Calico Printers Association. This industry has now completely disappeared. Lace making was introduced to the Irvine valley from Nottingham in 1876 by Alexander Morton, and flourished in a climate of low wages, traditional skill, and expanding home and export markets. India-rubber goods, which are often 'treated' textiles, were a speciality of several Glasgow firms. George McLellan & Co., the sole survivor, made machine belting, fire hose, valves, wringer rollers, rubber balls, fishing stockings, and hot-water bottles.

The Home Market

It is difficult to identify industries not involved directly or indirectly with exports. Some branches of food processing and retailing, and numbers of small firms in most industries, concentrated on the local market, which covered the whole of the West of Scotland. Flour milling, an historic industry, was revolutionized in the 1880s by the introduction of roller milling, leading to the concentration of the industry in Glasgow, accompanied by the centralization of bread baking in large mechanized factories. The pioneers were J. & B. Stevenson, of the Cranstonhill and Plantation Bakeries, Glasgow (founded in 1878), whose 'machine-made bread' (a phrase which appears on posters held by Milanda Bread Ltd, Glasgow) was distributed by carriers throughout the West of Scotland. Their example was followed by Beatties, Bilslands, and the United Co-operative

Baking Society. At about the same time, much of the retailing and wholesaling business of the West of Scotland was concentrated in new 'warehouses' which supplied the complete range of clothing and household goods to both retail shops and their customers by arrangement. This system has almost died out, but in its heyday one of the leading firms, Mann Byars & Co., had depots in Toronto, Sydney, and St John's, New Brunswick.

The emergence after the First World War of competing factories overseas, often behind tariff barriers, the weakening of ties with former British colonies during the 1950s and early 1960s, technical changes facilitating the concentration of production and distribution in larger units, and a decline in the demand for some products, or in the supply of raw material for their manufacture, have combined to make many of these industries in the West of Scotland less significant. Some which were carried on by a number of companies until recently are now only represented by one or two firms in the area. They have, however, been partly replaced by 'new' industries, such as the production of motor vehicles, electrical apparatus, and consumer durables, and partly by the expansion of some traditional industries, like the manufacture of ready-made clothes and hosiery.

From 1930 new industry has been attracted to the region by a variety of national and local government, and private enterprise incentives. In particular, the Scottish Industrial Estates Ltd, through its successful Hillington Estate (established 1937) and numerous other smaller estates, has brought many new firms to the region, both from south of the border and abroad. This policy of widening the productive base of the region was continued after the Second World War and confirmed by the Distribution of Industry Act, 1950. By then the Scottish Development Area, as designated by the Special Areas (Development and Improvement) Act of 1934, had received 13 per cent of all new industrial building undertaken in Britain. Although this 'regional policy' has succeeded in attracting investment from many companies, including such American firms as Euclid, Honeywell, IBM, and Marathon, their commitment to the region has always remained doubtful. One of the weaknesses of the regional policy has been its tendency to operate to the disadvantage of indigenous firms and talent. Moreover, its success has been qualified. Less than 10 per cent of the West of Scotland workforce are employed on industrial estates and the regional economy has continued to be characterized by its residual heavy industries.

Survey Techniques, References and Further Reading

Distinguishing Letters.	DESCRIPTION.
E T,	A VERY POWERFUL SCRAP CUTTING MACHINE, driven by a 15-inch Cylinder Engine. The Slide having a lift of 7 inches, any special scrap, such as Boiler Ends, Bridge Rails, &c. (which cannot be cut by Machines having the ordinary lift), may be cut by this Machine. It is specially designed for plate-scrap, and has a gap of 18 inches. The Steelings are 2 feet 4 inches long, and $2\frac{1}{4}$ inches thick. The ordinary double-headed rail may be cut into lengths up to 18 inches. This Machine is equal to cutting a section of 4 inches square iron (cold), and can be made with Cross Blades, if preferred, for cutting up Railway Carriage Axles, or the heaviest class of Rails, Tyres, or Puddle Bars.

Approximate Weight,   *Price,*

CHAPTER EIGHT

The Techniques of the Western Survey
of the National Register of Archives
(Scotland)

Finding and Listing Business Records

Figure 8.1   In the selection of business records catalogues and advertising literature should always be kept, even if originating from other firms. This typical nineteenth century catalogue sheet shows a 'very powerful scrap cutting machine' driven by a steam engine. Advertising literature usually includes details of construction, ice, and applications.

Much of the material used in the compilation of this volume has been discovered by the authors in the past four years, while working for the Western Survey of the National Register of Archives (Scotland). The Register, a branch of the Scottish Record Office, was begun in 1946 with the aim of locating and listing records of historical interest in private hands in Scotland[1]. In 1970, the Western Survey was established at the University of Glasgow with the aid of a Treasury grant, carried on the Scottish Record Office's vote, to extend the work of the Register in the West of Scotland. In terms of its general remit the Western Survey has listed a number of important family collections but one of its main tasks has been to discover new sources of business records. Although the Register and the Departments of Economic History at the Universities of Glasgow[2] and Strathclyde had already carried out many surveys and rescued several significant collections, much remained to be done. The problem was to decide the strategy of the Survey: which firms or industries were to be approached.

Obviously companies going into liquidation, moving premises or about to be taken over had to be contacted, but for the rest it seemed sensible to adopt a systematic industry by industry approach. The first chosen was ironfounding, in the mistaken belief that it is a simple homogenous industry with well-defined products, and on the correct assumption that it would provide a useful introduction to the more complex engineering and shipbuilding sectors. The ironfounding survey was conceived with the dual purpose of listing the records of individual companies, and at the same time photographing plant, premises, and machinery, making rough lay-out drawings, and interviewing the management and members of the workforce to discover details of the firm's antecedents, especially changes in location, product types, linkages, and production methods. The object was to attempt to create an historical picture of the industry at a moment in time by the use of a variety of complementary techniques. Such was the success of this ironfounding survey that the methods developed were used in the more significant surveys of the engineering and shipbuilding industries.

The problems of locating, selecting, and preserving business records from manufacturing companies were highlighted by Barry Supple in 1962 when analysing the subject of business history. He pointed out that business historians have tended to assume that an enterprise consists of separate departments, for example, purchasing, manufacturing, and marketing, independent of each other. He indicated that there were two dangers in adopting this approach. Variation in the relative importance of different departments can easily be overlooked and the significance of the firm as a corporate institution undervalued[3]. Similarly, the archivist in considering his academic audience must seek to create a balance between various interests and at the same time not overlook or diminish the significance of any department or firm in relation to the others. For instance, in the Western Survey it could have easily been assumed that the large collections of archives of the constituent companies of Upper Clyde Shipbuilders were representative of the industry on the Clyde. In fact, by exploring the record holdings of the other surviving companies it was evident that the industry had a much wider base than the records from the constituent companies of Upper Clyde Shipbuilders suggested. And within collections from individual companies it is tempting to look for and select items of particular current interest while neglecting others and so distort the balance of the collections.

As Professor Payne rightly pointed out in discussing his survey of business records, 'the most fruitful results were achieved in those cases in which it had been possible to gain some prior knowledge of the history and organization of the firm being approached and hence some idea of the sort of records that might have been kept'[4]. The range and type of records likely to be held by any firm tends to be a reflection of its product. Professor Mathias writing about the brewing industry pointed out that 'excise produced elaborate documentation'[5], similarly in the heavy engineering and shipbuilding industry one-off or small-batch products, repeat orders, and requests for spares have the same effect. The more sophisticated and individual the product, the greater the documentation becomes; whereas in an industry with simple products only those records required by law are to be found, and sometimes not even those. In the ironfounding industry the best records of the range of a firm's activities are found not in the manager's safe, but in the pattern store. Even within industries practice varies from firm to firm. In shipyards in the West of Scotland firms like Fairfield Shipbuilding and Engineering Co. Ltd and John Brown Shipbuilding and Engineering Co. Ltd, specialists in quality passenger tonnage, produced far more elaborate documentation than firms like Lithgows Ltd that build, largely, cargo tonnage.

Record-keeping practice, however, is rarely continuous throughout a firm's history. Indeed it would be strange if it was. New accounting techniques, the growth of the firm, takeovers, and changes in the range and complexity of the product, make for the introduction of new series of records. In the case of J. & G. Thomson Ltd, later John Brown Shipbuilding and Engineering Co. Ltd, the firm began in 1847 with the usual range of accounting records, ledgers, journals, and cash books, but as the firm grew new record groups, such as tender books, estimating books, and balance books, had to be introduced to control cash flows in the various departments. When the firm was taken over by John Brown & Co. in 1899, record-keeping practice was reviewed and a number of new documentary controls introduced, such as progressive and finished cost books, iron and steel order books, and weight books. Moreover, these changes do not only occur in the record-keeping practice of the general management, but also in that of technical departments, largely in response to a growth in complexity of the product or the structure of the firm, with the resulting need to create new controls to ensure quality and reliability.

In the location and selection of records from within a firm it is important to recognize that in most manufacturing firms there is an administrative division between general management and technical functions, purely as a matter of convenience. This is reflected in record-keeping practice. Since the disciplines of economic and business history have grown out of social and economic studies attention has been given to records that contain details of management decisions, particularly those relating to finance and labour. It has generally been assumed that the technical records are only of interest to the historian with engineering or scientific knowledge. Hence the general management records, often conveniently bound in volume form, are commonly preserved, while the technical records, which are difficult to handle and interpret, tend to be destroyed, or at best stored separately from the other records.

It is not possible to lay out firm criteria for location and selection of general management records, as record-keeping practice and nomenclature varies widely : each firm devising its own procedure. For example, in some firms details of all financial transactions for specific contracts are transferred from the cash books and journals to the principal ledgers, whereas in others they are not. So in the first instance it would be reasonable to discard the cash books and journals and in the other it would not. Similarly, the custodians of records vary from firm to firm, in some all the management records are under the control of the secretary; while in others each department has control of its own documentation. The general management records usually comprise records of the board of directors, the private and general accounts, contracts, materials, charges and costs, plant, property and equipment, wages, salaries and labour, and advertising (Figure 8.1). In the small firm these records are contained in a few simple sets of volumes, but the bigger the company and the more complex the management structure, the greater the tendency for each of these components, and sometimes subdivisions of them, to be contained in individual series. In locating these record types, even in a small firm, enquiries have to be made in every administrative department, as the central management is often unaware of the systems of documentation of subordinate departments.

Once the records have been located, such is their bulk, that some selection procedure must be adopted. In the Western Survey, when records were to be deposited in record offices, the process of selection was in two stages. First a rough list was prepared in the firm's offices and the more obvious rubbish, like vouchers, unidentified rough accounting records, and miscellaneous files on trivial subjects, discarded. Any material of doubtful value was retained for later review. After deposit the records were sorted, put in order, relisted, and a further more detailed selection made on the basis of comparison of material within the collection and with other collections. In making a selection the archivist must avoid pressure from academics to concentrate on particular functions of current interest to the detriment of others and the temptation of borrowing techniques of selection by date not suited to business records. If in a large run of business records that appear to be of a standard pattern datal selection is employed, the series may be rendered valueless for statistical analysis as in an economy characterized by cyclical fluctuations, this type of selection severely distorts the cycle. This is true even for the very bulky wages records, as small fluctuations in wages often aggravated the cyclical behaviour of an industry.

The large survey of the records of John Brown Shipbuilding and Engineering Co. Ltd, one of the constituent companies of Upper Clyde Shipbuilders Ltd, illustrates how this system worked in practice. The majority of the management records at Clydebank were held in the Secretary's safe: but a significant residue was held by individual departments, such as estimating, shipyard manager's, and engine works. The Secretary's safe was full to overflowing with records from 1847 to the present day in no particular order. Such was the variety of record types and their disorder that it was impossible to attempt any rearrangement at that stage. Each volume, bundle or file was allocated a running number and described briefly in a handlist. Although it was possible to draw on previous experience as a rough guide, selection was largely pragmatic. In general all records prior to 1900, except receipts for payments, were kept; thereafter cash books, bank books, journals (where detailed ledgers existed), and miscellaneous sundry-debtors records were discarded. All files relating to significant contracts, like the *Lusitania, Queen Mary,* and *Queen Elizabeth*, even if on a cursory examination they seemed of little interest, and all costing, policy, and technical files on individual contracts, were retained. If a file contained any records that seemed to be of possible interest the whole file was kept.

After the transmission of the records to the record store of the Department of Economic History at the University of Glasgow, they were put in order and relisted. All the volumes and files which belonged to obvious groups, like general ledgers, progressive cost books, general letter files, and wages books, were ordered and shelved. The residue of the filing material was placed in order of the running reference number of the original handlist boxed and shelved. In the completed list, all records relating to specific departments or functions, where possible, appeared together. Some categories of records which were common to all administrative departments, such as the general letter books and

Figure 8.2 *The layout of order books varies widely. Figure 8.2 (a) shows: a fine example of the detailed practice of Neilson & Co., Glasgow (later part of the North British Locomotive Co. Ltd), laying out the order, placed 1886, for the famous Caledonian Railway's locomotive no. 123, now preserved in the Glasgow Transport Museum. Drawing offices, like other departments, evolved their own practice to suit the requirements of the firm's particular product. Figure 8.2 (b) shows a pipework arrangement drawing for locomotive no. 123. In the late nineteenth century pipework drawings were the only general arrangement drawings made by some locomotive builders and marine engineers. Finished product photographs, like this (Figure 8.2 (c)) of locomotive no. 123, were taken primarily, for advertising purposes. The foreground in this print has been retouched and the background painted out to give clear illustration for blockmaking. Taken together these three types of record help create a balanced archive.*

the general particulars of vessels built, were arranged in separate categories. Although the residual filing material was not physically reordered, the list was rearranged so that each file appeared under a specific subject heading.

Technical Records

If the use and selection of management records is generally understood, that of technical records is not. However, the recent growth in the study of individual firms and of particular industries has been accompanied by a gradual understanding of the importance of the technical aspects of industry. Economic and business historians can make no proper evaluation of management and production problems, labour skill and demand, or capital and credit requirements without a consideration of the range and type of products manufactured by particular firms, and of the extent to which firms were inter-dependent for orders and components. Order books are valuable, but they need to be supplemented by at least a superficial study of the drawings, photographs, catalogues (Figures 8.2 (a)–(c)) and other technical records. In selecting and

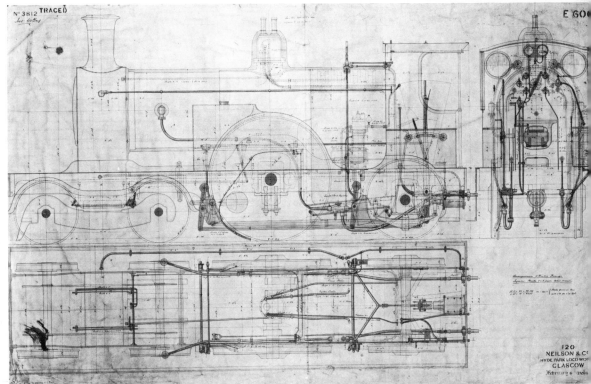

(b)

(c)

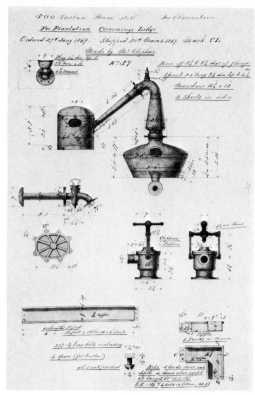

preserving technical records, care must be taken to create a balanced archive, as the preservation of one collection to the detriment of others can easily make for false impressions in the future. The preservation in bulk of the Boulton & Watt drawings has exaggerated the importance of that firm as a manufacturing enterprise. There is a temptation for the archivist to discard a group of poor quality drawings from one firm in favour of retaining a high quality group of drawings of identical products from another. Apart from catalogues (Figure 8.3), specifications, and data books, which are usually found with the general management records, there are two classes of technical records particularly at risk: engineering drawings and photographs.

The type, range, and quality of drawings varies from one firm to another, one period to another, and from one draughtsman to another. In the early nineteenth century often only design sketches were made, the exact dimensions of the finished product being left to the workers on the shop floor (Figure 8.4). Later in the century fully-dimensioned drawings were made, with detailed sketches of individual components often on the same sheets (Figures 8.5 (a)–(c)). As subdivision of labour progressed, and products became more complex, detailed working drawings were required. Even now, in firms where highly sophisticated products are not made, rudimentary sketches often remain adequate. In a firm with standard products, such as motor cars, one set of drawings may be used for thousands, or even hundreds of thousands of identical products. Heavy engineering, shipbuilding, and construction firms on the other

Figure 8.5 *These three drawings are unusually beautiful, and noteworthy for the absence of dimensions or scale. They were probably drawn as advertisements by Robert Napier, the famous shipbuilder and marine engineer. They show a set of two-cylinder simple side-lever engines for the P.S. King Orry, built for the Isle of Man Steam Packet Co. in 1842. Figures 8.5 (a) and (b) are front and rear elevations, and Figure 8.5 (c), a side elevation, with a section of the box boiler and funnel uptake at the right. The paddle casing and deckhouses are also sketched in. Points to note are the Gothic styling of the engine frame and the use of shading to indicate the materials of construction. Robert Napier's side-lever engines gained an outstanding reputation for reliability and economy in running costs.*

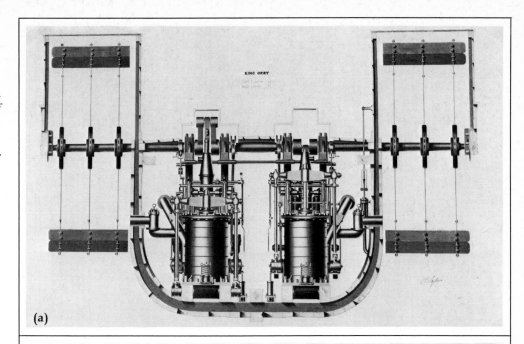

(a)

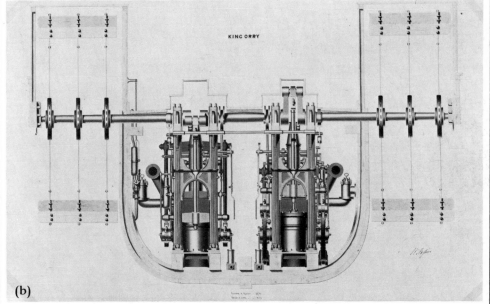

(b)

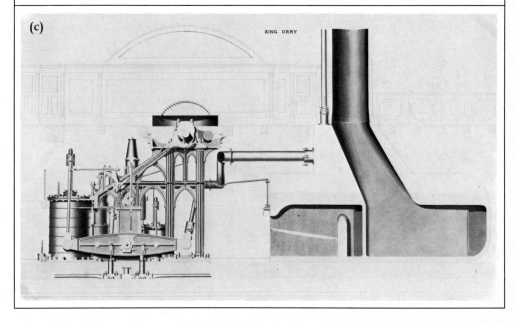

(c)

162

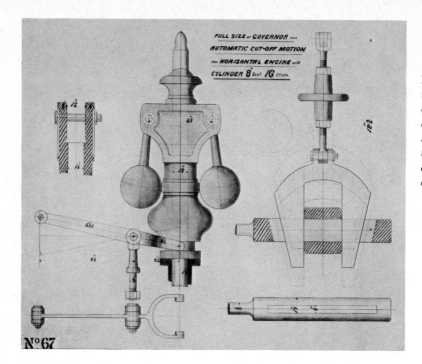

Figure 8.6 *A detail of special interest: a Porter governor (speed control) for a horizontal steam engine made by Andrew Barclay Sons & Co. Ltd, Kilmarnock, in the 1870s. The reference number and description on this drawing are typical.*

hand, prepare a set of drawings for each finished product as the capital outlay allows the customer to demand his own specification.

Drawings are retained initially by those firms where guarantee periods are long and the manufacturer, therefore, has a continuing interest in his product. Ability to quote for repair work is determined by the existence of drawings, showing not only general arrangements, but also details. Few firms know which of their products still exist, and whether orders for spares are likely. The more recent the drawings, therefore, the less willing a firm is to allow selection. Certain obvious criteria for selection can be applied, all drawings before perhaps 1880 retained and all large-scale details rejected. The optimum selection procedure is the retention of all general arrangement and sub-assembly drawings (Figure 8.6), covering both the demands of the technical historian and those of the model maker. In most firms this task is made easier as some weeding out of earlier drawings has usually taken place, and the arrangement, detail, and working drawings are often stored separately. As with general management records, selection is inevitably a two-stage operation, a rough selection is made on the firm's premises and then a more detailed one at a later date, dependent on evaluation by comparison with drawings originating in other firms.

In order that second phase weeding out can take place, lists of the first selection must be made. The difficulties of listing large quantities of technical records rapidly can be easily overestimated. The practical experience of the Western Survey is that the task is straightforward but laborious. Nearly all technical drawings are described and referenced by the firm of origin. There is, therefore, rarely any problem of identification and it is anyway not difficult to learn quickly how to distinguish different products and sub-assemblies. In any case most firms possess old drawing lists which can be related to the physical arrangement of the drawings and provide a useful starting point when compiling new catalogues.

Photographic Collections

The role of photographic collections within the firm is hard to ascertain. In the larger companies these collections contain negatives of every job and sometimes of various stages in its production. These were probably used to give an indication of the progress of manufacture to the customer, important in industries which produced an expensive complex product dependent on progress payments (Figures 8.7 and 8.8). In most firms, though, the photographic department exists to produce publicity literature, to demonstrate the firm's background of continuous reliable quality products and to display the current products to their best advantage (Figure 8.9). Depending on the type of the product, these photographs will be more or less technically informative. For example, a motor car manufacturer will be concerned with the aesthetic appeal of his product (Figures 8.10 (a) and (b)), whereas machine-toolmakers will be anxious to demonstrate clearly technical features and will be only marginally concerned with aesthetics (Figures 8.11 and 8.12). In addition, photography appears to have been used as a management tool to illustrate the layout of the shops and premises (Figures 8.13), and also items of equipment and methods of production (Figures 8.14 (a) and (b)). Naturally, works or outside photographers also took pictures of general interest, especially of employees, special occasions (Figures 8.15 and 8.16), such as launches in shipyards, and the dispatch of important contracts (Figures 8.17, 8.18, and 8.19).

The majority of these collections are in the form of glass negatives which pose few storage problems apart from weight. The draft British Standard Specification of optimum storage conditions[6] for glass negatives is compatible with present archive practice in humidity and temperature for paper storage. Because of the relatively small bulk of these collections there is no necessity to weed at the time of deposit. But at a later stage unidentified negatives of minor components can be safely discarded. The descriptive listing of negatives is not usually difficult as often they are in reasonable order, referenced, and old lists are available. However, the long-term management of such collections is more complex and costly. As negatives are fragile and deteriorate with handling, they cannot be produced regularly for researchers. Photographic opinion is agreed that the solution is wherever possible to make archive prints from the original negatives and to prepare copy negatives. This is accompanied by a certain loss in clarity in the copy negative, but not enough to outweigh the advantage of the operation. It is, however, expensive and can at present only be justified for significant well-used collections. The setting up of a national conservation centre with regional services for museums and galleries as suggested by the recent report, *Conservation in Museums and Galleries: A Survey of Facilities in the United Kingdom*[7] would allow its more general application.

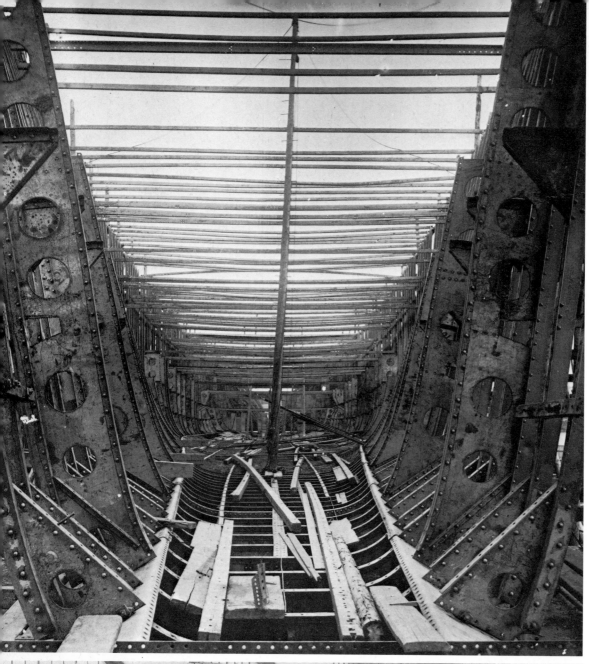

Figure 8.7 *Shipbuilding, more than any other West of Scotland industry, depends on progress payments. The accurate recording of the stages of construction of a ship from keel-laying to completion is necessary to secure payments and to ensure that specifications are met. This photograph shows the construction of the hull of the City of New York, built by J. & G. Thomson Ltd for the Inman International Line, in 1887. The frames of the vessel are virtually complete and the deck beams are in place. Note the pole derrick in the centre of the picture – a primitive crane.*

Figure 8.8 *Sugar-machinery makers use progress photographs to monitor the assembly of products in the erecting shop so as to safeguard themselves against customers' complaints. Here is a 15 roller sugar mill being erected at the Eglinton Engine Works of A. & W. Smith & Co. Ltd, Glasgow, in 1939. The sugar cane enters the mill on the left, and passes through five banks of rollers in which virtually all the juice is removed. The residue – bagasse – is used as fuel for the mill.*

Figure 8.9 When photographing finished products white sheets were often hung round them to make it easier to pick out the background of the negative for blockmaking. Here a compound side-by-side Corliss engine has been assembled (without its flywheel) in the workshops of Fullerton, Hodgart & Barclay, general engineers, Paisley. This engine was built in 1897 for Peter Jackson, Esq, probably for a textile mill. It would have to be dismantled for despatch.

(a)

Figure 8.10 These typical coachbuilders' photographs from Andrew Fleming Ltd, Rutherglen, Glasgow, in Figure 8.10 (a), a horse-drawn laundry van, representative of the light spring vans made until the beginning of this century by many West of Scotland firms for the service industries, and in Figure 8.10 (b), a motor laundry van, with a chassis made by the Glasgow firm of Albion Motors Ltd. With the introduction of motor vehicles, coachbuilders became body builders, and stopped assembling their own chassis and wheels. As arrangement drawings were rarely prepared by coachbuilders, such photographs were used to demonstrate various styles to prospective customers.

(b)

Figure 8.11 *An example of a photograph in which the non-essential parts of the negative have been blacked out before printing. This is of an end-milling machine for preparing the bases of ingot moulds at steelworks, made by Clifton & Baird Ltd, Johnstone, c. 1930. Clifton & Baird specialize in heavy metal-sawing and cutting equipment, largely for the steel industry.*

Figure 8.12 *Some photographs were taken to illustrate the methods of operating machines. This figure shows rails bent by a rail-bending machine built by Craig & Donald Ltd, Johnstone, for the Sao Paulo Railway in 1926. Craig & Donald were leading manufacturers of bending and cutting machinery for shipyards, railway companies, and structural and general engineers.*

Figure 8.13 *Many firms commissioned general views of their works in the early years of this century, and these were often included in catalogues. A typical view of this genre is this photograph of the fitting shop of the Bergius Co. in Dobbies Loan, Glasgow. Kelvin petrol-paraffin engines for fishing boats and launches can be seen at various stages of completion.*

(a)

Figure 8.14 *Novel techniques naturally attracted the attention of works' photographers. Figure 8.14 (a) shows a then-new portable hydraulic riveting machine in use on the hull of R.M.S.* Aquitania, *at the Clydebank yard of John Brown Shipbuilding & Engineering Co. Ltd, in 1911. This type of riveting machine could be used at various angles. Riveting was gradually displaced by welding from the early 1930s. The first all-welded ship built on the Clyde was the ferry* Robert the Bruce *(see Figure 5.24, on page 107), constructed by William Denny & Bros, Dumbarton, in 1933. Figure 8.14 (b) shows welders at work on the hull of this vessel.*

(b)

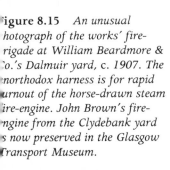

Figure 8.15 *An unusual photograph of the works' fire-brigade at William Beardmore & Co.'s Dalmuir yard, c. 1907. The unorthodox harness is for rapid turnout of the horse-drawn steam fire-engine. John Brown's fire-engine from the Clydebank yard is now preserved in the Glasgow Transport Museum.*

Figure 8.16 *A classic type of works photograph, in which the workmen were photographed with their product. This view, taken in the works of Aimers, McLean & Co. Ltd, Galashiels, c. 1900, shows a semi-portable single-cylinder horizontal engine and vertical boiler. Such engines were uncommon in Scottish practice. This example may have been used on a farm.*

Figure 8.17 *The despatch of a product is always an occasion in an engineering or shipbuilding works. Locomotives make particularly attractive photographs. Unlike most engineering products, they are shipped uncrated and usually fully assembled. In this figure, 2-6-2 tank locomotives, part of a batch of 40 for the Egyptian State Railways, are being loaded as deck cargo, by a Clyde Navigation Trust heavy steam crane, at Mavisbank Quay, Glasgow, in 1926.*

Figure 8.18 *Sometimes industrial photographic collections contain views of exported machinery under construction and in use. In many cases the plant illustrated was financed by Scottish capital. This view shows a copper converter being tapped into moulds at the Rio Tinto mines in Spain, in 1901. In the background are two roasting furnaces for the preparation of the 'matte' (a copper/iron sulphide mixture) for charging the converter. The converter removes the iron in a slag, leaving molten metallic copper. The heat for the process is obtained by burning off the sulphur.*

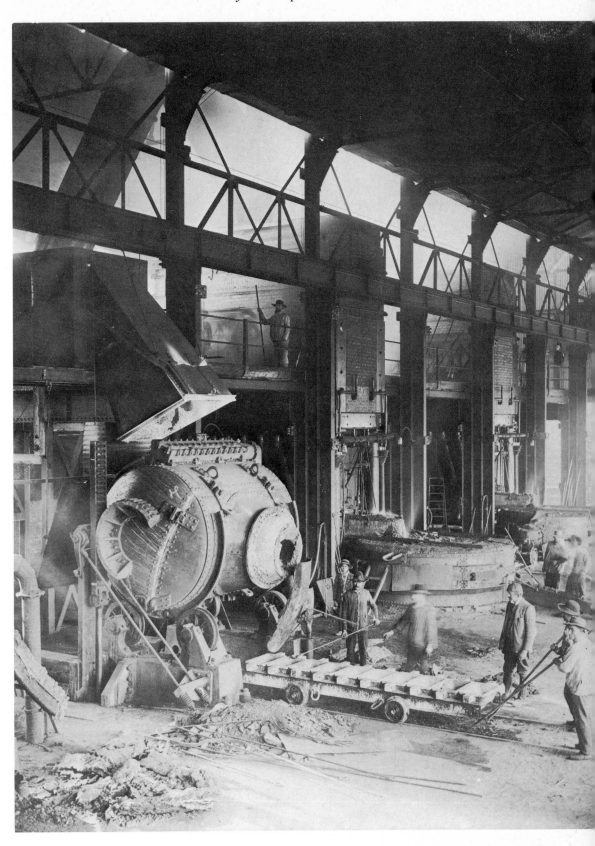

Recording the Working Environment

Although large quantities of business records have been located by the Western Survey, they remain only imperfect yardsticks by which to judge a particular industry or firm in the West of Scotland. To improve their quality some of the techniques of the industrial archaeologist were used in the Western Survey. Writing in 1970, Professor J.R. Harris observed that: 'Some economic historians who affect to despise industrial archaeology do so because their concept of their subject is one of abstract rationalization from factual data, preferably statistical, to them visual and tactile evidence is childish antiquarianism'[8]. Indeed the fortuitous survival of the records of one firm will

Figure 8.19 *Not all industrial photographs are to be found with manufacturing firms. Many commercial photographers take industrial subjects, either on commission or as a speculation. Here is a fascinating view of the old Glasgow Central Station of the Caledonian Railway at the New Year, taken by Thomas Annan, in 1899. Note the large number of hats. The locomotive is one of Connor's 2-4-0's for express passenger work.*

170

Figure 8.20 *Photographs of industrial premises tend to survive where written records do not. This view of the erecting shop at Duncan Stewart & Co. Ltd's London Road Ironworks, Glasgow, shows the trial assembly of a reversing plate-rolling mill built for the Appleby Iron Co., c. 1924. Few written records survive for this company, but photographs such as these give an excellent idea of the scale of work undertaken.*

tend to give rise to the mistaken assumption that it was more significant than a firm of similar magnitude but with no surviving records. Even in the case of firms like Andrew Barclay Sons & Co., Fairfield Shipbuilding & Engineering Co., and John Brown Shipbuilding & Engineering Co., the records contain little information about the layout of their works or their physical appearance. The systematic photography of industrial premises can both supplement the records of firms and also provide an indication of the scale of operations and relative importance of firms with few or no records (Figure 8.20).

The focus of much of what is called industrial archaeology has been on the period of the Industrial Revolution, with reaches into the late nineteenth century and includes items of special interest, such as early electrical equipment, more developed examples of steam engines, and early internal combustion engines. As

171

Figure 8.21 (a)-(c) *Three views of the Crownpoint Road, Glasgow, factory of Adam Knox & Co., general engineers, in 197 . Figure 8.21 (a) shows the woode framed, overhead travelling cran serving the main machine shop; Figure 8.21 (b), is a facing lathe made by John Lang & Son, Johnstone, and Figure 8.2 (c) a horizontal boring machine made by D. & J. Tullis Ltd, Clydebank The factory was almost entirely equipped with Scottish machine tools dating mainly from the tur of the century.*

(a)

(b)

(c)

a result the subject has an uneven quality, leaving it open to charges of obscurantism and antiquarianism. As Dr A. Raistrick has recently suggested, the main preoccupation of the subject must be 'to demonstrate and display the progress through the centuries of the material environment of man's working life and the increasing skills in manipulating the raw materials of that environment'[9]. In the Western Survey, the techniques of industrial archaeology have been used to record the whole development of the firms and industries surveyed from their origins to the present day and in some cases to arrange for the preservation of items of special interest.

In most manufacturing companies surveyed the plant, premises, and machinery were systematically photographed and the negatives stored in a photographic archive in the Department of History at the University of Strathclyde. The plant and property was dated either by reference to documentary material and, if this did not exist, by a rough estimation from the style of the architecture. General views were taken of both interiors and exteriors, with detailed views of special features (Figures 8.21 (a)–(c)), and rough sketch plans made of the layout of both the works and individual shops (Figure 8.22). Every attempt was made to discover from documentary evidence and by questioning the staff and workforce, whether the building was still in its original use and if not, what its previous history had been (Figure 8.23). Each machine was usually photographed separately and notes made of the maker and, where given, the date of manufacture. It was also possible sometimes to discover dates of acquisition from the plant registers and minute books. Where shops contained

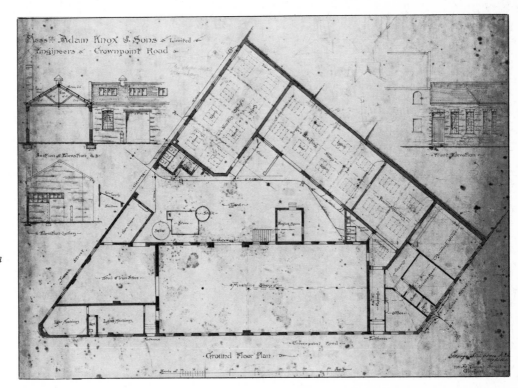

Figure 8.22 *Plant drawings can easily be overlooked, as they are not usually in the custody of a commercial department, but in the master of works' or millwright's department. This drawing details the layout of the premises of Adam Knox & Sons Ltd, in 1918, when the minor addition (at the top of the drawing) was made.*

Figure 8.23 *The foundry of Jeffrey Bros, Langholm, Dumfriesshire started as a brewery in the eighteenth century and later became a laundry. In this view, taken in 1971, the modern, home-made, cupola contrasts with the original masonry. No documentary evidence, so far as is known, exists for this site.*

large numbers of similar modern machines only general impressionistic photographs were taken, with example views of each machine type.

The most interesting photographs taken were those of techniques of production, which can only be adequately recorded in living firms, where the traditional and the modern are often employed side by side (Figures 8.24 (a) and (b)). It is, for instance, still possible to record hand riveting and machine welding in the same engineering shop. With the introduction of more mechanized plant and machinery, many industrial techniques, of sometimes quite recent origin, are being rapidly replaced. For example, in the ironfounding industry the traditional methods of greensand and drysand moulding are being discarded, together with the recent technique of CO_2 moulding, in favour of furane sand moulding. In most cases, series of still photographs, illustrating each stage in an operation, provide sufficient record, and only occasionally in the case of complex or particularly interesting processes, do they require to be supplemented by film, which is, anyway, an expensive and difficult medium.

Although the activity of recording industrial sites and artefacts is quite separate from their preservation, it is necessarily part of it. The majority of the machinery, plant, and premises recorded by the Western Survey neither suggested themselves for preservation nor could even have been considered, as they often lay in the heart of active firms. However, sometimes firms had interesting or unusual examples of certain machines, which they were prepared to offer for preservation for nothing or at a low cost. During the period of the Western Survey, the Scottish Society for the Preservation of Historical Machinery was set up with the object of acquiring representative examples of machines and machine tools made or used by Scottish industry. By liaison with

(a)

(b)

Figure 8.24 *Two views showing changing techniques in the ironfounding industry. Figure 8.24 (a) shows an open sand mould. The weights are placed on the sand cores to hold them in place. The molten iron is poured into the gate on the right. In the background is a finished casting of the same type. The photograph was taken at Russell & Co's Foundry at Carluke, Lanarkshire, (closed in 1971). By contrast, Figure 8.24 (b) shows machine-made moulds on roller conveyors at George Taylor & Co. Ltd, Larbert, Stirlingshire.*

Figure 8.25 *Now preserved by the Scottish Society for the Preservation of Historical Machinery, this brass finisher's lathe was discovered by the authors in John Glover & Sons' Bridgeton Brass Foundry, Glasgow. The lathe was donated by Mr Jack Glover, and is seen here in the works before closure.*

the Society, the Western Survey was able to arrange for the preservation of many items of interest (Figure 8.25).

In the preservation of both artefacts and, to some degree, records the professional and the amateur complement each other. The removal of large items of equipment and large collections of records is heavy work, which often has to be carried out at weekends, when firms are closed. Without the assistance of the amateur the task would either be physically impossible or prohibitively expensive. The Western Survey depended on the amateur and enthusiast, not only in this valuable rescue work, but also, in providing a regular source of information on firms worth approaching, and in identifying unfamiliar records, especially technical. In disparaging the enthusiast and amateur, the professional and academic tend to forget that they are professionals in their own work, which is often related to their interest in the industrial past.

Much recent discussion about industrial archaeology has centred on the problem of its proper definition; particularly whether it is legitimately separate from business, social, or technical history. In the Western Survey the skills of the subject were used, in the same way as those of the archivist, to record and preserve plant, premises, and machinery to cater for a multiplicity of academic disciplines. Although the subject does have a formal academic expression in the study of industrial sites and structures, its main emphasis must surely remain firmly on the activities of systematic recording and exploration to provide a second dimension to our historical perspective.

If industrial archaeology provides the second dimension, then oral evidence provides the third. No collection of industrial records or series of photographs can ever be so complete that it cannot be supplemented by the carefully scrutinized evidence of the staff and workforce. Most firms, which have a continuity in employment, management, and location, have their own folk lore. The recording of this requires a tolerance of the attitudes and opinions of the witnesses and a reasonable knowledge of the antecedents, structure, techniques, and current problems of the particular industry. In the Western Survey an attempt was made to record as much as possible by making notes of interviews with the managing directors and other members of the staff and workforce. The most useful evidence acquired was: details of linkages and relationships with other firms, especially in terms of the capital formation and the nature of the products; outlines of management structures; and descriptions of production techniques.

By the careful and systematic use of these three techniques it is possible to come nearer to achieving a balanced archive of particular firms and industries and by so doing reduce the possibility of misinterpretation and misconception in the future. However, the task is an urgent one. Inevitably, during periods of rapid reconstruction and recapitalization of industry, much will be destroyed. If techniques similar to those developed in the West of Scotland are not employed in other areas, the damage will be irreparable and historians will have occasion to regret a missed opportunity.

References

Abbreviations used in References

UCS   Upper Clyde Shipbuilders collection of records, all applications for access should be made to the Keeper of the Records of Scotland, Scottish Record Office, P.O. Box 36, H.M. General Register House, Edinburgh EH1 3YY. The collection comprises the records of:

UCS/1   John Brown Shipbuilding & Engineering Co. Ltd

UCS/2   Fairfield Shipbuilding & Engineering Co. Ltd

UCS/3   Alexander Stephen & Sons Ltd

UCS/4   Simons-Lobnitz

SRA   Strathclyde Regional Archives, Glasgow District Office, City Chambers, P.O. Box 27, Glasgow G2 1DU

SRO   Scottish Record Office

UGDEH   University of Glasgow Department of Economic History (business history collection). Requests for access should be addressed to the Archivist, University of Glasgow, Glasgow G12 8QQ.

Chapter 2

1. *Glasgow Herald,* 19 September 1853.
2. John Sharp, *Modern Foundry Practice,* Spon, 1900, p. 50.
3. *The Engineer,* 1866, Vol. 22, p. 117.
4. *Glasgow Herald,* 8 January 1849, 15 June 1849.
5. John Mayer, 'The Engineering Industries of Glasgow and the Clyde', in *Some of the Leading Industries of the Clyde Valley,* Glasgow: Blackie & Son, 1876, p. 69.
6. *Industries of Glasgow,* Historical Publishing Co., 1888, p. 129.
7. Mayer. loc cit., p. 68.
8. Ibid, p. 65.

Chapter 3

1. *Memoirs and Portraits of 100 Glasgow Men,* Glasgow: MacLehose, 1886, p. 267.

2. Robert Harvey, 'The History of the Sugar Machinery Industry in Glasgow', *The International Sugar Journal,* 1916, p. 60,

3. Ibid, p. 112.

4. R. Mayer, *Some of the Leading Industries of the Clyde Valley,* Glasgow: Blackie & Son, 1876, p. 118.

5. Ibid, p. 116.

6. *Record of the International Exhibition 1862,* William Mackenzie, 1862, p. 227.

7. *Engineering,* 1896, vol. 61, p. 534.

8. Mayer, loc. cit., p. 117.

9. *Engineering,* 1896, vol. 61, p. 535.

10. John Scott Russell, *On the Nature, Properties and Application of Steam and on Steam Navigation,* Edinburgh, 1841, p. 245.

11. 'Memoir of David Elder', *Transactions of the Institute of Shipbuilders in Scotland,* 1886–7, vol. 9, p. 92.

12. *Two centuries of Shipbuilding by the Scotts at Greenock,* 2nd Edn, 1920, p. 22, published by Scott, Sinclair & Co.

13. 'Memoir of David Tod', *Transactions of the Institute of Shipbuilders in Scotland,* 1858–9, vol. 2, p. 61.

14. F.C. Marshall, *Proceedings of the Institute of Mechanical Engineers,* 1881, p. 454.

15. Mayer, loc. cit., p. 159.

16. *The Engineer,* 1895, vol. 59, p. 92.

17. Mayer, loc. cit., p. 84.

18. Ibid., p. 105.

19. Ibid., p. 127.

20. Ibid., p. 105.

21. *The Economist,* 24 January 1903, vol. 61, p. 153.

22. Mayer, loc. cit., p. 106.

23. James Napier, *The Life of Robert Napier,* William Blackwood & Sons, 1904, p. 30.

24. Harvey, loc. cit., p. 59.

25. Mayer, loc. cit., p. 85.

26. Ibid., p. 87.

27. Ibid., p. 88.

28. Frank Taylor, *Johnstone and Co-operation,* Johnstone, 1916, p. 71.

29. *Glasgow Herald,* 8 April, 1803.

30. *Bridges, Structural Steel Work and Mechanical Engineering Productions,* by Sir William Arrol & Co. Ltd, published by *Engineering* London, 1909, p. 150.

31. William Beardmore & Co. Minute Book No. 2, 1919.

32. William Beardmore & Co. Minute Book No. 6, meeting 25 January, 1934.

33. William Beardmore & Co. Minute Book No. 7, meeting 26 November, 1935.

34. William Beardmore & Co. Minute Book No. 7, meeting 26 February, 1936.

Chapter 4

The sequestration records of Andrew Barclay, Barclays & Co., and the North British Iron and Hematite Co., are in the Scottish Record Office (trs 1, 2, 4–17). The records of Andrew Barclay Sons & Co. Ltd are held by the company in their Kilmarnock offices (trs 18–38).

1. *Notes on Andrew Barclay,* printed by Dunlop and Brennan, 1880 (available in Kilmarnock public library).
2. From the titles of the works held by Messrs Bannatyne, Kirkwood, France & Co., solicitors, Glasgow.
3. *Kilmarnock Standard,* 22 August 1874.
4. Minute Book No. 1 of Andrew Barclay Sons & Co. Ltd.
5. *Kilmarnock Standard,* 16 July 1870.
6. SRO/CS318/$\frac{1878}{21}$/364.
7. SRO/CS318/1878/32.
8. SRO/CS318/1884/57.
9. SRO/CS318/1889/32.
10. Minute Book No. 2 of Andrew Barclay Sons & Co. Ltd.
11. Minute Book No. 5 of Andrew Barclay Sons & Co. Ltd.

Chapter 5

1. T. Scott Russell: 'On the Late Mr. John Wood and Mr. Charles Wood, Naval Architects of Port Glasgow', *Transactions of the Institute of Naval Architects,* 1861, vol. 2.
2. Barclay Curle & Co. Ltd, Minute Book No. 1, SRA, TD265/1/1.
3. *R. Napier, 1791–1876 Father of Clyde Shipbuilding,* a B.A. dissertation submitted to the Department of History, University of Strathclyde in 1973 by G.T. Kennison, p. 29.
4. UCS 1/38/1.
5. c.f. T.E. Milne; 'British Shipping in the Nineteenth Century: a study of the Ben Line papers', in P.L. Payne: *Studies in Scottish Business History,* London: Cass, 1967.
6. *The Engineer,* 1867, vol. 24, p. 201.
7. SRA, TD265/1/1.
8. Papers in possession of A. Gilchrist, Esq., National Register of Archives (Scotland), survey No. 955.
9. Professor Sir J.H. Biles, 'Relative Commercial Efficiency of Internal Combustion and Steam Engines for high speed passenger vessels,' *Transactions of the Institute of Naval Architects,* 1925, vol. 67.
10. Richard Hough, *First Sea Lord,* London: George Allen & Unwin, 1969, p. 244.

11. UCS 2/1/6.
12. UCS 4/1/2.
13. UGDEH/D4/3/10 Letter to Lord Inchcape from F.J. Stephen, September 1920.

Chapter 6

1. P.N. Davies, *The Trade Makers*, London: George Allen & Unwin, 1973, pp. 52–7.
2. John Bourne, *A Treatise on the Screw Propeller*, 1852.
3. British Association Handbook, *Some of the Leading Industries of Glasgow and the Clyde Valley*, Glasgow, 1876.
4. Chief Engineer King, U.S.N., *The War Ships of Europe*, Portsmouth: Griffin & Co., 1878, p. 203.
5. British Association Handbook, 1876.
6. *The 'Building of the Ship'*, p. 25 (see suggestions for further reading).
7. H. Fry, *The History of North Atlantic Steam Navigation*, Sampson, Low, Marston & Co., 1896, p. 78.
8. Sederunt book of G. Thomson vol. 2 held by Messrs. McGrigor Donald & Co., Glasgow.
9. Manuscript *History of Clydebank Shipyard 1847–1953* by H. Brown p. 58.
10. UCS 1/38/1.
11. *West Highland Steamers* by C.L.D. Duckworth and G.E. Langmuir, 2nd ed., London: Richard Tilling, 1950, p. 68.
12. Chief Engineer King, loc. cit., p. 78.
13. H. Fry, loc. cit., p. 196.
14. Correspondence of Charles Gairdner held by the Head Office of the Bank of Scotland, Glasgow N.R.A.(S) survey No. 1110.
15. *Glasgow Herald*, November 25, 1888.
16. H. Fry, loc. cit., p. 125.
17. UCS 1/38/1, p. 332.
18. UCS 2/20/1.
19. *The 'Building of the Ship'* loc. cit. p. 15.
20. Sir George Grant, *Steel and Ships*, London: Michael Joseph, 1950, p. 58.
21. UCS 2/1/3.
22. UCS 1/5/18, March 1919.
23. UCS 1/5/18, December 1919.
24. UCS 1/5/20, April 1921.
25. UCS 1/5/20, June 1921.
26. UCS 1/5/20, July 1921.
27. UCS 2/1/5.
28. UCS 1/5/24, 1 May 1925.
29. UCS 1/5/24, 29 May 1925.

30. A.C. Hardy, *History of Motorshipping*, London: Whitehall Technical Press, 1955, p. 53–54.
31. UCS 1/5/35, February 1937.
32. UCS 1/2/1.
33. UCS 2/1/6.
34. UCS 1/2/2.
35. George Brown's speech in the House of Commons, 22 December 1965.

Chapter 8

1. For a general account of the origins and development of the Register see John Imrie, 'The Modern Scottish Record Office', *Scottish Historical Review*, vol. LIII, 2: no. 156, 1974, pp. 207–9.
2. See *Studies in Scottish Business History*, edited by P.L. Payne, Part 1, London: Cass, 1967.
3. B. Supple, 'Uses of Business History', *Business History*, 1962, vol. 4, p 84.
4. *Studies in Scottish Business History*, loc. cit., p. 42.
5. P. Mathias. *Historical Records of the Brewing Industry*, Archives vol 7, 1965, pp. 3–40.
6. A constant relative humidity with a range of 40 per cent to 50 per cent, and a constant temperature of 15–20 °C.
7. *Conservation in Museums and Galleries: A Survey of Facilities in the United Kingdom,* published by the United Kingdom Group of the International Institute for Conservation of Historic and Artistic Works, 1975.
8. J.R. Harris, 'Industrial Archaeology and its Future, a review article', *Business History*, 1970, vol. 12, p. 130.
9. A. Raistrick, *Industrial Archaeology, an Historical Survey*, London: Eyre Methuen & Todd, 1972, p. 93.

Suggestions for further reading

Chapter 1

T. Devine: *The Tobacco Lords*, Edinburgh: John Donald, 1975

A. Slaven: *The Development of the West of Scotland 1750–1960*, London: Routledge & Kegan Paul, 1975.

Chapter 2

John Sharp: *Modern Foundry Practice*, London: Spon, 1900.

R.H. Campbell: *Carron Company*, Edinburgh: Oliver & Boyd, 1961.

Chapter 3

M.C.V. Allchin: *A History of Highland Locomotives*, Railway Hobbies Ltd, 1947.

Bridges, Structural Steel Work and Mechanical Engineering Productions by Sir William Arrol & Co. Ltd, published by *Engineering*, London, 1909.

James Cleland: *The Rise and Progress of the City of Glasgow*, Glasgow: James Brash & Co., 1820.

David Dehane Napier (ed): *David Napier, Engineer*, Glasgow: MacLehose, 1912.

A.E. Durrant: *The Garratt Locomotive*, Newton Abbot: David & Charles, 1969.

The Engineer and Machinist's Assistant, Blackie & Son, 1849.

An Engineering Record of the Glasgow Exhibition, 1901, published by *Engineering Times*, London: P.S. King & Son, 1901.

The Glasgow & South Western Railway, London: The Stephenson Locomotive Society, 1950.

J.D. Gillies and J.L. Wood: *Aviation In Scotland*, Glasgow Branch, Royal Aeronautical Society, 1966.

John Guthrie: *A History of Marine Engineering*, London: Hutchinson, 1971.

Half a century of Shipbuilding, Mercantile and Naval, with a description of the Clydebank Works of James and George Thomson Ltd, partly reprinted from *Engineering*, published by *Engineering*, London, 1896.

A History of the North British Locomotive Co. Ltd, 1903–1953, Glasgow: North British Locomotive Co. Ltd, 1953.

D.F. Holland: *Steam Locomotives of the South African Railways*, Vol. 1, 1859–1910, vol. 2, 1910–1955, Newton Abbot: David & Charles, 1971 and 1972.

A Hundred Years of Howden Engineering, Glasgow: James Howden & Co., 1954.

The Manufacture of Locomotives and Other Munitions of War, during the period 1914–1919, Glasgow: North British Locomotive Co. Ltd, 1920.

A. Craig Macdonald and A.S.E. Browning: *History of the Motor Industry in Scotland,* Inst. Mech, Eng. Automobile Division, 1961.

The Marine Number of Cassier's Magazine, The Louis Cassier Co. Ltd, 1897.

W.S. Murphy, *Captains of Industry,* published by the author, Glasgow, 1901.

James Napier, *The Life of Robert Napier,* Edinburgh: William Blackwood & Sons, 1904.

The Practical Mechanic and Engineer's Magazine, Vol. 2, Glasgow: W.C. Pattison, 1842–3.

Sir Robert Purvis: *Sir William Arrol,* Edinburgh: William Blackwood & Sons, 1913.

L.T.C. Rolt: *Tools for the Job,* London: Batsford, 1965.

E.C. Smith: *A Short History of Marine Engineering,* Cambridge University Press, 1937.

Some of the Leading Industries of Glasgow and the Clyde Valley, Glasgow: Blackie and Sons, 1876.

John Thomas: *The Springburn Story,* Newton Abbot and London: David & Charles and Macdonald, 1964.

Chapter 5

John R. Hume and Michael S. Moss: *Clyde Shipbuilding from Old Photographs,* London: Batsford, 1975.

John Shields: *Clyde Built,* Glasgow: William MacLellan, 1949.

Leslie Jones: *Shipbuilding in Britain,* Cardiff: University of Wales Press, 1957.

Chapter 6

The 'Building of the Ship' being an historical and descriptive narrative of the works of the Fairfield Shipbuilding & Engineering Co. Ltd, partly reprinted from *Engineering,* published by *Engineering,* London, 1891.

Half a Century of Shipbuilding, Mercantile and Naval, with a description of the Clydebank Works of James and George Thomson Ltd, partly reprinted from *Engineering,* published by the offices of *Engineering,* London, 1896.

The Fairfield Shipbuilding and Engineering Works: History of the Company; review of its production; and description of the works, published by *Engineering,* London, 1909.

Sir Allan Grant: *Steel & Ships, the History of John Brown's,* London: Michael Joseph, 1950.

K.J.W. Alexander and C.L. Jenkins: *Fairfields,* London: Allen Lane the Penguin Press, 1970.

Chapter 7

The Third Statistical Account, City of Glasgow, Glasgow: Collins, 1952.

J.R. Hume: *Industrial Archaeology of Glasgow,* Glasgow: Blackie, 1974.

A. Slaven: *The Development of the West of Scotland, 1750–1960,* London: Routledge & Kegan Paul, 1975.

Charles Oakley, *Scottish Industry To-day,* Edinburgh: The Moray Press, 1937.

Industries of Glasgow, The Historical Publishing Co., 1888.

Stratten's Glasgow and Its Environs, Stratten & Stratten, 1891.

F.H. Young: *A Century of Carpet Making 1839–1939,* Glasgow: Templetons, 1943.

The Carpet Makers, A.F. Stoddard & Co. Ltd, 1962.

The Faithful Fibre, The Linen Thread Co. Ltd.

George Blake: *The Gourock,* Port Glasgow: The Gourock Ropework Co., 1963.

Chapter 8

Studies in Scottish Business History, edited by P. L. Payne, Cass, 1967.

Scottish Industrial History, the Newsletter of the Scottish Society for Industrial Archaeology, Scottish Society for the Preservation of Historical Machinery, and the Business Archives Council of Scotland, available from C. Munn, Esq., Joint Editor, Department of Finance and Accountancy, Glasgow College of Technology, 20 North Hanover Place, Glasgow G.4.

Journal of the Business Archives Council, available from 37–45 Tooley Street, London SE1 2QF.

J.P.N. Pannell: *Techniques of Industrial Archaeology,* Newton Abbot: David & Charles, 1966.

Industrial Archaeology, a journal published by Bratton Publishing Ltd, 1 West Street, Tavistock, Devon.

Index

[References to illustration captions are set in italics.]

ABC 'DRAGON FLY' AERO ENGINE, 64
Abercorn Ropeworks, 147, *148*
Aberdeen, 12
Aberdeen Steam Navigation Co., *114*
Abyssinia, 118
Admiralty, 40, 65, 86, 101, 102, 105,
  119, 126, 131, 136
Aero-engines, 63
Aeroplanes, 48, 64–66
Africa, *25*
African Royal Mail Co., 113
Agamemnon, H.M.S., 63, *103*
Ailsa Shipbuilding Co., 41
Aimers, McLean & Co. Ltd, *168*
Aircraft Carriers, *110*, 139
Airdrie, *17*, 45
Airships, 64, 66
Alaska, 118
Alaunia, 134
Albion Motors Ltd, 165
Alexandra Docks & Harbour Co., *81*
Algeria, 118
Alisa, *143*
Allan, F.G., 75, 76
Allan, James, Senior & Sons, 55
Allan Line, 99
Aller, 119
Alley & MacLellan, 41, 64
Allied Ironfounders Ltd, 26
America, 119
American Civil War, 115
Anchor Line, 95, 105, 138
Anchor-Donaldson Line, *135*
Anderson Rodger, 105
Anderston Cotton Works, 56
Anderston Foundry, 12, 27
Annan, Thomas, 170
Aorangi, 135
Appleby Iron Co., *171*
Archer-class torpedo cruisers, 119
Andersonian University, 29, 63
Anniesland, 64
Aquitania, *96*, 129, *167*
Architectural ironwork, *1*, *5*, *19–21*, 24
Arethusa, H.M.S., 114
Argentine Navy, 139
Argos Foundry, 26
Arizona, 39, 118
Armitage Shanks, 149
Arrol Brothers, 60

Arrol, Sir William, 123, 125
Arrol, Sir William, & Co., *3*, 55, 57,
  58–60, 62, 63, *99*
Arrol-Johnston & Co., 63
Ashington Coal Co., *81*
Atlas Works, 43, 48
Atlas Works, Sheffield, 126
Auchengree Foundry, 56, 149
Aurania, 119
Australia, 46, 49, 114, 117, 136, 138
Australia, H.M.A.S., 102
Austro-Daimler aero engines, 63
Automobiles, 64, 65
Ayr, 12
Ayrshire Dockyard Co., 109

BABCOCK & WILCOX & CO., 40
Baird, H. & R., 12
Baird, William, & Co., 13
Bairnsfather, Mr, 73, 74
Baking, 151
Bank of England, 65, 66, 109, 138, 141
Bank of Scotland, 126, 138
Ban Righ, 114
Barclay, Andrew D., 75
Barclay, Andrew, junior, 75
Barclay, Andrew, senior, 68
Barclay, Andrew, Sons & Co., *22*, 41, 45,
  56, 68–84, *162*, 171
Barclay, Curle & Co., *3*, 86, 89, 93, *95*,
  96, 97, *100*, 107, *108*, 109, 110, 131
Barclay, John Galileo, 75
Barclay, James Wilson, 72
Barclays & Co., 70
Barham, H.M.S., 131
Barnwell, Richard, 123, 125
Barrowfield Foundry, *19*
Battlecruisers, *102*, 134
Battleships, 63, *102*, 122, 126, 139, *140*
Beagle, H.M.S., 137
Beardmore, Isaac, 62
Beardmore, William, senior, 62
Beardmore, William, & Co., 41, *43*, *44*,
  48, 62–67, 90, 95, 101, 102, 103,
  105, 109, 128, 139, 141, *167*
Beardmore, Sir William, later Lord
  Invernairn, 62–67, 97, 101, 102
Beattie, W. & D., 151
Beith, 149
Belfast, 97, 109, 131

Belfast Harbour, *79*
Bell, Henry, 86
Bennie, James, & Co., 55
Berenice, 36
Bergius Co., *166*
Berwick, H.M.S., 134
Bessemer steel making, 44
Betts & Co., 68
Beyer, Peacock & Co., 46, *52*
Biles, Sir John, 92, *100*, 101, 119
Birch, John, & Co., 84
Bilsland Brothers, 151
Birkenhead, 128
Birmingham, 12
Blackfriars Bridge, 60
Blackwood & Gordon, 40, 93
Blair, Campbell & McLean, 42
Blairs Ltd, 42
Blantyre Engineering Co., 29
Blenheim, H.M.S., 121
Blockade runners, 115–16
Blue Riband, 97, 117, 118, 119
Blythswood Shipbuilding Co., 106, 131
Bodnant, 133
Bogata, 114
Boiler making, 40, 54, 55, 57, 67, 68, 77
Bombs, *23*
Bonawe, 11, 27
Bonnybridge, 54, 160
Bonar Bridge, 57
Bothnia, 117
Boulton and Watt, 29, 30, 36, 160
Bour and Wetzell evaporating pans, 35
Bow & McLachlon, 40
Boyd, J. & T. Ltd, 18, 26, 56
Braby, Frederick, & Co., 60
Brandon, 37, 114
Brandon Bridge Building Co., 60
Brassfounding, 42
Brazil, 31
Brazilian Government, *99*
Bremen, 112
Bridge building, *3*, 57–60
Bridgeton Brass Foundry, *177*
Brisk, H.M.S., 128
Bristol, 37
Bristol *BE2C* aircraft, *48*

British & African Steam Navigation Co., 113, 117
British India Steam Navigation Co., *3*, 90, *95*, 99
British Iron and Steel Federation, 65
British Mariner, 106
British & North American Steam Packet Co., 113
British Petroleum Ltd, *106*
British Rail, 49, *51*
British Workman, 106
Brown, John, & Co., 122
Brown, John, Engineering (Clydebank) Ltd, 141
Brown, John, Shipbuilding & Engineering Co., 40, *60*, 88, 95, 97, 101, 102, 110, 111, 113–44, 156, 158–9, *167*, 171
Brown, John, Shipbuilding (Clydebank) Ltd, 141
Brown-Curtis turbine, 100, *101*, 128
Brownlie, William, 37
Brunel, I.K., 57
Bryce Blairs, 68
Bullard King & Co., 99
Burmeister & Wain diesel engines, *100*
Burns, G. & J., 113, 128
Burrakur, Coal Co., *81*
Buruyeart Brown & Co., Cardiff, *81*
Bury, Edward, 43

CABLE SHIPS, 134
Caernarvon Castle, 89
Caird & Co., 37, 40, 43, 93, 105, 149
Caledonia, 120
Caledonia Foundry, 68–84
Caledonian Railway, 44, 45, 57, *158*
Caledonian Steam Packet Co., *120*
Calico Printers Association, 151
Calico printing, 151
Callendar Coal Co., 73
Camlachie Foundry, 12, 14, 19, 28, 51, 52
Cammell Laird & Co., 128, 141
'Camp Coffee', 147
Campania, 40, 91, 123, *124*, 125
Canada, 136
Canadian Pacific Line, 89, *90*, 99, 125, 126
Canadian Pacific Steam Ship Co., 118, 133
Canadian Pacific Steam Ship Line, 89
Canal Foundry, 12
Cape Government Railway, 46
Capital structure, 6
Carlisle Citadel Station, 60
Carlisle-class cruiser, 130
Carluke, 175
Carmania, 126
Caronia, 126
Caronia (II), 140

Carpet loom, 68
Carpet weaving, *148*, 149
Carron Co.,*11*, 11–13, *15*, 19, *23*, 30
Castle Line, 99, 125
Catrine Mills, 29
Central America, 60
Central Station, Glasgow, 57, 60
Chatham Dockyard, 116
Chemical manufacture, 150–1
Chenille axminster carpets, *148*
China, 53, 117
China, 118
China Navigation Co., *93*
Christian, 86
City of New York, 91, 119, 120, 123, *124*, *164*
City of Paris, 91, 119, 123, *124*
Clan Galbraith, 94
Claymore, 116
Cleland, James, 30, 36
Clephan, Mr, *160*
Clifton & Baird Ltd, *166*
Clockmaking, 27, 51
Clyde, 36, *120*
Clyde Bank Foundry, 113
Clyde Foundry, 26
Clyde Iron Works, 12, 109
Clyde Locomotive Works, 46
Clyde Navigation Trust, *59*, *120*, 168
Clyde Structural Steel Co., 60
Clydebank, *96*, 97, 100, *101*, 102, *103*, *111*, 112, 117, *120*, *121*, 123, 126, 136, *167*
Clydebank Engineering & Shipbuilding Co., 122
Coast Lines, 99
Coasters, 40, 91
Coatbridge, 54
Cochrane, John, (Barrhead) & Co., 83, 84
Cold blast, 13
Colombo, H.M.S., *130*
Colossus, H.M.S., 102
Coltness Iron Co., 69
Columba, 118
Columbian Stove Works, *160*
Colville, David, & Sons, 109
Colvilles Ltd, 62, 65, 66, 109
Comet, 4, 36, 86
Commonwealth, H.M.S., 126
Compagnie Générale Transatlantique, 108
Compound engine, 23, 37, 92, *114*, *115*, 119
Comus-class corvettes, 118
Confederacy, the, 115–16
Connell, Charles, & Co., 90, 96, 111, 112, 133, 142
Constance, H.M.S., 114
Cook, David, & Co., 31
Cook, James, 12, 30, 31, 35, 36, *88*
Copenhagen, *100*

Copper smelting, *169*
Coppersmithing, 42
Corliss valve gear, 32, 35, *81*, 165
Cornish drop valve gear, 69
Cornwall, H.M.S., 64
Coronel, battle of, *125*
Cotopaxi, 115
Cotton industry, 4, 27, 28, 53, 56
Coventry Syndicate, 126, 128, 131
Cradock, Admiral, *125*
Crackleckan, 11, 27
Craig, A.F., & Co., 56
Craig, Sir John, 109
Craig & Donald, 54, *166*
Craigellachie, 57
Craigiehall, 99
Cranes, *59*, *60*, *80*
Cranstonhill Bakery, 151
Crawhall & Campbell, 54
Cressy, H.M.S., 126
Cruisers, 63, 65, 119, 121, 122, *125*, 126, 130, 134, 139
Cuba, 31
Cunard, Samuel, 88, 89
Cunard & Co., *89*, 95, *111*, 113, 117, 118, 123, 134, *137*, 138, 140, 142, 150
Cupolas, 13–15, *29*, *174*
Currie, Donald, 90
Cutty Sark, 88
Cygnet, 113

DALE, David, 27
Dalmarnock Ironworks, 57
Dalmuir Naval Construction Works, 63–65, 102, *103*, 105, 128, 139, 167
Dalry, 26, 84
Darjeeling & Himalayan Railway, *4*
Davie, James, & Son, 18
Deanston Mill, 27, 29
Dempster, John, 113
Dempster Moore & Co., 54
Denny & Co., 39, 40
Denny, William, & Bros, 40, 86, *88*, 90, 92, *100*, 107, 110, 149, 167
Depreciation, 35
Depressions, 6 ff., 35, 105–9, 110, 112, 128, 129, 134–5, 136, 137–8, 141
Destroyers, 63, *110*, 131, 138, 139
Devon Ironworks, 12
Devonshire, 94
D'Eynecourt, Sir Eustace Tennyson, 128
Diesel engine, 35, 64, 66, *99*, 135, 136
Diesel locomotives, 49, *51*, 83, 84
Dilution, 8, *128*
Distribution of Industry Act, 152
Dodwell, G.E., 89
Dominion Line, 99
Donaldson Bros, 89
Donaldson, W.A., 122
Doulton & Co., 149
Doxford, William, & Sons, 131, 134

Doxford Diesel Engines, 97
Drake-class cruiser, 125
Dreadnought, H.M.S., 103
Dreadnoughts, 102, *103*
Dredgers, *95*, 110, 112
Dron & Lawson, 54
Drysdales & Co., *39*
Dübs & Co., 46
Dübs, Henry, 46
Duchess of Hamilton, 120
Duchess of Rothesay, 120
Duke of York, H.M.S., *140*
Dumbarton, 86, 88, 110, *167*
Dumfries, 63–65
Duncan, Sir Andrew, 65
Duncan, Robert, & Co., 105
Dundee, 29, 43, 97
Dundee, 90
Dundee Perth London Shipping Co., 90
Dunera, 95
Dunlop, C., and Partners, 122
Dunlop, James, & Co., 109
Dunlop, John Gibb, 122
Dunlop Bremner, 105
Dunn, William, 27
Dunsmuir & Jackson, 40

EAST ASIATIC STEAMSHIP CO., *100*
Edinburgh, 12
Edinburgh & Glasgow Railway, 43, 44
Edington, Thomas, & Sons, 19, 43, 44
Eglinton Engine Works, *31, 164*
Egypt, 60, *81*
Egyptian State Railways, *168*
Elder, Alexander, 113
Elder, David, 28, 29, 36, 52, 113
Elder, John, 29, 88, 89, 92, 96, 113, 114
Elder, John, & Co., *39*, 40, *115*, 116–9
Elder Dempster Lines, 99, 113
Electric motors, *39*
Elizabeth, 36
Elliot, John, 29
Emancipation Society of Glasgow, 115
Empress of Asia, 129
Empress of Britain, 126
Empress of Britain (II), 136
Empress of Japan, 90, 140
Empress of Russia, 129
Empress of Scotland, 90, 136, 140
Endeavour, H.M.S., 129
England, North East of, 91
English Electric Co., 131
Ermine, 128
Etruria, 118
'Export' products, 147
European Economic Community, 10

FAIRBURN, Sir William, 29, 92
Fairfield (Glasgow) Ltd, 111, 141, 144
Fairfield Shipbuilding and Engineering
  Co., 23, 40, 62, 67, 88, 89, *90*, 91, *99*,

101, 102, *104*, 105, 106, *110*, 111, 112,
  113–44, 149, 156, 171
Fairfield-Rowan Ltd, 141, 142
Fairfield-Sulzer diesel engine, 135
Fairlie, modified-, locomotive, 51, *52*
Fairy Queen, 44
Falkirk Iron Works, *24, 25*
Fans, 40
Federated Foundries Ltd, 26
Ferries, 99, *107*, 110, 125
Fife, H.M.S., 112
Finlay, Alexander, & Co., 60
Finlay, James, & Co., 27, 29
Finnieston, 117
Firebrick manufacture, 151
Fireless locomotive, *82*
Firhill Iron Works, 20
First World War, 8, 9, 23, 48, 50, 63, 64,
  79, *82*, 97, 99, 101, 102, 106, *128, 130,
  133*, 52
Firth, Thomas, & Sons, 136
Fisher, Admiral Lord, *102*
Fishing boats, 40, 86
Fleming, Andrew, Ltd, *165*
Fleming, P. & R., & Co., 60
Fleming & Ferguson & Co., 95
Flour milling, 151
Forced draught, 40
Forge pig iron, 13
Forrest & Barr, 56, *58*
Forth Bridge, *3*, 57, 58, 60
Forth and Clyde Canal, 20
Fowler, Sir John, *3, 58*
Franconia (1922), 134
Franconia (1963), 111
Frederica, 121
Froude, William, 92, 119
Fry, Henry, 124
Fuerst Bismarck, 99
Fullerton, Hodgart, Barclay & Co., *22*,
  56, 58, *59, 165*
Funchal, 114
Furnaces, 11–13, 19, 63
Fyfe Donald & Co., 51

GAIRDNER, Charles, 119, 121
Galashiels, 168
Gallia, 118
Garden Roller Association, 24
Gartsherrie, 13
Gas generators, 83, 84
Gear cutting, 27, 51
Gear wheels, 51
Geddes, Sir Reay, 142
Geddes, Committee, 111, 112, 142
General Ship Co., 117
Generating Equipment, 40
Germany, 48, 97, *99*, 119
Girdwood & Pinkerton, 56
Glasgow Central Station, *170*
Glasgow Iron & Steel Co., 64, 109

Glasgow Locomotive Works, 48
Glasgow, Paisley, Kilmarnock & Ayr
  Railway, 43, 44
Glasgow Railway Engineering Co., 44, *44*
Glasgow & South Western Railway, 43,
  49, 120
Glasgow Steel Roofing Co., 60
Glasgow Water Co., 19
Glen Line, 99
Glen & Ross, *42*
Glen Sannox, 120
Glenbuck Iron Works, 11
Glenfield and Kennedy & Co., *39, 80*
Glengarnock, 149
Globe Shipping Co., 134
Glover, Jack, *177*
Glover, John, & Sons, *177*
Glynwed Ltd, 26
Good Hope, H.M.S., 125
Gourock Ropework Co., 147
Govan, 63, 86, 96, 97, 102, 105, *106*,
  113, 116, 117, *143*
Govan Shipbuilders Ltd, 112
Gracie, Alexander, 126
Graham, Wellington & Co., 113
Grahamston Iron Co., *14*
Grant, John, 117
Grant, Sir Allan, *126*
Great Eastern, 41
Gregory Thomson & Co., 68
Greenhead Engine Works, *42*
Greenhead Foundry, 36
Greenock, 12, 37, 86, 93, 95, *102*, 105,
  108, 112, 147
Greensand moulding, 16, 18
Guion Line, 118, 119, 125

HAMBURG-AMERICA LINE, 99
Hamilton, William, & Co., 105
Handyside, 60
Handyside & Henderson, 105
Hanna, Donald and Wilson, 41, 57
Hardy, A.C., 135
Harland & Wolff & Co., 26, 97, 102, 105,
  106, 109, 128–9, 131, 141, *143*
Harris, Professor J.R., 170
Harvey, G. & A., 53, 55
Harvey, Robert, & Co., 54
Hatry, Clarence, 106, 107, 109, 131, 134,
  136
Hawthorn, R. & W., 43
Helmsdale Steamship Co., *94*
Henderson, D. & W., 105
Henderson, James, & Son, 120
Hercules Foundry, 14
Heritage Securities Investment
  Association, 71
Hillington Industrial Estate, 152
Hindustan, H.M.S., 126
Hoey, David, 70, 72
Hogarths, 107

Holland, 53
Holland-America Line, 99
Hood, H.M.S., 131, *133*
Hot blast, 5, 13
Houldsworth & Fairbairn, 12
Houldsworth family, 27, 56
Howden, James, 40
Howden, James, & Co., 40
Hudson, J.G., 35
Hull design, 92
Hutcheson, D., & Co., 118
Hydepark Foundry, Finnieston, 44, 45
Hydepark Works, Springburn, 45, *49, 52*
Hydraulic machinery, 35, *43*, 49

IMPERIAL PAPER MILLS LTD, Gravesend, *82*
Inchcape, Earl of, 106
India, 45, 46, 49
Indian State Railways, 65
Industrial Archaeology, 170–7
Inflexible, aeroplane, 66
Inglis, A. & J., *3*, 40, 90, 105, 120
Inland Revenue, 64, 65
Inman Line, 91, 99, 119, 120, 125, *164*
International Mercantile Marine Co., *99,* 119
Invernairn, Lord, *see* Beardmore, Sir William
Inverness & Perth Junction Railway, 57
Inverted vertical direct acting engine, 37
Iona (I), (II), and (III), 116, 118
Iron, 5, 11–27, 29
Iron shipbuilding, 86, *89*
Iron smelting, 11, 13, 27, 29, 30
Iron and Steel Institute, 92
Iron-framed buildings, 56, 57
Ironfounding, 11–27, 41, 56, 155
Ironstone, 5
Ironworks, 5, 11, 12, 71–2
Irrawaddy Flottila Co., 90
Isle of Man Steam Packet Co., 118, *161*
Italy, 45, 53
Ivernia, 111

JACKSON, Brown & Hudson, *21*
Jackson, Peter, Esq., *165*
James Watt, 86
Japan, 46, 53
Java, 31
Jeffrey Bros, *174*
Johnstone, 51, 54, *59, 147,* 166
Jutlandia, 100

KAISER WILHELM DER GROSSE, 97
Kelvin, Lord, *150*
Kelvin and James White Ltd, *150*
Kelvinhaugh, 97, 117
Ker, Henry, 73
Kerr, Neilson & Co., 44
Kilmarnock, *16, 22, 39, 45,* 68–74, *162*

Kilmarnock and Troon Railway, 42
Kincaid, J. & G., & Co., 41, 103, 112
King, Chief Engineer, 114–5
King Edward VII class battleships, 126
King Edward, 100
King George V class battleship, *140*
King Orry, 161
Kingston Yard, 112
Kinning Park Foundry, 13, 16
Kinning Park pumping station, *39*
Kirk, A.C., 39, 93
Kirkintilloch, 21
Kirkwood, David, M.P., 138
Knox, Adam, & Co., *172, 173*
Knox, W. & J., 147
Kungsholm, 112
Kylsant, Lord, 107

LACEMAKING, 151
Laidlaw, R., & Sons, 19, 57, 60
Laidlaw, Sons & Caine, 57
Lamport & Holt, 99
Lanarkshire Steel Co., 109, 134
Lancashire Iron & Steel Co., 134
Lancefield Forge, *28*, 29, 41, 53, 63
Lancefield Works, 113
Lang, John, & Sons, 54, *172*
Lang, W.J. & W., *147*
Langholm, *174*
Larbert, *175*
Lawson & Co., 68
Leith, 43
Letitia, 135
Letterkenny & Burtonport Extension Railway, 78
Leven, 36
Leven, river, *88*
Linen industry, 28
Linthouse, 97
Lion Foundry Co., 21, 26
Liskeard & Caradon Railway, 78
Lithgow, Henry, 104, 108, 138, 141
Lithgow, Sir James, 65, 66, 104, 108, 109, 138, 141
Lithgow, W.T., 94, 104
Lithgow, Group, 112, 141
Lithgows Ltd, 104, 105, 107, 110, 156
Liverpool & Great Western Shipping Co., 118
Liverpool-Hamburg Steamship Co., 89
Lloyd Saubado Shipping Line, 90
Lloyds, 86
Lloyd's Bank, 65
Loam moulding, 14, 16
Lobnitz & Co., *95*, 105, 110
Loch Katrine, 131, 134
Lochwinnoch, 149
Locomobiles, 73
Locomotive building, 5, *22*, 42–51, 64, 65, 68–84
Locomotive Manufacturers' Association, 79

Locomotives, industrial, 46, 70–84
London, 12, 30, 60, *88*, 91
London & Glasgow Shipbuilding & Engineering Co., 101, 105
London & Limerick Steamship Co., 114
London Midland & Scottish Railway, 4, *82,* 83
London Road Ironworks, *171*
London & South Western Railway, 45
Looms, 4, 68
Loudon Brothers, 54–56
Lowther Iron Hematite Co., 71
Lucania, 40, 91, 123, *124,* 125
Lusitania, 40, 100, *126,* 158
Lyle Shipping Co., 117

MACHINE TOOLS, 27, *28, 39,* 41, 51–52, 77, 120, 125, *155, 166*
Machine-tools building, 1, 23, 36, 37, 41, 48, 51–56, 83
McArthur, Duncan, & Co., 36
MacBrayne, David, & Co., 116
McDowall, John, & Sons, 56, 68
McDowall & Steven, 72
McCulloch, Thomas, 68
Macfarlane, Walter, & Co., Saracen Ironworks, 1, *5*, 20, 21
Macfarlane, Strang & Co., 19, 20
McGregor Laird, 113
Mackintosh, Charles Rennie, *99*
MacKinnon, William, 119, 120, 121
MacLaren, Robert, & Co., 26
McLellan, George, & Co., 151
MacLellan, P. & W., & Co., 60
McNeil, Duncan, & Co., *81*
McOnie, Peter, 30, 31
McOnie, P. & W., 30, 31
McOnie, Sir William, 122
McOnie, W. & A., 31, 34, 41, *160*
McOnie & Mirrlees, 31
Madeira, 114
Main, A. & J., & Co., 62
Mallet, Robert, 31
Manchester, 12, 29, 46, 52, 113, 126
Manganese, 13
Mann, John, 74, 75
Mann Byars & Co., 152
Marathon (UK) Ltd, 112
Margery, 88
Maria Rickmers, 94
Marine engineering, 28, 30, 36–42, 91, 111, 112
Marshall, John, & Sons, *59*
Martyn, William, & Co., *17*
Maschinenfabrik Augsburg Nuremberg, 35
Mass production, 6
Mathias, Professor P., 156
Mauretania, 40, 126
Mauritius, 31
Mayer, John, 21, 37, 41, 42

Meadowside, 105
Media, 140
Mersey, river, 91
Michell bearing, *121*
Middle East, *25*
Milanda Bread Ltd, 151
Millwrighting, 4, 27–28, 30, 36
Mining, 4, 5, 10, 29, 68–70
Mining machinery, 5, 29, 30, 68, 69, 72, 75, 79
Mirrlees & Tait, 31
Mirrlees, Tait & Watson, 32, 35
Mirrlees, Watson & Co., 34
Mirrlees, Watson & Yaryan, 35
Mirror, 134
Mitchell & Neilson, 44
Mo-Car syndicate, 63
Monklands, 5
Monmouth Shipbuilding Co., 131, 134
Montrose, 133, 136
Moore, H.S. & W., 83
Morton, Alexander, 151
Morton, Thomas, 68
Mossend Steelworks, 63, 65
Motherwell, *44,* 60
Motherwell Bridge & Engineering Co., 60
Moulding, 12, 14–18, 26
Muir & Houston, 40
Muirkirk Ironworks, 11, 30
Multitubular boiler, 40
Murdoch & Aitken, 42
Murray & Paterson & Co., 54

NAPIER, David, 12, 36, 113
Napier, John, 12
Napier, Robert, 12, 19, 28, 29, 36, 37, 62, 86, 88–90, *106,* 113, 116, *161*
Napier, Robert, & Sons, 39, 40, 41, 63, 97, 102, 117
Napier family, 12
National Government, 139
National Light Castings Association, 24
National Line, 119
National Register of Archives (Scotland), 155
National Shipbuilders Securities Ltd., 105, 108, 109, *110,* 138, 139
Nationalization, 9, 10
Nederland Steam Navigation Co., 113, 117
Neilson, John, 44
Neilson, J. Beaumont, 13, 44
Neilson, Walter Montgomerie, 45, 46
Neilson & Co., 30, 44–46, *158*
Neilson Mitchell & Co., 44
Neilson Reid & Co., 46
Nelson, H.M.S., 118
Nelson Line, 99
Netmaking, 147
New Lanark, 27, 28

New York City, 40
New Zealand, 135, 136, 138
New Zealand Shipping Co., 118, 125
Newark Sailcloth Works, 147
Norddeutscher Lloyd, 97, 119
Norman, Montagu, 65, 66
Norseman, 134
North American Royal Mail Steam Navigation Co., 88, 89
North Bridge, Edinburgh, 60
North British Diesel Engine Works, *100*
North British Iron Hematite Co., 71
North British Locomotive Co., 4, 23, *42,* 46, 49, 50, *52,* 56, 62
North British Railway, 43, 57
Northumberland Shipbuilding Co., 106, 109, 131, 134, 136
Nuffield Trust, 84

OAKBANK FOUNDRY, 44
Octavia, H.M.S., 114
Oil, offshore industry, 10
Old Kilpatrick, 108
Omrah, 123
Oral evidence, 177
Ord, Lewis Craven, 64
Oregon, 118
Orient Line, 123
Oronsay, 134
Ottawa Agreement, 138
Owen, Robert, 27

PACIFIC STEAM NAVIGATION CO., 99, 113, 114, *115,* 117
Paddle Steamers, 23, 36
Paisley, *22,* 56, 63, 147, 148
Para, 99
Parkhead Forge, 41, *43,* 62–67, 86
Parsons, Charles A., *100*
Parsons, C.A., & Co., 51
Partick, 113
Paton, William, *147*
Payne, Professor P.L., 156
Pearce, Lady, 131
Pearce, Sir William, 89, 116, 119, 122, 125, 131
Pearce, Sir William G., 122, 123, 125
Peninsular & Orient Line (P. & O.), 99, 106, 141
Penn, John, & Sons, 53
Persia, 89
Perth, 90
Phosphorous, 13
Photographic collections, 163
Picken, James, & Son, 147, *148*
Pickering, R.Y., & Co., *44*
Pier construction, 57, 60
Pig iron, 12, 13, 23
Pipe founding, 19, 20, 24
Pirrie, Lord, *106,* 129, 131, 134
Plantation Bakery, 151

Plas Kynaston, 57
Pleasure steamers, 99
Plymouth, 114
Pointhouse, 105,
Polmadie, 45
Pompero, 115
Poplar, 97, 99
Port Glasgow, 86, 94, 104, 105, 108, 112 120, 147
Portland Foundry, 68
Post Boy, 36
Princess Kathleen, 134
Princess Marguerite, 134
Princess Marguerite (II), 140
Princess Patricia, 140
Proctor, David, *80*
Propontis, 39, 119
Pumping engines, 5, 29, 30, 34, *39,* 69, 75

QUEEN ELIZABETH, *96,* 138, 140, 158
Queen Elizabeth 2, 112, *142*
Queen Mary, 96, 133, *137,* 138, *139,* 140, 158
Queen Street Station, Glasgow, 60
Queens Park Works, *3, 42,* 48, 49

RAISTRICK, Dr A., 173
Ramsay Pit, Midlothian, 29
Randolph, Charles, 29, 113
Randolph & Elder & Co., 37, 39, 60, 88, 113–16
Randolph, Elliot & Co., 29, 52, 113
Rankin & Blackmore, 40, 41, *94,* 103, 112
Rankine, Professor William MacQuorn, 92
Rasmara, 3
Rationalization, 10, 26, 48, 65
Rebouças, André, 95
Record surveying, 155 *et seq.*
Record-keeping practice, 156–7
Reid, James, 45
Reid, John, & Co., *120*
Reid, Joseph, 75
Reincke, H.A., 65
Renfrew, 95, 105, 110, *120*
Renown, H.M.S. 131
Reoch Bros & Co., 62
Repulse, H.M.S., 131
Rigby, William, *42,* 62
Ringarooma, 121
Rio Tinto Mines, *169*
Ritchie, David, 121
Riverbank Works, 70, 74, 75
Robert the Bruce, 107, 167
Robertson, John, 86
Roebuck, John, 30
Rolls Royce Ltd, 10
Ropemaking, 147, *148*
Ross, R.G., & Co., 36, *42*

Ross & Duncan, 40, 41
Rothesay Dock, *120*
Rotomahana, 92
Rowan, David, & Co., 39–41, 103, 112
Rowan, J.M., 39
Rowan, John M., 43, 44
Royal Mail Shipping Group, 99, 105, 107, 109, 131, 134
Royal Mail Steam Packet Co., 134
Russell & Co., 94, 104
Russell & Co., Carluke, *175*
Russell, John Scott, 36
Russia, 45, 53
Russia, 117

SAALE, 119
Sailing ships, 39, 85, 93, 94
St Enoch Station, Glasgow, 60
St Rollox Chemical Works, 151
St Rollox railway workshops, 44
Sanitary appliances, 1, *5,* 21, 149
Saracen Foundry, 1, *5,* 20, 21
School of Mines, South Kensington, 63
Scientific instrument makers, *150*
Scotland Street Ironworks, 35
Scotstoun, 97, 99, *100*
Scotstoun Marine Ltd, 112
Scott, John, 37
Scott, Sinclair, & Co., 37, 43, 52
Scott & Linton, *88*
Scottish Co-operative Wholesale Society, *18*
Scottish Development Area, 152
Scottish Development Council, 105
Scottish Ice Rinks, Crossmyloof, 64
Scottish Industrial Estates Ltd, 152
Scottish Ironfounders' Association, 24
Scottish Machine Tool Corporation, 55
Scottish Society for the Preservation of Historical Machinery, 175, *177*
Scotts Shipbuilding & Engineering Co., *86,* 93, 95, *100,* 101, 112
Scout, H.M.S., 119
Scythia, 117
Seaward and Maudslay, 37
Second World War, 49, 50, 56, 66, *83,* 84, 109, 152
Seedhill Tannery, *147*
Selandia, 100
Sentinel Works, 64
Servia, 118
Sewing machine manufacture, 18, 67
Shanks' Patent Water Closets, 149
Shanks, Thomas, & Co., 53, 54, *59*
Shanks, William, 53
Sharer, Edmund, 123, 125
Sharp, John, 13
Sharp, Roberts & Co., 56
Sharp, Stewart & Co., 46, 56
Shaw & McInnes & Co., 20

Shaws Water Spinning Co., 27
Shearer & Co., 108
Sheffield, *126*
Shipbuilding, 1, 10, 53, 55, 85–144
Shipbuilding, wooden, 6, 86, 93
Shire Line, 99
Shotts Iron Co., 11, 19
Side-lever engines, 23, 34
Siemens, C.W., 96
Simons, William, & Co., *95,* 110, 147
Singer Manufacturing Co., 26, 55, 66, *123*
Siraia, 108
Slumps, *see* Depressions
Small-arms manufacture, 6
Smeaton, John, 30
Smith, A. & W., & Co., *31,* 32, 34, 36, 56, 60, *164*
Smith, George, & Co., 21, *149*
Smith, Hugh, & Co., 55, 56
Smith, James, 27, 29
Smith Brothers, 55, 56
Smith & Naysmith, 60
Smith & Rodger, 40
Smith & Wellstood, Ltd, *160*
South Africa, 46, 48, 49, *50, 52*
South America, 45, 46, 60, 114, 117
South Queensferry, 58
Spain, 49, 60
Special Areas (Development and Improvement) Act, 152
Special Areas Reconstruction Association Ltd, 84
Spinning, 151
Springburn, 45, 46
Stained glass, 149
Standardization, 50, 51, *79, 80,* 94
Star Foundry Co., 21
Stark and Fulton, 30, 43, 44
Steam navvies, 72
Steamboat, development of, 6, 29, 36, 37, 86
Steel Company of Scotland, 65, 109
Steel industry, 109
Steel making, 6, 10, 62, 65
Steel shipbuilding, introduction of, 92
Steel works machinery, 34, 54, 66
Steeple engine, 36
Stella Coal Co., Blaydon-on-Tyne, *81*
Stephen, Alexander, 97
Stephen, Alexander, & Sons, 40, *48,* 96, *97,* 105, 106, 107, 109, 110, 111, 142
Stephen, F.J., 109
Stephenson, Robert, 57
Steven, Hugh, 76
Steven, Thomas, 72–76
Steven, Thomas, junior, 76
Stevenson, J. & B., 151
Stewart, Sir Iain, 111
Stewart, Duncan, & Co., 34, 35, 41, *171*
Stewart, D.Y., & Co., 19

Stirling, David, 68
Stirling, Gordon, & Co., 31, *86*
Strachan, George, 123, 128
Strang, W., & Co., *16*
Structural engineering, *3,* 56–62
Submarines, 63, 112, 123, *130,* 131
Sudan, 60
Sugar machinery, 1, *11,* 12, 23, 30–36, *164*
Sulzer diesel engines, 97
Sun Foundry, 21, 149
Supple, Professor B., 156
Surface condensers, 36
Sutlej, H.M.S., 126
Swan, Hunter & Co., 97, 107, 109, 136
Sweden, 45
Swire, John, & Co., *93*
Symington, William, 29
Szarvasy, F.A., 64

TANCRED, ARROL & CO., 58
Tank landing craft, 110, 139
Tank testing, 119
Tankers, 106, 134, 136, 140
Tanks, 48–49
Tannery, *147*
Tauranga, 121
Taxicabs, 64
Tay Bridge, 57
Taylor, George, & Co. Ltd, *175*
Technical records, 159–63
Telford, Thomas, 57
Templeton, J. & G., 28
Templeton, James, & Son, 148
Tennant, Charles, & Co., 151
Terpsichore, H.M.S., *121*
Textile industries, 147
Textile machinery, 4, 12, 18, 27, 28, 34, 53
Thames, river, *88,* 91
Thomson, George, 113, 117, 122
Thomson, George, P., 122
Thomson, James, 113, 117
Thomson, James Roger, 117, 120, *121,* 122
Thomson, J. & G., & Co., 37, 40, 88, 91, 95, 113–25, 149, 156, *164*
Thomson, Robert, 113
Thread manufacture, 151
Tiger, H.M.S., 129
Titchfield Foundry, 68, 74, 77
Tod & MacGregor Ltd, 37, 86, 88, *89*
Tongland, 63–65
Tosi diesels, 64
Tower Bridge, 60
Trade cycle, 9
Trade Facilities Act (1921), 64, 134
Trade Facilities Act (1926), 138
Tramp ships, 40, 94, 103–05, 136
Transport Museum, Glasgow, *165, 167*
Transylvania, 100

Trave, 119
Treasury, The, 109
Trinidad, 31
Triple expansion engine, 39, 92–94, 101,
   103, 119, 120, *124*, 134, 139
Troon, 41
Tullis, D. & J., 56, *172*
Turbines, 39, 51, 100, *101*, 102, 126,
   130, 135
Turner, Thomas, 75–78
Tyne, 97, 107
Tyrrhenia, 95

UMBRIA, 118
Union Bank of Scotland, 117, 119
Union Canal, 57
Union Castle Line, 99
Union Line, 99
Union Steamship Co., *135*
United Co-operative Bakery Society, 151
United States of America, 48, 51, 53, 54
United States Navy, 114
United Turkey Red Co., 151
University of Glasgow, 29, 155
University of Strathclyde, 155, 173, *177*
Upper Clyde Shipbuilders Ltd, 10, 110,
   111, 112, 142, 144, 156, 158
Ure, William, 68

V-CLASS DESTROYER, *133*
Vale of Leven, 151
Valiant, H.M.S., 131
Vanguard, 86
Vassaras Sugar Mill, *32*
Venomous, H.M.S., *133*
Venty, H.M.S., *133*
Veteran, H.M.S., *133*
Vickers Ltd, 63, 128
Vulcan Foundry, *22*

W-CLASS DESTROYERS, *133*
Waddell, John, 73, 74
Wages, 9, 23, 24, 91
Wallace, Patrick, 90
Wallsend Shipbuilding & Engineering
   Co., 97
Wanlockhead, 30
Washington Treaty, 134, 138
Water tube boilers, 40, 119
Water wheels, 4, 12, 27, 28, 29
Watson, Laidlaw & Co., 34
Watt, James, 30, 114
Wear, 131
Wear, River, Commissioners, *70*
Weardale Coal Co., *81*
Wearmouth Coal Co., *69*
Weaving, 147, *148*, 151
Weir, First Viscount, 138

Weir, G. & J., & Co., 26, *48*, 110
Weir, James, 40
Welding, 24, 66
West Indies, 114
Western Centrifugal Separator, 35
Western Survey of the National Register
   of Archives (Scotland), 155 *et seq*.
White, R. Saxton, 123
White, Thomas, & Sons, 56
White Star Line, 99
Whitelegg Baltic Locomotive, 49
Whiteworth & Co., 45
Wilkinson, William, 13
Wilson (Pipe Fittings) Ltd, *19*
Winding and hauling engines, 5, 29, 69,
Windsor Castle, 134
Wishaw, *44*
Wood, John and Charles, 86
Wood, J.R., & Co., *80*
Woodworking machinery, 56
Workington, 71
Workman Clark & Co., 109, 131
Workshops, construction of, 56, 57, 60
Wrought iron, 13, 57, 60, 62

YARROW & CO., 40, 97, 99, 111, 112, 142
Yarrow Admiralty Research Department,
   112
Yaryan evaporator, 35